Four Funerals and a Wedding

(Journeys in Creative and Life Writing)

by

Neil Bradley

**Grosvenor House
Publishing Limited**

First published in Great Britain in 2014
by Kindle Direct Publishing

Copyright © Neil Bradley, 2014

The moral right of the author has been asserted.

This book is published by
Grosvenor House Publishing Ltd
28-30 High Street, Guildford, Surrey, GU1 3EL.
www.grosvenorhousepublishing.co.uk

A CIP record for this book
is available from the British Library

ISBN 978-1-78148-853-9

WITH THANKS

Throughout the years of writing this book there have been a host of people that have influenced and encouraged me, as well as offering me the kick up the backside I so very much needed to finally get it finished.

First and foremost, I would like to thank my wife, Sharon, for her love, determination, and her unflinching belief in me, especially during all those times I took to my bed and was unable to face a world I'd grown far too weary of.

I'd like to thank my dad for his encouragement, love and understanding.

I would like to thank Joe Baden, Fiona Taylor, Silver-Sue Hallissey, and Lord James Carney, as well as everyone connected with the Open Book Project at Goldsmiths College. I'd especially like to thank Joe for his ridiculously kind offer of a teaching position with the project and for convincing me to tackle the MA, and Fiona for her proofreading and editing skills, and her wonderful determination in seeing me finally put this bleedin' thing to bed.

I'd like to thank Maura Dooley for her wonderful support and continued encouragement. I'd like to thank Francis Spufford and Stephen Knight for their 'good cop, bad cop' routine, their generosity and good humour. I'd like to thank Maria MacDonald for her wonderful smile, and for helping see my wife across the finishing line of the London Marathon. And I'd like to especially thank Professor Blake Morrison for his most generous foreword, his sense of humour, and for always being happ to talk with me about the 'dead.' I'll make a South London lad of him yet!

I'd like to thank the Class of 2009 (MA in Creative and Life Writing) at Goldsmiths for all of their advice and friendship.

I'd like to thank Paul Casella and Carl Prosser (RIP) of *The Lion Roars*, for first offering me a platform to vent my journalistic spleen.

I'd like to thank Paul Swift for the hours he spent drinking coffee at the Royal Festival Hall and listening to this story unfold.

I'd like to thank Joan for constantly asking after "that book about the angels?"

I'd like to thank Mick Flaherty (Millwall's Most Famous Cab Driver) for his friendship.

And finally I'd like to thank ZerkaaHD for convincing me that I should go it alone!

For Sharon

Foreword

As he tells us early on in this book, Neil Bradley has done a lot of different jobs in his time: worked in a plastic bags factory, painted railings, cleaned toilets, operated a goods lift, sold sandwiches out of the back of a van. He has also occasionally delivered eulogies at family funerals. To honour the dead without being pious requires a special talent, and to me the most moving parts of *Four Funerals and a Wedding* are those where he speaks of the deaths of those he has loved, in particular his mother, whose presence dominates the latter half of the book – just as her absence dominated Neil's mind for a decade.

The obvious thing with this book would have been for Neil to make it a family memoir pure and simple. But he's someone who always avoids obvious things. So as well as being a record of his south London working-class family, full of comic vignettes, larger than life characters, and a keen political awareness, it's also the story of Neil's struggle to become a writer. Much of it is focused on the two years he spent doing an MA in creative writing at Goldsmiths, with accompanying portraits, not always flattering, of some of his tutors, myself included.

Though his mother encouraged it and his father came to accept it, Neil's ambition to be a writer puzzled some in his family, who didn't consider writing a proper job. And surrounded as he was at Goldsmiths by students from more privileged backgrounds, Neil himself sometimes felt like a fish out of water. But in the end – partly by accident and partly because his tutors pushed him in the direction of life writing – Neil discovered a genre he could thrive in, got his MA and was transformed by the experience. Writing became a journey of self-discovery for him and this book documents the various stumbling blocks and forward leaps along the way.

In tutorials I used to complain Neil seemed to be writing several books at once. Now he has made a virtue of that. *Four Funerals and a Wedding* makes room for all sorts: fiction extracts, journal entries, family anecdotes and reflections of what writing is or ought to be. But at its heart is the story of a man coming to terms with loss and finding, if not 'closure' (a word he associates with factories, not psychoanalysis), then a kind of peace and redemption. Knowing Neil, he will probably now go on to write the airport novel his tutors discouraged him from writing. But I'm pleased he wrote this book first. It's a true story, and *his* story, and he needed to get it told.

Blake Morrison, Professor of Creative and Life Writing, Goldsmiths

Content

The Big Freeze

Friday 22nd February 1963

Just off the Old Kent Road – cheapest street on the *Monopoly* board – there once stood a non-descript little stretch of road by the name of Ruby Street. These days it stands no more than an ill-thought-through industrial estate, its industrial units clawing back the street by stealth rather than as a result of some grand design. In fact, today, if you were to ask direction of this tiny stretch of tarmacadam you'd probably be confronted by a collection of blank looks, furrowed brows and scratched heads. For many, even those familiar with the Old Kent Road, they'd be hard-pressed to even acknowledge its existence, let alone make reference to or point in the direction of. No surprise then that in 1963 Ruby Street was one of the Old Kent Road's best-kept secrets. In 1963 Ruby Street, the street to which this opening gambit lends itself – Ruby Street on the edge of the, romantically-named, 'Ruby Triangle' - was actually playing host to the future. In 1963 Ruby Street - penned in by the Old Kent Road Gasworks at one end and the (old) Surrey Canal at the other - simply sat there waiting to be discovered, as if some Shangri-La or New Jerusalem.

In 1963 my Father, James Lloyd Bradley, was 28, and was married with two children - an anti-nuclear family living in an attic room in Austral Street (SE11). This was just off of West Square, and sat midway between the Elephant and Castle and Westminster Bridge. Although many of the houses in West Square had retained their grandiose splendour, and remained in the hands of the rich, a few in and around the square had been claimed in the form of cramped social housing, and had once boasted residence to an unknown, at least at the time, Charlie Chaplin, who, like my family, was more than familiar with the harsh reality of working class life.

At the south western corner of West Square could be found a giant wall on the opposite side of which sat Geraldine Mary Harmsworth Park, which, in the 1920s, had been bequeathed by Harmsworth - Viscountess Rothermere, to give her her official title - to the London County Council for use as a public park. Although the park still retains the title of Geraldine Mary Harmsworth, who was the mother of Lord Rothermere - proprietor of the Daily Mail and often cited as the inventor of today's tabloid-style sensationalism – to all those that lived locally it has always been referred to as 'Bedlam Park,' as a result of it housing the Bethlehem Hospital, more infamously known as 'Bedlam Hospital.' In later years this would become home to the Imperial War Museum, as well as home to – before the big guns were set down in front of its entrance – my grandfather's allotment.

My parent's modest accommodation in Austral Street consisted of one room, including a double bed. Outside on the landing stood a cooker, as well as just enough room for a small collapsible dining table accommodating three people – as long as the third person was very slim and did not attempt leaning backwards in their chair, less they fell backwards down four flights of stairs all of which led to the backyard and an outside toilet shared by the five or six families that shared occupation of the house. This accommodation, whilst homely, was obviously not ideal, at least not for a family of four, and so in 1963 my parents managed to secure a 'move' to a new build just off the Old Kent Road. Even so, this was not without its difficulties, with their move to Ruby Street, intended for the early part of the new year, delayed by the 'Big Freeze,' when Britain found itself in the grip of snow, when the ground had been so hard that the government had been forced to bring the army in to help dig out the frozen solid potato harvest; when the Thames had frozen over in the middle of London; when the milkman, if you were one of the few lucky households to receive a daily pint, delivered frozen solid milk in clinking bottles.

Throughout this period, as the days turned to weeks and the weeks turned to months, my parents sat waiting patiently for the snow to thaw, the building of their new home delayed by a freak cold snap that arrived on Boxing Day 1962 and stubbornly lingered right through to March of the following year. Of course, in reality, there had been no 'building' to speak of. The houses, based on a Canadian design, were actually prefabricated: erected elsewhere and then transported on the backs of lorries, before being set down in grids to form instant new communities.

My parents were one of the first families to receive keys to these new dream homes – 58 Ruby Street was the house they chose – which was why my dad found himself, on that cold day in 1963, sat in the middle of the living room floor waiting for an electrician and a plumber, both of whom would connect him to the power and the water supply respectively. On that cold day in 1963 The Beatles topped the charts with *Please, Please Me*, and were about to conquer America. On that cold day in 1963, despite the irony, *Summer Holiday*, starring Cliff Richard, was the box-office cinema hit. On that cold day in 1963 the USA had just instituted a trade embargo on Cuba following the 'missile crisis.' On that cold day in 1963 my dad could be found sitting crossed-legged on the floor of our new home - his coat, gloves, scarf and hat still firmly in place in a futile attempt at keeping warm. Unfolding that day's newspaper to the pages offering further details of the big freeze, he reached for the brown paper bag containing his packed lunch. "There's a flask in there," my mother had said, kissing him on his way earlier that morning, "and an apple, and a round of sandwiches." When he reached into the bag however, instead of finding the promised pack lunch, he discovered a bottle containing baby milk and half a dozen towelling nappies (mine). Cursing, he returned the contents to the bag and folded his arms against the freezing interior of our new home. He was in for a long, cold wait.

Mrs Robinson, you're trying to seduce me?

Interview with Maura Dooley
Programme Coordinator for the MA in
Creative and Life Writing

Not that I knew it at the time, but Maura Dooley would prove to be one of the nicest people I've ever had the good fortune to meet - not just for granting me a place on her course, but in terms of the encouragement she would offer in the two years I was under her department's supervision: I think, even from our first meeting, she knew what it meant to me to be on the course – to be a 'writer.' More importantly, I think she knew, even better than I did, that there was a story I was desperate to tell, even if, at the time, again, I didn't quite understand exactly *what* that story was. Despite having worked at Goldsmith's College as a clerical officer for some seven years prior to my interview for the course, our paths had never crossed – I had no idea what she looked like or who she was.

According to the Goldsmiths College Website:

Maura Dooley *has published six collections of poetry, including 'Kissing a Bone,' and recently 'Life Under*

5

Water' (2008) both of which were shortlisted for the T S Eliot Prize. Maura is also an anthologist, has worked as a script consultant and been involved in numerous initiatives to enhance the profile of poetry in the United Kingdom.

The person that greets me at the door looks every inch the poet – pale skinned, and with a flock of, long flowing, dark hair: her overall appearance puts me in mind of the muse for every single English folk song ever written. Pulling back the door and bidding me entry, Maura's smile takes immediate effect, and I find myself instantly at ease.

Her office on the fifth floor of Warmington Town - a building on the Goldsmith's campus which one could easily mistake for a block of council flats - offers panoramic views of London, including many of the locations, unbeknown to me then - I will eventually write about.

During the first ten minutes or so she guides me through, what she describes as, the "bread and butter stuff," explaining the course requirements – she's already seen my hefty, over-compensatory, portfolio - all the while, no doubt, attempting to get a handle on the somewhat apprehensive man hiding behind the application. Having enquired as to the reasons for my applying she then attempts delving a little deeper, demanding to know a little bit more about me, including my reading habits. "What books have you read?" she asks.

Despite the fact that it is *I* that has approached her, rather than the other way round, I viewed the question with suspicion, so worn down was I by my experience of the 'real world,' worried that this might be a trick question. "*Books?*"

"What books do you *like* to read?"

"Oh, detective novels mostly."

"Agatha Christie?"

"No," I laugh. "American writers usually: Joseph Wambaugh? Richard Price? There's this guy, Tim Ernshaw, that wrote this brilliant Los Angeles trilogy."

"I'm not sure I've heard of him." She makes a note (all writers are constantly making lists of writers they never heard of and of books they've never read).

"He's great, really."

"How about classic books?"

"At school they had us reading Robinson Crusoe, which I never really got on with. In fact the closest we got to literature were brief flirtations with the likes of *Kes* (*A Kestral for a Knave* by Barry Hines) and *A Clockwork Orange* (Anthony Burgess). All the other stuff though, just left me cold. I mean, at my school, it wasn't exactly *The Dead Poets Society*!"

She nods her understanding. "What else did they make you read?"

"To be honest, they didn't really attempt introducing us to too many works of a classic nature. If you want to know the truth, I think they were more concerned with preparing us for a life of work."

"What, no further and higher education?"

I shake my head. "I don't know one person, from any of the schools that I attended, that ended up at university. If you were bright they tended to steer you towards working in a bank or in an office somewhere. As for the rest of us we, well, were just factory fodder as far as I could make out. We were never really asked what it was we wanted to do. Not that any of us would have known, even if we had been asked. Most of us just accepted the fact that a job would probably be chosen for us. We didn't really have any say in the matter. To be honest, if you claimed you wanted to be a painter and decorator they'd accuse you of being pretentious!"

Maura laughs, nodding her understanding again, and I suddenly remember an interview I had with the school's careers master a few months before I left school – this must have been nearly thirty years ago now.

Of course, the title, 'careers master,' was a bit of a red herring. Sure, the sign of the door may well have read as much, but the guy sitting behind the desk, the guy in the brown warehouse coat, was actually the woodwork teacher: I knew he was the woodwork teacher because he taught me *woodwork* - I remember I made a pipe rack for my dad. My dad never smoked a pipe.

"So, lad," he'd said to me by way of an opening gambit, "what's all this stuff and nonsense about you wanting to dance with the Royal Ballet?"

There had obviously been some mistake. You could get beat up listening to David Bowie, so the Royal Ballet was definitely out of the question. "The Royal Ballet, sir?"

"The ballet, lad, the *ballet*? All this stuff and nonsense about you wanting to dance *Swan Lake* with the Royal Philharmonic?"

Again I have no idea what he's talking about.

He looks at me over the desk. "I must say, lad, you've certainly got the legs for it. Even so, I can assure you there's no future in it. I should know; my wife and I won the southern area finals, ballroom dancing, 1957."

"Congratulations, sir," I said.

"In the semi-finals we danced the foxtrot. In the finals though, we danced the tango. Have you ever danced the tango, lad?"

"No, sir, I can't say I have."

"Full of Latin passion, the tango."

"I'm sure it is, sir," I say, looking down at my legs.

"Anyway, this nonsense about you wanting to dance with the Royal Ballet?"

"Well, that's just it, sir, I don't."

"Changed your mind, have you, lad?"

"No, sir," I laughed. "I've never wanted to dance the ballet. In fact, I think, sir, you might have the wrong boy!"

"The wrong boy, lad?" he looks confused.

"The name's Bradley, sir. Neil Bradley." I'm sure if he'd read the file properly he would've quickly established that I was no ballet dancer. In fact, I was probably more likely to be described as a somewhat average student, and that my career prospects were probably not good.

For the next few minutes he rummaged through the debris on his desk, before finally locating the correct file. "Here we go," he said triumphantly holding the file aloft, before reading the inscription on the front of the file. "Bradley . . . Neil James . . . average student . . . career prospects . . . not good."

"There you go, sir," I said, suddenly buoyed by the efficiency of it all.

However, it soon becomes clear from his long sigh that he's not as confident as I am in terms of career prospects. He lets out another sigh, and then another. "Tell me then, Bradley," he asks, "what is it exactly you want to do?"

"*Do*, sir?"

"Well, in terms of a job? In terms of a career?"

Maura Dooley smiled at the story. "And what did you say?" she asked.

"What did I say?" I offered her a resigned smile. "I didn't say anything."

"No?"

"It was a bogus question," I said. "He wasn't expecting an answer. He didn't *want* an answer. Not really. He was just going through the motions, that's all it was. A few months before I'm due to leave school they finally got around to asking the question. During a five minute interview he was asking me to make this snap decision about the next fifty years of my working life."

"Well, lad, any ideas?" the career's master prompted.

"I'm not really sure, sir."

"Well, how about working in a shop or a factory perhaps?"

And that was the crux of it: a shop or a factory. As such my answer was somewhat unsurprising. "I'm not really bothered, sir."

Of course, what I really wanted to say was that I want to be an astronaut or a shepherd. I wanted to be Marc Bolan or David Bowie. I wanted to be that bloke from Led Zeppelin with the long hair . . . *I am a golden god.* Failing that, I wouldn't have minded something along the lines of television criticism or bed testing – I was even prepared to combine those two. Instead I say nothing, other than not really being bothered.

"Tell me, lad," the career's master leaned forward in his chair, "have you ever considered plastics?"

"Plastics, sir?"

"Believe me, there's a big future in plastics."

Plastics? It certainly sounded familiar. *Plastics?* Wait a minute; it's that scene from *The Graduate.* This woodwork teacher thinks I'm Dustin Hoffman. This careers master, he thinks I'm Benjamin Braddock –

anti-hero – who, as the film title proclaims, is "A little worried about *his* future." Trouble is, I'm more concerned with my *own*.

"Well, what do you think, lad?"

"Mrs Robinson, you're trying to *seduce* me?"

"Seduce you, lad?" he demands an explanation, a curious look on his face.

I can see it now, an illicit rendezvous with Mrs Robinson in the bar of the Taft Hotel. We'll order drinks. I'll be a little nervous, and she'll be wearing that leopard-print coat of hers. Later, upstairs in the room, she'll unbutton my white shirt. She'll be wearing that zebra-print underwear set.

The next day I'll float in my parent's pool, and I'll tan beneath the southern Californian sunshine, happy to bask in the secret of the Robinson's affair . . .

"Seduce you, lad? What the devil are you talking about?"

"Mrs Robinson, *please* say you're trying to seduce me?"

"It's a factory in the Tower Bridge Road. They make plastic bags!"

"Plastic bags, sir?"

"Let's give them a ring, shall we, see if we can't get you fixed up?"

Maura laughs out loud and offers me a sympathetic look suggesting *you poor thing, you.*

"School was . . . well . . . school was school," I said with a shrug of defeated shoulders. "I couldn't say it was a pleasant experience . . . and from there I was sent to work in a plastic bag factory," I point off in the direction of Tower Bridge Road way off in the distance through her office window.

"Ah," is all she says.

"I think it was at work that I first started taking an interest in books . . . when I really started reading seriously."

"Have you read *The Great Gatsby*?" she asks.

"Yes," I said sheepishly.

"And what did you think of that?"

"Well . . ."

"Did you like it?"

"It was one of the most boring things I've ever read, if you want to know the truth."

"*Really?*" she looked crushed.

"How I managed to get to the end of it I'll never know." In forty-odd years it's my first contribution to the world of literary criticism.

I can tell she's disappointed. "You do realise, if you're accepted onto the course, that there's a long list of books you'll have to read?"

"Yeah, of course."

"These books, they're required reading."

"I understand that."

"And how do you think you'll cope?"

It's not as if I hadn't read a book before. I probably haven't read many of the same books *she's* read. But that doesn't mean I haven't read the odd classic. "I'm sure I'll be fine," I lie.

"Have you read any other classic works?" she prompts again.

"One or two, sure."

"And what was your favourite?"

"*The Catcher in the Rye*, I suppose. Although I'm sure everyone says that."

"And what was it you liked about *The Catcher in the Rye*?"

"I'm not sure . . . just the tone of it, I suppose. To be honest, I always thought Holden Caulfield would've benefited from a bloody good hiding, although, deep down, I think I identified with him . . . I've always liked anti-heroes . . . rebel without a cause, that was me . . . a rebel without a clue if I'm at all honest. Yeah, I liked Catcher in the Rye . . . not enough to kill John Lennon though."

"Any other books?"

"Oh, Dickens . . . *Oliver Twist* . . . *Hard Times* . . . my granddad once lived in *Little Dorrit's* house."

"Really?" she says surprised, although it's clear she thinks I'm pulling her leg.

"According to my mum, they lived in the house that Charles Dickens envisaged for Amy Dorrit."

"Really? She says again, although this time she appears to smile at the wonder of the notion.

"That's what my mum always claimed, although how true that is I have no idea."

"Were there any other books you liked?"

"I loved *Dracula*," I said, almost by way of final mitigation.

"And what was it you liked about Dracula?"

"Just the way the whole thing was laid out in that diary and letter form. I'd never seen it done like that before. It was really fantastic . . . Bram Stoker's description of the Count . . . him crawling down the castle walls . . . him bringing back that baby in the bag." It's the most animated I've been the entire interview. "Did you know he hid one of his coffins in Walworth Road?" I said, pointing off in the general direction. "I lived there for years."

Even with Dracula, I'm still not sure I've convinced her. In fact, I still wasn't sure whether or not I was wasting my time sitting there. Throughout the interview Maura had been really nice. No, that's not true. She'd been *more* than nice - really attentive, really interested. Even so I still had the feeling she was weighing up the risks involved in offering me a place on the course: no qualifications, no first degree, no literary background, hates *The Great Gatsby*.

"Can I ask?" I said, biting the bullet. "What are the chances of me being accepted?"

Maura laughed though "Oh, I was always going to offer you a place," she said.

"Oh, right," I admit, I was somewhat taken aback. I return the smile.

"I just wanted to make sure you knew what it was you were letting yourself in for, that's all?"

"I wouldn't let you down, if that's what you're thinking?"

"I'm sure you wouldn't," Maura reassures me. "I just worry about you working full time, studying, really, it's an awful lot of work."

I smile again. I've worked in a plastic bag factory. I've cleaned out water tanks on top of buildings to prevent Legionnaire's disease. I've crawled through air conditioning tunnels, scraping congealed ink from the walls. I've sold sandwiches out the back of a van. I've cleaned toilets. I've painted railings. I've operated a goods lift, where all I did was go up and down all day. I've been blacklisted. I've been threatened with arrest in support of the coal miners. I've been knocked down by a police horse, and attacked by riot police. I've been through a divorce and experienced the tragedy of the family court system. I've seriously contemplated suicide on more than one occasion, and suffered such bouts of depression that I've often had to rely on other people to confirm the days when I actually looked happy. *Creative writing.* How hard could that be?

The Brass Angel (novel extract)

Above the screaming sirens, Jimmy was suddenly aware of the cell phone ringing again - even from his prone position in the seat well, squeezed down in-between the front seat and the back - aware of Jack Nicholson bringing the phone to his ear with one hand, snapping the seat belt into place with the other.

'Hello?' Nicholson said calmly into the mouthpiece. 'Yes, I understand.' He checked his wristwatch again. 'Estimated time of transformation one minute and fifteen seconds.'

Closing the phone and placing it back in his pocket, Nicholson looked back through the rear window at the distant pack of police cars. 'James,' he said calmly, without panic, 'I need you to listen to me very carefully.

'Yes?'

'This car is about to crash.'

'*What*?'

'Now, you need not be alarmed.'

'What do you mean, *crash*?' Jimmy said alarmed.

'You must remain calm.'

'What?'

'James, I'm afraid our two friends here have already chosen their destiny.'

'What?'

'However, for you there is an alternative. There is a way out.'

'What are you talking about?' Jimmy demanded. 'What the hell's going on?'

'Upon my signal,' Nicholson continued, 'the passenger door will open.'

'What?'

'The passenger door will open and you will need to jump.'

'What?'

'You will need to jump,' he confirmed calmly, smiling down at Jimmy. 'You will need to make a leap.'

'What?'

'A leap of faith, so to speak,' he said, smiling down at him.

'Are you mad?' Jimmy said, trying to free himself from the seat well. 'I'm not jumping from a moving car.'

'James, rest assured, you will come to know harm, I guarantee you that.'

'I'm not doing it.' Jimmy proclaimed, clear terror in his voice now.

'I assure you, it will be painless,' he said, checking his watch again.

'*No*, I'm not doing it.'

'James your time is almost up,' Nicholson said. 'You must be ready.'

'Come on Ed, let's just call it a day, eh mate?' Oliver Hardy pleaded again from the driver's seat. 'Let's just pull over, give ourselves up?'

'No, just keep going,' his accomplice demanded. 'Just a little bit further we should reach the railway bridge. If we can get to the other side we can escape underneath it.'

'Almost time to make that leap I'm afraid James,' Nicholson said, suddenly grabbing Jimmy by the scruff of the neck. 'You must be ready.'

'No!' screamed Jimmy. 'I won't do it!'

The young doctor continued to press down rhythmically on the old man's chest. 'Come on Charles,' he said. 'Stay with us old son.'

'Come on Charlie,' demanded Sergeant Harrison. 'Don't go like this you old sod.'

'Charging doctor,' the nurse said handing him the paddles again.

'Okay everybody, stand back please,' the doctor said taking the paddles and placing them on Charlie's chest. 'Clear!'

Zap.

'There!' screamed Stan Laurel, pointing in front of him. 'The bridge, it's there up ahead.'

'Ed, we're not gonna' make it,' Stan Laurel said, resigned to his fate, suddenly thinking about *Thelma and Louise*.

'Just put your foot down.'

'Ed, hold my hand'

'What?'

'Hold my hand.'

'Fuck off, what're you talking about?'

'Not much further now James.' Jack Nicholson prompted.

'What?'

'Not much further, I'll tell you when.'

'Stupid fucking film,' Stan Laurel said to no one in particular, suddenly reaching across and squeezing Oliver Hardy's hand.

'Almost there,' Jack Nicholson coaxed.

'No, I won't do it.' Jimmy cried.

'Too late I'm afraid,' Jack Nicholson said.

Without another word he opened the rear passenger door and with, what Jimmy thought was surprisingly relative ease, lifted Jimmy from his prone position by his feet, and somehow manoeuvred him towards the open door.

The doctor looked in Sergeant Harrison's direction, barely making eye contact. 'I'm really sorry,' he said. 'Truly.'

'Please doctor; just one more time, just give him one more go?'

'It really is quite hopeless.'

'Please doctor,' Harrison stepped forward and gently grabbed the sleeve of the doctor's white coat. 'Do it for me, I'm begging you?'

The doctor looked down at the dead man lying in the bed, knowing that it was futile, yet equally knowing that it could do no harm to either the patient or this desperate man standing in front of him, this retired policeman, begging for one more chance – *Do it for me, I'm begging you.*

'Okay, charging again everyone,' the doctor said, resigned, exhausted by the effort of it all. 'Let's give it one more go shall we.'

'Thank you doctor,' Harrison said. 'Thank you.'

'Stand well clear everyone,' the doctor said, rubbing the paddles together and then placing them on the dead man's chest once again.

Zap.

For Jimmy time suddenly seemed to have stopped; the violent vacuuming wind calming to a mere breeze, the terrifying sight of the blurred road surface now appearing like clouds to him. In fact, the last thing he remembered was Jack Nicholson smiling down at him benevolently; just moments before he gave him an almighty shove, propelling him through the door, 'Take care James,' were the last words he heard.

Reaching the brow of the bridge the car suddenly swerved uncontrollably, mounting the pavement, hitting the bridge wall, violently flipping over onto its roof; Laurel and Hardy's last fine mess, their screams and the screeching of metal drowning out the police sirens.

For a few moments Jimmy felt as if the whole world had suddenly stopped, as silence, for the briefest seconds reined. But then just as quickly his ears - his brain – filled with noise, as his body, just as suddenly, collided with the tarmac - his body rolling over and over again. It was at that moment that he knew that his life was over, dead, no second dates, no meetings beneath big clocks, no brief encounters or Waterloo sunsets, dead, an end to it. As his propulsion continued unabated he was struck by the sudden realisation that he didn't have to try any more, knowing that his life had always been destined to end this way, in tragedy like some bloody circus routine, the high-wire act gone wrong, the smell of the grease paint the roar of the police siren.

It had been a gallant attempt, not even Sergeant Harrison would've denied that. Even so, in the silent calm of the room, even he had to admit defeat.

'Thank you, everyone,' the young doctor declared.

For the next few moments everyone stood around in silent reflection of the battle fought and lost.

'I'm sorry,' the doctor said, reaching out his hand to Sergeant Harrison.

'Thank you for trying,' Harrison appreciated the gesture. 'Thank you for that.'

'I'll give you a few minutes alone with your friend,' he said, motioning the old man lying dead on the table.

'Thanks, doctor.'

Just how far he'd travelled, how far he'd been propelled, he had no idea, far too preoccupied with those thoughts of death to notice - the sudden inevitability of death clouding any other thoughts. Besides, his brain was far to scrambled for any hope of logical thought – the effects of his body rolling and spinning over and over again, across the gravel and tarmac for the briefest of moments, yet seeming like, feeling like, an eternity. He remembered colliding with the kerb on the opposite side of the road, but could equally remember that he did not stop, or come to rest, or die. In fact, for some peculiar reason – a reason he simply could *not* reason – he suddenly found himself taking off again, up into the air, rising higher and higher, his body spinning over and over once again. This time though, instead of colliding with concrete or tarmac or brick, he'd simply fallen, until his body once again hit terra firma, only this time landing with a far softer thud – he'd landed in shrubbery, which didn't make much sense.

Dazed, he lay hypnotised by the reflective glimmer of blue flashing lights of the police cars, up above now, yet could no longer hear the sirens or the sickening scraping of metal upon brick. Instead, he was left with the feeling that a giant shell had been pressed to his ear, the sound of the sea echoing through his tangled brain, bringing weird comfort to the agonising pain he felt, pain that seemed to dissipate with the arrival of each new police car, until he felt a wave of tiredness, serenity almost, suddenly creep over him.

'James, you must resist the temptation to sleep,' a voice somewhere, somewhere close by, or in his head even, he was no longer sure - *James please, you must resist the temptation to sleep.* Was it in his head? Was he really being attended to? He certainly hoped so; that would mean that he was still alive, that there was still a chance. 'James, you have been in a road traffic accident.' Yes, a paramedic, he was sure of it now, certain of it.

'James,' the voice said again, closer now; down by his side, pulling the giant shell away from his ear, replacing the sound of the sea with his own, 'James, can you hear me?'

'Yes,' Jimmy gasped, desperate now to be saved, desperately wanting to be alive. 'Yes, I can hear you.'

'Good,' the voice said, 'James, we need to leave this place now.'

'Yes,' said Jimmy, 'I need to go to the hospital, I need to go in the ambulance.'

'James, listen to me?' the voice said again, 'There is no need for an ambulance.'

'What?'

'There is no need for hospitals.'

'What?'

'James, I'm afraid you're dead.'

'*What?*' he said, opening his eyes wide, suddenly aware of a man crouching in front of him; a youngish man, dressed all in black and wearing a bowler hat. 'Leaving the vehicle like that,' the man said. 'Your chances of survival were always going to be pretty slim.'

'What?'

'My colleague, the gentleman in the car, was forced to make a risk assessment.'

'What?'

'Calculating your chances of survival, had you remained in the vehicle," the man continued. 'The risk was too great I'm afraid. In fact, your only real hope of survival was to leave the vehicle in the manner in which you just left it.'

'What do you mean, *I'm dead*?'

'Yes, that was rather unfortunate, I must agree,' the man said embarrassed.

'Unfortunate?'

'James, I want you to drink this,' the man said, holding up, what appeared to be, a glass of milk.

'What?'

'Please James, I need you to sit up, and I need you to drink this.'

It took all of his effort for Jimmy to move, to raise his head from the ground, fearful that his neck was broken, knowing that one should not attempt moving in situations like this. Besides, the paramedics were meant to do that, it was their job, they were the ones that did the moving, *they* would be the ones doing the moving on your behalf. 'James?'

'No!' *They* were the ones that moved you. They certainly wouldn't ask you to sit up and drink; that wasn't how it was done; they had equipment, like on the television, equipment to secure the neck and back, and every other area of the body that they suspect is broken or damaged; he'd seen enough medical dramas to know all of these facts, to know that you *never* attempted moving anyone following a road traffic accident.

'James, I need you to sit up now,' the voice again, clearly not a doctor or a paramedic, clearly someone that had never seen a medical drama. 'I need you to sit up and drink this?'

Jimmy suddenly found himself annoyed by the request, this ridiculous demand; the persistence of the voice, demanding that he sit up and drink. The whole thing was ridiculous; a ridiculous dream probably, a dream, which, if he were to ever truly live again, he knew he had to wake from. 'No,' he said again.

'James, I need you to drink this,' the voice persisted. 'I need you to sit up, to *stand* up.'

'*No!*' he gasped the words again, blood filling his mouth, pouring out down his chin and onto his chest.

Tutorial – Stephen Knight

I've always been fascinated by their rooms - the tutors - the precious space where they hold their *Goodbye Mister Chips* type chats. Stephen Knight always looks busy, as though he's got a million and one things on his mind.

He reaches for the brown A4 envelope and removes the thin bundle of papers contained within: I recognise the typeface, the label, my own meticulous style of correspondence. This I sent him a week before – my first submission. For the next few minutes he leafs through the pages, giving the piece one last cursory glance.

Looking at him now, on his home turf, he looks every inch the mean and moody poetic image of his press photograph: the hair's not as dark as it obviously once was though. But then neither is mine.

According to the British Council's list of Contemporary Writers:

***Stephen Knight** was born in Swansea in 1960. He read English at Jesus College, Oxford, after which he studied at the Bristol Old Vic Theatre School to become a freelance director with a particular interest in new writing. He has worked extensively as a creative-writing tutor in schools, colleges, and for the University of Glamorgan and Goldsmiths College, University of*

London. In 1987 he received an Eric Gregory Award and in 1992 won first prize in the National Poetry Competition. He is the author of three main poetry collections: Flowering Limbs (1993), a Poetry Book Society Choice, shortlisted for the Mail on Sunday/John Llewellyn Rhys Prize and the T. S. Eliot Prize; and, for younger readers, Sardines and Other Poems (2004).

Stephen Knight has also published a novel, Mr Schnitzel (2000), which won the Arts Council of Wales Book of the Year in 2001. His fiction and poetry reviews appear in the Times Literary Supplement and the Independent on Sunday. He lives in London.

This is my first tutorial with Stephen, and I'm obviously eager to get the verdict on my novel. Even so, I'm still slightly nervous. When I'm nervous I tend to joke. Stephen Knight doesn't get my jokes.

"It's full of clichés," he says.

"What?"

"It reads like an airport novel."

"Ooh, thanks very much," I say, genuinely pleased with his description of it.

"That wasn't meant as a compliment."

"Oh."

"Anyone can write an airport novel," he says disdainfully, leaning forward in his seat.

"Yeah?"

"You should be striving for something . . . better . . . something more than . . . *this*," he holds up my submission.

"Like what?"

"Literature," he smiles. "You should be attempting to write a proper piece of literature."

"This isn't literature?"

"No. As a first effort, it's fine."

"Oh, right."

"However, you should be attempting to write a work of proper literature," he says. "You should be striving for that."

"Stephen, I live in the real world," I say. "Perhaps if I can write a best-seller, I'd have enough money to sit down and write a work of literature."

"Not with this," he holds up my submission.

"And why's that then?"

"Like I said, it's full of cliché. Most of it doesn't make any sense whatsoever."

"*Really*?" I'm genuinely surprised. "What bits are you talking about?"

"All of it," he says. "All of this stuff about Laurel and Hardy?"

"They were wearing masks," I say. "They'd just robbed a bank."

"Laurel and Hardy had just robbed a bank?"

"No, two men wearing Laurel and Hardy *masks* had just robbed a bank."

"I see," Stephen said, even though it was clear he *didn't*. "And Jack Nicholson, was he wearing a mask?"

"No."

"So it really was Jack Nicholson in the back of the car?"

"No," I say. "He just looked like Jack Nicholson."

"What?"

"Although, his name is *Jack*."

"Hang on," he says. His 'hang on' will become a common theme of our tutorials. Hang on means back up a little bit, which means I'll need to explain something to him – an aspect of the story or my motivation for revealing certain bits of information to the reader.

He brings his hands up to his head despairingly, flattening down his hair, his mind working overtime. I can tell from his reaction that I'm in for a rough ride: his tutorials, like his workshops, are delivered at breakneck speed - a two-hour summation of my work is delivered in one. "It's fine as a first draft," he says again.

"Thanks," I say, although I have neither the heart nor the energy to tell him that the piece has been written and re-written over and over again (ten times at least).

"However, you need to go away and re-write it."

"Okay," I say.

Upon his desk my original piece of, neatly-typed, prose lies like the victim of a serial killer. Thin red pen marks are splattered all over it. There are whole paragraphs crossed out and carelessly discarded. If he's attempting to make me become less precious about my work then he's failing miserably. In fact, I'm insulted if you want to know the truth. I mean, just who the hell does he think he is, this theatre director, this novelist; this award-winning poet?

The Party

Workshop Submission – Life Writing

Wednesday 25th December 1968

Christmas Night and the snow had been falling heavily over London for several hours. So much so that immediately after having set out that evening - navigating our way across the Ruby Triangle, round into Sandgate Street, and then on towards the Old Kent Road - we were already finding the walk heavy going.

That evening we were off to a family gathering at my Aunt Nora's flat, just off Lambeth Walk. Being a Christmas Day there was no public transport, and my dad didn't drive a car – not many people we knew drove cars in those days, let alone owned one – and so we were forced to walk the two miles or so from door to respective door.

Not that my dad seemed concerned at either the prospect of a long walk or the fact that we'd be forced to do so in the middle of an unexpected snow blizzard. "How are we getting there?" my brother, Lloyd, had asked as we busied ourselves with winter coats and scarves and hats and mittens.

"Shank's pony," my dad had replied, laughing, as he always did, which, in layman's terms, meant we we'd be walking.

At the time, I wasn't sure why my brother was making such a fuss: we *always* walked everywhere, so I'm not quite sure why today, even with it being Christmas Day, he should have thought it would be any different. By the time we reached the Old Kent Road though, with the four of us covered in snow, even I was beginning to have my doubts as to the merits of my dad's favourite mode of transport, a complaint echoed by my brother again. "It's freezing," he said.

"Stop moaning," my dad said, demanding this be an end to any further debate – we didn't usually have to be told more than once.

My mother meanwhile, who looked even colder than the rest of us, perhaps sensing an escalation of the mutiny in her midst, attempted a more conciliatory tone. "It won't take us long," she said cheerily. "Not if we walk quickly." Gently she grabbed my hand, and then my dad, following her lead, held a reconciliatory hand out towards my brother. "The sooner we get walking, the sooner we'll get there." This was a lie, of course - a snow white lie, perhaps, but a lie all the same. Even so, my brother and I, as part of the compromise, allowed the lie to stand, and we all set off again without any further complaint. Besides, *it's Christmas Night*, we both told ourselves. *We're going to a party*

As luck would have it though, the walk, which was rapidly turning into a 'trek,' was about to be cut much shorter than we first feared. Having walked only fifty yards or so along the Old Kent Road a London Black Taxi suddenly pulled along beside us, and the taxi driver, who'd obviously seen us struggling through the snow, rolled down his window and beckoned my dad over to the side of the road. My dad, being my dad, naturally assumed that the cabbie was going to ask him for directions, so he was a little taken aback when the chap demanded to know "Where are you going?"

"Sorry, mate?" my dad said, not sure that he'd heard correctly.

"Where are you going?" repeated the cabbie.

"No, it's alright, mate," my dad replied. "We're not going far." He obviously didn't want to tell him he'd got no money – certainly not money for black cabs, especially not on Christmas Night at double fair.

"Where are you *going*?" the cab driver, obviously reading my dad's mind, demanded again.

"Lambeth Walk," my dad said embarrassed.

"Get in," the cab driver said.

The journey was short, despite the snow enforcing a ten-mile an hour speed limit. There was certainly no traffic to speak of. Throughout the journey my dad chatted amiably to the cab driver, whilst my mother sat rigid in the back seat, worrying that we'd drip melting snow onto the floor of the cab.

At Lambeth Walk my dad reached into his pocket. "How much do I owe you, mate?" he asked.

"It's on the house," the cab driver smiled, giving him a little nod. My dad offered him a tip, but he just smiled again. "Merry Christmas," he said, before carefully pulling away from the kerbstone.

"What a nice man," my mother said (I thought she was going to cry). "That was such a nice thing to do."

"It's nice to know that there are still people around like that," my dad said in agreement.

"Wasn't that nice of the man?" my mother demanded of my brother and I.

"Yes, mum," we replied in unison.

And then it was my dad's turn. "I want you both to remember what that nice man did for us, okay?"

"Yes, dad," we said again: it was like a scene from Charles Dickens, only in a modern day setting – as modern as 1968 would allow.

"Off to a party?" the cab driver had asked of my dad during our careful progression along the Old Kent Road.

"Something like that," my dad had replied, although not really elaborating any further. Under normal circumstances it would indeed have been described as a party: in the years since it has certainly been described in such terms. Looking back now though, *party* seems a somewhat odd description, even if the mood at that particular festive moment had indeed appeared somewhat party-like. In fact, in terms of the day, Christmas Day – Christmas Night to all intents and purposes – one could perhaps be forgiven for thinking that particular description apt. In reality though, the party - we'll call it a party for argument's sake - was actually being held in memory of my Uncle Mike who'd died a few weeks previous: his slumped body had been discovered prone behind his front door. This had been locked, although one suspects that it not had been done so in prevention of him opening it in welcome of carol singers. The Christmas party then - this same Christmas party to which the Good Samaritan had offered us carriage - was actually being held in belated wake.

On arrival at Aunt Nora's flat, we found the crowded living room filled with boisterous greeting. All the men shook hands and slapped each other on the backs - my dad was telling everyone about the cab driver. All the women kissed each other – my mother was telling everyone, along similar lines to my dad, about the journey to the party and our Christmas Good Samaritan. All of the children chatted excitedly with each other – what we'd received for Christmas, what we were planning to do during the remainder of the school holidays.

Having made all the appropriate greetings, my mother ordered our coats removed, and then proceeded to give our hair a quick comb, and to lick her lace hanky and give our faces a quick wipe with it. After that we were made to go over and greet my Aunt Nora, widow of my not-so-long-departed Uncle Mike. She was sat in the corner of the room, waiting to greet each new arrival – Don Corleone style – a smouldering cigarette held between the fingers of her right hand, a glass of ale in her left; her hair tightly sculptured into a beehive, held together with hundreds of hairpins and enough spray to render a considerable sized hole in an ozone layer that no one was familiar with in 1968 – certainly not in Lambeth Walk. With each new guest she'd shed new tears over her recent sad fortune, which saw all the women proffering handkerchiefs in her direction, and the men offering to top up her glass.

"Let's get a look at you," Aunt Nora said, and with that my brother and I were ushered towards her, as if being granted audience with the Papal Father or some visiting head of state. For a few moments she inspected us, whilst my parents stood anxiously awaiting approval of our appearance.

The week before Christmas my parents had taken my brother and I to *Fred Harris'* in Lower Marsh, just along from the Old Vic Theatre. *Harris'* described itself as a 'young gentlemen's outfitter,' which, in layman's terms, meant it sold 'trendy' clothes at exorbitant prices: hipster trousers, wet-look shoes, Ben Sherman flower power shirts, and machine knitted tank tops – something George Best might wear or Michael Caine on a trip 'Up West.'

Standing before my Aunt Nora there was complete silence. She took a long drag of the cigarette, and then a sip of ale. "Oh, don't you look smart, the pair of you," she said. "Like little princes." This provoked new tears.

From my mother there was an audible sigh, even if the importance of the decree was completely lost on my brother and I. For my parents though, it was a matter of pride – if necessary they were prepared to walk us miles through the snow, yet no expense was spared when it came to our Christmas outfits. "Little princes," my Aunt Nora said again, although this only prompted further tears.

"Give your aunt a kiss," my mother commanded the pair of us, in order to show our gratitude for the compliment.

"Go on," my dad encouraged. "Give your aunt a big kiss."

Reluctantly we leant into Aunt Nora's open arms, our eyes closed, holding our breath against the onslaught of bright red lipstick, tobacco smoke and stale beer.

Escaping her clinches, we both quickly wiped the lipstick from our cheeks. Aunt Nora dabbed at her eyes with the handkerchief again, and then motioned my mother towards the bedroom next door. "Put the coats on the bed, Doreen," she said.

"Can I do it, mum?" I asked excitedly, grabbing back my coat, and my brothers, and waiting while my mother removed hers.

"Don't just throw them," my mother demanded, handing me her coat and shoving me off in the direction of the bedroom, in which stood a large double bed, covered by the mountain of coats already left there. Despite my mother's warning though, as soon as I saw the collection of coats piled high upon the bed, I simply threw our coats in the general direction, eager to get back to the main event in the living room, where the men were all preparing to leave.

"Don't bother taking your coat off, Jimmy," I heard one of my uncle's call out, "we're going over the pub." It had always been like this, the men going off to the pub, the women, other than my Aunt Nora, staying back at the flat.

Ten minutes later, with the men all gone, we were all charging around the living room, over-excited: the girls were dancing, the boys were all happily stamping their feet on those pieces of floorboard not covered by a large fake Persian rug. Between songs we all hid beneath the dining table, as the women, my mother and my aunts, laid out the spread of food: cheese sandwiches, ham, pickled onions, crisps. Everyone was giggling. My cousin, Gary was monopolising the record player: playing *Lilly the Pink,* by The Scaffold, over and over and over again. No sooner had the song begun to fade Gary would grab the arm on the record player and unceremoniously drop the needle back at the start of the record - the vinyl spinning, the needle crackling its way towards the label. Over and over it played, until the women could bare it no longer. "For gawd'sake, Gary, turn that bleedin' record off," my Aunt Vera demanded. "It's giving me a bleedin' headache." Naturally, this had us all in stitches, which suddenly made all the women laugh in turn, and which only served to make us laugh even louder. Truly, it was a magical time. All of the women were smiling – my mother, my aunts, my grandmother, my great aunts – everyone seemed so innocent.

An hour or so later the men started drifting back from the pub – all of them full of medicinal compound. Uncle Alf was the first one to arrive back, his pocket full of sweets – as if we needed any more sugar. Immediately, he started teaching us all the swear words, which had us laughing even more than before. In fact, as more of the men arrived back from the pub, the louder the laughter got, until everyone was laughing: the men folk, some already the worse for wear, the women - their mascara running down their cheeks. For us this was a time of wonder: we didn't know it at the time, but these were the best years of our lives.

"Gary, put that record on, *Lilly the Pink*," someone demanded.

"Nooooo . . ." Aunt Vera screamed, threatening to snap the 45 in half.

"What's the problem, Vera?" someone asked.

"We've only just convinced the little bugger to turn it off," she said, which had everyone laughing again, with all of the men making sport with Vera, in unison, breaking into drunken song, mimicking the record.

"Sing us a song, Alf," one of my aunts demanded, before the men could break into another chorus of *Lilly the Pink*. Immediately, my uncle broke into song, not really remembering the words, as if that mattered, but giving it sufficient enough gusto to encourage others to break into song also: my Uncle Tim, his daughters, my dad's cousins, Susan and Eileen.

By now everyone was laughing again. Everyone was yelling encouragement. Some of the women were dancing. All of the children were charging around, screeching with excitement.

If only the moment could have lasted forever. For most of the children present though, the party would end just as it was really getting going. In fact, as the night wore on, and as the party became more raucous, our young eyelids suddenly grew heavy, as we fought to stave of the inevitable sleep, until, one by one, like the Von Trapp Family children, we bid all the adults a fond farewell and goodnight. In turn the adults responded with cries of "Night, night, darlings," from all the aunts, and "Sleep tight," from all the uncles. One by one we headed off in the direction of Aunt Nora's bedroom, climbing up on her giant bed, and finding room beneath the mountain of coats that would keep us warm throughout the long, cold, Christmas night.

For the next thirty minutes or so we all chatted excitedly in the darkness. Every now and then we'd all burst into fits of giggles, safe and secure with the sounds emanating from the living room, where my grandfather Jim was about to take to the stage in the form of the fake Persian rug. Having witnessed numerous such renditions over the years, I'd always been struck by the manner in which he allowed the alcohol to disguise the fact that he *couldn't* actually sing – *carry a tune*, is how the family would have described it. Even so, it still doesn't prevent various cries of encouragement ringing out through the Christmas night.

"Tell 'em, Jim," my Uncle Tim cried, which had my grandfather taking further heart, singing, performing even; dancing, as if upon the stage of *The Sands*, Las Vegas, with a new-found gusto.

At the start of the evening he'd looked immaculate, as he always did: subtle check, brown three-piece suit, yellow shirt with enormous collars that a gust of wind could allow take off, cufflinks, a rich brown tie, a yellow handkerchief in his top pocket – in reality, a three-pointed cloth stuck to a piece of card. Like us, his shoes had been polished to a high shine – we've always known how to wear shoes in our family. As the night wore on though, as the party got into its stride, and generous levels of alcohol passed his lips, he became more dishevelled: his jacket had been removed, his waist-coat undone, his tie hanging at half-mast, the first few buttons of his shirt ripped open - at some stage he'd removed the cufflinks, which he'd given to my grand-mother to put in her handbag for safe keeping, along with his gold tie clip - and his shirts sleeves were rolled up in anticipation of some heavy lifting duty he might need to perform.

Just how long the police have been waiting for their cue to enter is anyone's guess. Indeed, just why they choose to come crashing through my Aunt Nora's front door just as my grandfather's none-too melodic Christmas party piece is reaching crescendo, surely only they will know. Whatever the reason for their timing though, it still amazes me, even to this day, how my grandfather, according to family folklore, still managed to carry on his performance, still managed to maintain that Tony Bennett cool, and yet still found time to throw one of those hay-making punches often seen delivered by John Wayne in *The Quiet Man*.

What followed, again, according to family folklore, was a mass brawl, with varying members of the

Metropolitan Police trading punches with varying members of the recently bereaved. In fact, the only one not involved in the melee was my Uncle Joe, who, having neither the stomach for the booze or my grandfather's off-key singing, and having long since passed out in the armchair, remains blissfully unaware of these incredibly chaotic events going on around him. And yet, it is Uncle Joe who will soon find himself the centre of everyone's attention. In fact, for one young copper, who appears straight out of Hendon and somewhat soaked behind the ears, the sight of my uncle, happily snoozing in the corner of the room, is obviously a sight for sore eyes – as is proved by the fact that he suddenly aims a shaking finger in his direction, before letting forth a cry to his commanding officer, something along the lines of, "There he is Guv; there's Biggsy!"

The 'Biggsy' to whom the policeman is referring to is *Ronnie* Biggs, the escaped Great Train Robber, although just why he's pointing in the direction of my Uncle Joe is not entirely clear. In fact, it only really makes sense when one considers the fact that Ronnie Biggs is indeed a Great Train Robber and that he had *indeed,* earlier that year, escaped from prison. What doesn't make sense however, is why such a declaration is being made in my Aunt Nora's living room, or just why that shaky finger accompanying the declaration, is being pointed in the direction of my sleeping uncle.

At first, no one is quite sure as to what the hell it is the young copper's pointing *at* or making identification *to.* Indeed, not even his colleagues, despite the fact that they're actually there in apprehension of the Great Train Robber, can comprehend the reason for his excited shouts and crazed gesticulation.

Sensing that everyone else is missing both the suspect and, much more important, the *point*, he suddenly attempts the old pantomime approach, with cries of, "Behind you," which finally stops everyone in their tracks, including my grandfather who isn't quite sure whether to plough on with another chorus, or simply throw another right-hander in the direction of the nearest policeman. "Over there, over there," again the policeman lets cry, again pointing in my Uncle Joe's direction. "In the armchair," this time leaving everyone in little doubt as who it is he's making identification to. "It's Biggsy!"

Naturally, this bold statement, especially when one considers that it's being made in connection with my Uncle Joe, gets a big laugh. In fact, it evokes such mass hysterics that the police officer in charge, so enraged by the wanton laughter, is forced to declare, in what has since been described as a BBC news reader's voice, "Any more of this laughing and you'll all find yourselves under arrest." This threat though, only serves to provoke even more laughter and ridicule, leaving the officer to further warn. "I mean it." In fact, good to his word, arrests promptly follow.

For some bizarre reason, my Aunt Mary is the first on the list, although not as a result of her baring any resemblance to the escaped fugitive, but rather by way of desperate attempts at protecting my Uncle Joe - at least according to the police - the *real* escaped fugitive. As far as the family can make out, the very fact that my Uncle Joe looks nothing like Ronnie Biggs no longer seems to be a deterrent to the police, who now seem convinced that he's undergone some kind of plastic surgery! In fact, so determined are they to get their man, whether the right man or not, that they suddenly attempt clamping him in irons and carting him off to the nearest police station with a blanket over his head.

As has often been the case though, especially in a family full of matriarchal figures it is Aunt Mary that actually manages to bring a hint of sanity to the proceedings. In fact, amidst the chaos and confusion of the fake Persian rug massacre, it is my Aunt Mary that lets forth her own rallying cry, even more significant than the one made earlier by the young policeman. "That's not Ronnie Biggs," she said dismissively, the pale ale giving her voice extra tenor. "That's my Joe, from Bermondsey."

It's only now that the commanding officers suddenly realises that they might be on somewhat shaky ground. "I'm sorry, madam, what did you just say?"

"I said, that's not Ronnie Biggs, that's my Joe, from *Bermondsey*," Aunt Mary declares proudly, giving my Uncle Joe - the still snoozing Uncle Joe it should be added - an affectionate little pat on the head. "He's my husband."

And it's only now, along with all charges, that the penny finally drops: the police, on mass, attempting a hasty retreat from the living room with cries of a "Merry Christmas" and a "Happy New Year" and "I'll get you next time, you bastard."

In their wake they leave my Aunt Nora crying her eyes out, whilst the rest of the women amass around the bedroom door in protection of the sleeping children within.

For the next few moments there is silence, interspersed with the occasional sob from Aunt Nora's direction, and the odd threat to the last few retreating policemen. Until suddenly my grandfather, newly replenished drink in hand, staggers toward the centre of the fake Persian rug once more, and declares in comedic tone, "Another song anyone?"

Again, there's massed hysterical laughter as the pressure valve is released and those gathered attempt making sense of exactly what it was that had just happened. It's also only now that my Uncle Joe, stirring from blissful Christmas slumber, opens his eyes and attempts taking in the decreasing scene of post-pandemonium taking place in the living room, suddenly declaring, in a similar voice to that of Professor Jimmy Edwards, "Hello, hello, hello. What the bleedin' 'ell's going on 'ere then?"

Writing Workshop with Francis Spufford

Student Submission – *The Party*

The classroom is sparse. As usual I'm the first to arrive. I'm excited today because a piece of my writing is to be work-shopped by the class.

A few minutes after ten o'clock, Francis Spufford arrives. This is his first year teaching at Goldsmiths. Immediately he struggles to take off this enormous jumper with holes in it, which he discards on the table, along with a battered briefcase and a packet of chocolate biscuits – "Tuck in, tuck in," he urges everyone.

Francis Spufford, (taken from the Faber and Faber website) a former Sunday Times Young Writer of the Year (1997), has edited two acclaimed literary anthologies and a collection of essays about the history of technology. His first book, I May Be Some Time, won the Writers' Guild Award for Best Non-Fiction Book of 1996, the Banff Mountain Book Prize and a Somerset Maugham Award. His second, The Child That Books Built, gave Neil Gaiman 'the peculiar feeling that there was now a book I didn't need to write'. His third, Backroom Boys, was called 'as nearly perfect as makes no difference' by the Daily Telegraph and was shortlisted for the Aventis Prize. In 2007 he was elected a Fellow of the Royal Society of Literature. He teaches writing at Goldsmiths College and lives near Cambridge.

Francis picks up his copy of *The Party* – all the other students have copies in front of them – and waves it in my direction. "And so, was it Ronnie Biggs?" he asked.

"No," I laughed – I'm sat down the end of the classroom

"But was Ronnie Biggs meant to be at the party?' I thought he was going to give me a nod and a wink – *go on, you can tell me.*

"No," I laughed again.

He looks confused. "But then why would the police turn up like that?"

"God knows," I said. To be honest, it's a question that's remained unanswered for more than forty years now. In fact, my dad even went to Kennington Police Station to demand answers, only they denied having any knowledge of the raid, or at least they'd claimed that it was nothing to do with them.

"They're still there," my dad had raged at the sergeant manning the front desk. "They're all standing around at the bottom of the flats. They've been there all night. The sergeant though, he'd just shrugged his shoulders in a manner that suggested there was nothing he could do.

"My dad said they were still waiting there when he returned to the flat, with the party having only just concluded – not even a police raid was enough to prevent the family drinking on through until dawn – with most of the partygoers, when they did eventually decide to call it a day, forced to walk past them as they set out on their respective journeys home."

"He must have had a theory though, about why the police did what they did?" Francis asked, obviously fascinated by the story.

"There were one or two theories. My dad's cousin, June, was actually married to Buster Edwards, who was another one of the Great Train Robbers, and who was also on the run. He owned an illegal drinking club not far from Lambeth Walk. That could have been a reason. The truth is though, most people in the family thought it was simply a neighbour complaining about the noise."

"A neighbour?"

"Sure."

"But why would they mention Ronnie Biggs?"

I laughed at that one. "What better way to get a noisy party stopped, but to phone the police and drop in the name of Britain's most wanted man?"

"Extraordinary," Francis exclaimed.

"All I know is that it's a pretty good story, whatever the reason behind it."

"I have one observation from reading your piece," Francis holds up the submission again. "It reads as if it's being delivered by someone standing in the saloon bar?"

"That's good, isn't it?" I say.

"Only if that was your intention."

"Well, that was my intention."

"Oh."

"It was meant to be one of those "Do you remember when?" stories," I offer by way of an explanation.

"Do you remember when?" Francis looks confused – it's obvious this won't be the first time.

"All the family stories seemed to begin with such a question. "Do you remember when?" That's how I remember that Biggs story so well. Every wedding, funeral, Christening I've ever been to that story has been retold, along with a million others."

"Family folklore?" Francis offers.

"Exactly. Family folklore."

"There was this big family trip to Brighton they all talk about, when my grandfather had a heart attack and my Uncle Mike nearly drowned," I laugh at the instilled memory of it.

As soon as they hit the beach my uncle stripped down to his vest and pants -apparently he'd been drinking throughout the journey down to the south coast –runs and dives headfirst into the sea. Well the story goes, he swam out a bit before succumbing to the lethal tidal force; almost drowning; needing to be plucked from beyond the spume and the waves beyond that.

Throughout the telling of the tale Mike's drinking was only really mentioned in passing or by way of adding to the humour of the story, which actually concerns the fact that he was so drunk that he nearly ended up drowning. This fact though, is merely mentioned as an aside. Of most amusement to everyone seems to be the fact that he was plucked, semiconscious from the sea, wearing only his underwear.

"He was gonna' swim the channel," someone said.

"About fifty yards out, he started waving," someone else said.

"We all waved back," chimed another.

"Only, he wasn't waving," someone else laughed. "He was drowning!"

When they finally managed to drag him back to the shore he was gasping for breath; his woollen underwear was sodden wet and had doubled in size. "My life, you could see all of his three-piece-suite," my uncle laughed.

"His three-piece-suite?" Francis asked.

"Yeah, you know, his tea and sugar?"

"Tea and sugar?"

"His nether regions."

"His private parts?"

"Exactly. His private parts," I laugh again. "My dad recalled another time – twenty minutes before his daughter's wedding. Everyone had left the flat, and were heading for the church, and Uncle Mike found himself alone with his daughter. This, one would think, was an opportunity for him to pass on a few words of wisdom; comment upon how lovely she looked; pull down the veil over her face and tell her she was the best daughter in the world. Instead, he picked up a bottle of brandy and drained it to its last.

"As the congregation sat waiting in anticipation of witnessing the happy union, the bride's brother was forced to return to the flat to collect his sister, before travelling back to the church in the wedding car and then, somewhat belatedly, giving her away at the altar in substitute for her father.

"Uncle Mike meanwhile lay unconscious on the living room carpet, his buttonhole still in place, the brandy bottle still gripped firmly in his hand."

The classroom looks stunned.

It is Francis Spufford that eventually breaks the uneasy silence that appears to have descended upon the room at the telling of this particular story. "There was something you wrote in your piece that I didn't quite understand?"

"Oh, yeah?"

Francis quickly scans through the first few pages, until he stumbles upon the paragraph to which he's confused. "You mention the fact that your uncle . . . your uncle Michael . . ."

"Uncle Mike, yes."

"This is the same Uncle Mike that nearly drowned? The same Uncle Mike you've just spoken about?"

"That's right."

"You said he was locked in?"

"That's right."

"In fact, to quote your piece, *"his slumped body had been discovered prone behind the front door. This had been locked, although one suspects that it not had been done so in prevention of him opening it in welcome of carol singers"*. Is that right?"

"Yes."

"He was locked in?"

"Yes."

"And who was it that locked him in?"

"Oh, the family."

"But why did they lock him in?"

"They were all going to the pub."

"And they didn't want uncle Mike going to the pub with them?"

"No, of course, not."

"And why was that?"

"No one's ever come right out and said it, but, I assume, because he was an alcoholic."

"I see," Francis says, although I'm not sure he does – not really. "So this Christmas party really was a family wake?"

"Yes," I smile. "Although, considering the nature of the man . . . a man's man . . . a man who liked the simple things in life . . . a man who liked his drink . . . perhaps *party* was an apt description after all? I mean, what better way then to celebrate his life, his death even, but with a great big family piss-up? All this on Christmas Night, as well - the festive season only really adding to the justification for mass family alcoholic bereavement. For those there, those not already put to bed as a result of tender age or lightweight drinking capacity, there was little in the way of eulogising, save for a raising of respective glasses; each family member in turn tipping a nod and wink in the direction of Uncle Mike's photographic image on the mantle."

"It's a great story," Francis smiles.

"Thanks," I say, "although, I was never really quite sure how to write it up . . . this stuff about Uncle Mike, this stuff about family secrets. It's clear to me, at least I suspect it to be the case, that uncle Mike had a drink problem, although I've never actually heard anyone confirm that fact. I mean, no one's ever come right out and said . . . you know . . . that he was an *alcoholic*. According to most family members he dropped down dead in the kitchen. No one ever mentions the fact that he was slumped behind the front door in a desperate attempt at escaping."

"You just have to be honest," Francis said.

"But what if it upsets people? What about his family?"

"That's always been the writer's dilemma, which stories to tell, which stories to 'gloss over;' which stories to leave untold." I think he could tell that I still wasn't confident with my telling of the story. "I think as long as you can handle the subject matter respectfully, and without malice; without having any axe to grind, you can pretty much write what you like. Besides, there's always humour in your writing."

"I hope so."

"Humour plays a big part in your writing; why'd you think that is?"

"It's just the way we are," I smiled.

"Even when you're writing about the more serious topics?"

"Absolutely," I leaned forward in the chair. "It's how we operate, my family, the working classes, I think, with humour."

"But much of what you write seems to concern death?"

"Where better to find humour?" I smiled again, although I'm not sure Francis could see the funny side. "Look, take my Uncle Alf, for example . . ."

When Alf died, his funeral (a cremation) had been a raucous affair, full of the black humour that typified the man. Towards the end of his life Alf was in a care home. He still had all his faculties, his mischievous nature, and his sense of humour, although he was minus his sight and both his legs (through diabetes). Even this though, provoked laughter amongst the family, with tales of him riding around the nursing home, his radio blaring, constantly bumping into furniture and other residents – the last time I saw him alive, at another funeral ironically, he arrived late, turning up at the wake claiming that he'd just come straight from a theatre in the West End, where he'd been auditioning for the part of Toulouse Lautrec in a forthcoming production of *Moulin Rouge*!

At the crematorium, as his coffin was carried down the aisle towards the altar, my Uncle Brian commented, "It's a bit long," in reference to its full size, which set the tone for the whole service. "In fact, it's a bit of an extravagance, if you ask me!"

I can tell Francis Spufford is horrified.

As with most funeral services these days, Uncle Alf's was a short, simple affair. The vicar, for his part, put on a good show, with a nice reading and kindly words, and as a parting shot we were all treated to Frank Sinatra singing *My Way* over the PA, prompting genuine tears amongst the congregation. Alf though, not surprisingly, and despite his daughter's reluctance, had saved the best for last. As the coffin made off on its way along the conveyor belt, slowly approaching the heavy red velvet curtains, the opening strains of the *Rawhide* theme tune suddenly filled the chapel.

For the briefest moment there was complete stunned silence, with most in the congregation unsure as to just how to react. A few moments later though, most were roaring with laughter, Alf going out with one last hysterical hoorah.

Of course, just what the next funeral party must have made of it is anyone's guess, especially when Alf's congregation came filing past them en route to the gardens of remembrance, what with people crying, literally, with laughter, everyone slapping each other on the back, wiping hysterical tears from their eyes, one or two even going as far as to declare it was the 'funniest thing they'd ever seen."

Francis, along with the rest of the class, looked aghast. "The theme from *Rawhide*?" he said.

"Yeah . . . you know . . . *Rolling, rolling, rolling . . .*"

It seems clear to me with the telling of these stories, the reactions they evoke - the reaction of Francis and my fellow students to my submission, that they don't really 'get me.' It certainly seems clear that they don't really understand my background or the family to which so many of these stories are attributed.

"What about your mother?" Francis asks. "Did she work?"

"She was a dinner lady in a school. She was a house-wife, obviously. And she spent most evenings threading elastic bands through large pieces of cardboard."

"Elastic bands?" Francis asks.

"It was those old pieces of board, which you found in chemists and shops on the high street, which had combs attached, or sceptic pencils in barber shops, or *Pacamacs* (fold-up plastic raincoats)," I offered, although I'm not sure if he or anyone else in the room understood what it was I was talking about. "Every Sunday evening a man would drop off hundreds of these boards, thousands, even, along with giant boxes of elastic bands. These my mother had to thread through little holes in the cardboard."

The classroom is silent. I'm not really sure any of them get the significance of the act.

"My mother's friend had nuts and bolts dropped off at her house, along with hundreds of five or six inch strips of copper wire. These were threaded around the nuts and bolts and then formed into a hook. Later, they would be hung on rails in preparation for dipping."

"And she was paid for doing this?"

"The nuts and bolts paid more than the cardboard and elastic bags routine, but my mother complained that the nuts and bolts ruined your nails and left dozens of tiny pin-pricks in the tips of your fingers."

"Was it hard work?" Francis asks, although I'm sure he already knows the answer.

"It was *work*," I said. "Sure, it was hard. It was monotonous, also. But then I don't suppose my mother, or her friend had very much choice in the matter. I remember Sunday evenings were always frantic, what with the man expected to collect all the threaded cards and drop off a new batch. If my mother ever got behind my brother and I, and my dad, would be pressganged into helping out, just in case my mother couldn't finish and she'd be paid short."

"And your father?" Francis asks. It's clear he's fascinated by the stories.

"He was a moonlighting typewriter mechanic, so he had his own problems."

"A moonlighting typewriter mechanic? That sounds very exciting."

"Believe me, it wasn't." I say, shaking my head at the naivety of everyone in the room. "His real job was in the 'ink,' which is a section of the printing industry. By day he worked for the Empire Printing Inks factory, which usually meant he went to work clean and then came home looking like a coalminer . . . only it was ink, not coal dust, that had made him so dirty."

"And what was his job?"

"Believe it or not, part of it required him being lowered into a giant ink tanker by rope, which was tied around his waist. Once inside, he washed out the insides with a mop and bucket, which was filled up with paraffin," I shake my head at the thought of it.

"Funnily enough, years later, I ended up doing the same job, only I was crawling through air-conditioning ducts, and scraping congealed ink from the walls with a giant wallpaper scraper."

"But why did you have to do this?" Francis asked.

"I don't know if you know this, but ink, once it starts to dry, congeals and becomes almost treacle like? It also becomes highly combustible, hence the reason for it needing to be cleaned and removed at regular intervals."

"And so where do the typewriters come into all of this?"

"That's what he did of an evening," I said. "My dad was a qualified typewriter mechanic, but he'd lost his job with the Stationery Office, and so he fixed and maintained typewriters on the side."

"Do you know what sort of typewriters?"

"*Imperials*, mostly."

Francis smiled. "I had an *Imperial* typewriter. They're great machines."

"Just like the cardboard and the elastic bands, another chap would drop off all these typewriters at our house, and my dad would sit up all night fixing them."

"And was he well paid for doing this?"

"I wouldn't have thought so. I'm sure the owners of the typewriters were paying a pretty penny, but I doubt that my dad was seeing much of that."

"So your parents did lots of different jobs?"

"It wasn't through choice."

"No, I suppose not."

"My mother also worked at the local biscuit factory making Christmas puddings."

"Christmas puddings," Francis lets out an excited gasp. "How wonderful."

"She stood on her feet all day, in soaring heat, wrapping thousands of Christmas puddings as if her life depended on it, which I suppose it did in a way."

For a few moments the room is silent again, although I'm not sure whether this is as a result of embarrassment or that they're all simply in awe of the story.

"Life sounded quite tough for your parents?" Francis offers up by way of observation.

"Of course it was tough. But they weren't downtrodden, if that's what you're thinking? None of the family were like that. They were all smart; all of the men dapper, and all of the women well presented. Everyone took pride in their appearance, and the appearance of their kids. We were South Londoner's. It's always been like that. All of their lives were hard . . . really hard, in some cases. But they weren't drudges. Even as a child, I can't remember seeing any scenes of drudgery, not like you see on those old black and white films and documentaries from the time.

"To be honest, it was all very socialist. Proper socialists, I mean. Not like here (in reference to Goldsmiths). Not any of this left-wing liberalism, or middle class socialism of the soul. We were all pretty rebellious, if you want to know the truth. We had it drummed into us from an early age. "No one's better than we are," my dad always said, even when I was tiny. "No one's better than us." Only he realised that sometimes, often, in actual fact, you had to fight for those things. "Always stand up for yourself," he'd always demand. "Never let anyone take the piss out of you.

"So, yes, life was tough. Those times I wrote about were really tough. But then I only know that now," I smile. "At the time I thought that life was wonderful. I mean; they seemed to make life wonderful, my parents and my grandparents, for my brother and I. We were poor, certainly, although no poorer than anyone else we knew. Even so, I had a fantastic childhood, I really did."

"That comes out in your writing," Francis motions the piece I submitted. "That childhood wonder."

"Those were wonderful times," I smile again.

"And this other stuff . . . your uncles . . . these funerals . . . have you written any of it down?"

"Some of it, yes."

"You need to write it *all* down," Francis said.

I nod, knowing he *means* it.

Reading List – Course Handbook 2007/2008

MA in Creative and Life Writing – Goldsmiths, University of London

Required Reading

Hermione Lee, *Body Parts: Essays on Life Writing*, Chatto & Windus

Richard Holmes, *Footsteps*, Flamingo

Henry James, *The Turn of the Screw/Daisy Miller*, Penguin Modern Classics

Blake Morrison, *And When Did You Last See Your Father?*, Granta

Jackie Kay, *The Adoption Papers*, Bloodaxe Books

Don Patterson, *101 Sonnets*, Faber

Graham Greene, *The End of the Affair*, Vintage

Seamus Heaney, *Finders Keepers*, Faber

Nicole Kraus, *The History of Love*, Penguin

Suggested Reading

Virginia Woolf, *A Writer's Diary*, Harcourt Paperbacks

Nadine Gordimer, *Writing and Being*, Harvard University Press

Julia Swindells, *The Uses of Autobiography*, Taylor and Francis
Toni Morrison, *Playing in the Dark*, Picador
WN Herbert and Matthew Hollis (eds), *Strong Words: Whiteness and the Literary Imagination*, Bloodaxe Books
Simon Armitage and Robert Crawford (eds), *The Penguin Book of Poetry from Britain and Ireland Since 1945*, Viking
Neil Astley (ed), *Staying Alive*, Bloodaxe Books
Richard Ford (ed), *The Granta Book of the American Short Story*, Granta
Alice Munro, *Selected Stories*, Vintage
Fuentes and Ortega (eds), *The Picador Book of Latin American Stories*, Picador
Joyce Carol Oates (ed), *The Oxford Book of Irish Short Stories*, Oxford
Zadie Smith (ed), *The Burned Children of America*, Hamish Hamilton

John Gardner, *The Art of Fiction*, Vintage Books
David Lodge, *The Art of Fiction*, Penguin
Peter Sansom, *Writing Poems*, Bloodaxe Books
Ruth Padel, *52 Ways of Looking at a Poem*, Vintage
Jeffrey Wainwright, *Poetry: the basics*, Routledge
Mark Strand and Eavan Boland, The Making of a Poem, Norton

Peter Ackroyd, *Chatterton*, Penguin/Avalon
Caryl Phillips, *A Distant Shore*, Vintage
Robert Lowell, *Life Studies*, Faber
Ted Hughes, *The Birthday Letters*, Faber
Carol Shields, *Stone Diaries*, 4th Estate
Andrea Levy, *Small Island*, Headline

John McGahern, *Memoir*, Faber

Eudora Welty, *One Writer's Beginnings*, Harvard University Press

Lorna Sage, *Bad Blood*, 4th Estate

Seamus Heaney, *Reading in the Dark*, Vintage

Isabelle Allende, *Paula*, Flamingo

Blake Morrison, *Things My Mother Never Told Me*, Granta

Paula Fox, *Borrowed Finery*, Flamingo

Hanif Kurishi, *Intimacy*, Faber

Francis Spufford, *The Child That Books Built*, Faber

Funeral One –
Joseph William Newman

Tutorial with Stephen Knight

Tuesday 12th February 1985

We'd all been surprised to discover him sat up in bed, his tiny frame almost lost as it sank into a mountain of recently plumped-up NHS pillows. At eighty-two Joseph Newman, my maternal grandfather, was by no means the eldest on the ward, although he certainly appeared to be the most popular.

According to the nurses he'd become a bit of a cause celebre on account of the manner in which he arrived at the hospital. "Excuse me doctor," he'd asked of the young casualty doctor tentatively listening to his rather erratic heartbeat, "do you think my car will be alright outside?"

"Your car?"

"Yes, doctor. It's parked just outside the entrance." My grandfather should have stopped driving years ago: he was always a bit of a nightmare driver at the best of times. These days he drove himself around town in this enormous estate car, perched up on a sofa cushion in order to see over the steering wheel.

"Surely, you didn't drive *yourself* here?" the doctor had asked, incredulous.

"Well, it was too far to walk, doctor, what with the chest pains and all." I think it was probably one of my grandfather's proudest moments. Retelling his story, with everyone gathered around his bed, it was clear he was in his element. We all laughed, of course, yet no one had the heart to tell him his that driving days were probably over now.

The pains in the chest to which he'd referred were actually as a result of the heart attack he'd suffered the previous day, although he was of an age, and from an era, which dictated that he hadn't liked to 'bother' anyone with the condition – hadn't liked to 'cause a fuss.'

Having rarely required the services of a hospital or doctors or any form of medical attention during his eighty-two years on the planet – a few cuts and bruises during the Blitz; a broken leg following a motorcycle accident in the late 1950s; a gash on his head following a car crash in 1980 – he'd not been quite sure of the protocol. In fact, as he sauntered into the casualty department at Guy's Hospital that morning he'd still not been quite sure as to whether he'd needed an appointment or not.

It was the receptionist that had spotted him first, walking through the automatic doors, despite his condition, looking like he'd not got a care in the world. "Can I help you?" she'd asked.

"Morning, miss," my grandfather said, raising his cap to her (he was from that generation), "I don't want to bother you, but I think I'm having a heart attack."

A few minutes later he'd been stripped down to nakedness and a hospital gown had been flung around his shoulders to protect his dignity. Doctors probed him. Nurses flittered around his bed. Questions were fired in his direction. "How old are you Joseph?"

"Eighty-two," he'd declared proudly.

"And just how long have you had the pains in your chest?"

"A couple of days now, thank you, doctor."

"A couple of days?"

"Give or take."

"Can I ask why did you not come to see us sooner?" the doctor asked.

"Oh, I didn't want to bother anyone."

"I see."

A nurse slipped an identification band around his wrist "Does anyone know you're here, Joseph?" she asked.

"I wouldn't have thought so," he smiled.

"Would you like us to call anyone for you?"

"That's very nice of you," he said. "If you'd be kind enough to pass me my trousers I'll give you 10p for the phone call."

"Are you having the pains now, Joseph?" the doctor interjected, bringing him back to the problem at hand.

"Not at this very moment, no," he reassured him.

"Well, I think we'll probably have to keep you in," the doctor informed him. "Keep an eye on you, just to be on the safe side."

It seems an odd thing to say now, of course, but throughout his telling of the tale - despite the heart attack that had prompted it - he'd looked as happy as he'd ever been. He smiled. He laughed. He told stories. He told silly little jokes. He passed around the Quality Street and the large bowl of fruit. "Take a banana," he said. "Take some grapes or an orange." Every time a nurse passed by he called for refreshments, "A nice cup of tea with six sugars, please, nurse," he said. "When you've got a minute. No rush." There was certainly no sign of a heart attack. Even so, he knew it *was* a heart attack, no matter how well his smile disguised it; he knew that his time was nearly up; *he* knew that the net was finally closing in.

Ironically, my grandfather had never really been one for visiting people. Even when he did he'd usually turn up unannounced – he was the complete opposite to my dad's parents, who visited anyone and everyone: "The hospital visitors," my dad called the pair of them. My grandfather Joe though, would usually turn up once in a blue moon. "I'm not staying," he'd declare, keeping his coat on as if in conformation of this fact, although his flat cap would be removed from his shiny, bald head, folded in half, and stuffed into his coat pocket like some gunslinger holstering his gun. "I'll have a nice up of tea though," he'd smile, taking root in the armchair.

Three hours later, having drunk an Empire's worth of tea harvest, he'd still be there, his coat still on; still talking: filling us in on the things he'd seen, the people he'd met on his travels around London: he loved London, and had never really hankered for anywhere else – he thought the Isle of White was 'abroad.' In many ways, despite the rarity of his visits, he was the perfect visitor: engaging, comical; requiring little in the way of enter-taining, save for a permanently boiling kettle, a full box of tea bags, a large bag of sugar, and an extra pint of milk. But then, just as quickly as he'd arrived, he'd be off again - off to we-knew-not-where. "Back to his other family," my dad always said: *he* had a theory that my grandfather had another family hidden away some-where, and that he divided his time equally between the two of us: he was certainly never home.

It was clear that Stephen Knight was fascinated by the story. "Is that true?" he'd asked during a tutorial to discuss this particular piece. "Did he lead a double life?"

"Who knows?" I gave a shrug of the shoulders. "Everyone always half-joked that he did."

"Which means they could have been half-serious?"

"I suppose."

"What do think?"

"Probably not." I can tell Stephen's disappointed. "I think he just couldn't sit still, that's all. I think he always needed to be doing something; he was always working; always turning a coin somewhere. I can remember, whenever we'd visit, he'd always offer to give us a lift home. Not because it was the right thing to do, but because he just loved being out; he just loved driving the car." I couldn't help but laugh. "My dad always refused. I think he was scared on account of the fact that my grandfather was a terrible driver." Stephen laughed with me. "He was worse before he had the car, and we had to rely on his motorbike and sidecar combination. You should have seen the state of us, all piling in and on this contraption . . . my mum and my brother and I . . . the weekly shopping in bags all crammed into the sidecar, my grandfather, on the motor-bike, wearing his crash helmet, despatch rider gloves, goggles, gripping on to the handlebars, my dad, the reluctant pillion, gripping on to my grandfather"

Stephen laughed again. "Have you written any of this down?"

"Bits and pieces," I reply, the germ of an idea already formulating. "Years ago, I'm not even sure I was born at the time, my parents, and my elder brother, were holidaying down the coast somewhere . . . I think it was in a caravan . . . anyway, my grandfather had driven them down in the motorbike and sidecar. On arrival he'd driven off again with my dad to get the weekly provisions. Only they didn't come back.

"My mother, back at the caravan, was none the wiser . . . there were no mobile telephones in those days . . . although as time went on she became more anxious. In fact, it wasn't until much later in the day that she discovered that the pair of them had driven off the road and landed upside down in a ditch: she later found out that my dad, who was fortunately not too badly injured had been forced to pull the motorbike off my grandfather, who was face down in muddy water. "I thought he was dead," my dad later said. I remember him shaking his head at the memory of it. He said that my grandfather had a big gash on his forehead and was unconscious. He'd also broken his leg, which they didn't know about at the time."

Throughout the telling of this particular story Stephen Knight sat listening intently, a mild look of astonishment on his face. "He sounds like a bit of a character, your grandfather?"

"Oh, he was certainly that," I laughed.

"A bit of a wanderer, too, by all accounts?"

"Yeah," I smiled. "But then he always came back, eventually. He was like some racing pigeon, always turning back up in the coop."

"It would have made a great story, though, him leading a double life?"

"I suppose so."

"And where was your grandmother in all of this?" Stephen asked. "Was she still alive then?"

"Oh, she was usually sat at home, with the television and the dog and the lovebirds and her knitting."

The truth was, she was oblivious to his whereabouts, "Who knows where he goes or what he gets up to," she would often say in a high-pitched voice that appeared similar in tone to a silent dog whistle – at least as far as we could tell from the look on the dog's face. The poor dog would lay cowering beneath my grandfather's armchair like Quasimodo tortured by the bells. Only it was the volume of the television, which was usually turned up to an ear-shattering high, that it was seeking sanctuary from. In fact, it was so loud that whenever we turned up for a visit we'd always demand a cup of tea, which would see my grandmother, eager to please, shuffle off down the passage to perform a routine of lighted match to North Sea Gas and the reuniting of a whistling kettle to the stove. This demand for tea though, was just a rouse, a distraction; an attempt at luring my grandmother from the armchair and out of the living room so that we could make a dramatic anticlockwise turn of the television knob.

Over the years my grandmother had become almost completely deaf, although she appeared to be the only one in the family not actually aware of that fact – my dad though, always claimed that she had selective deafness. "She hears when she wants to," he always said.

Whenever my grandfather returned to the house, he never seemed quite sure what all of the fuss was about, although he'd usually declare, "That telly's a bit loud, Beat (her name was Beatrice, but everyone called her 'Beat')." Even so, he'd never make any attempt at turning it down. He'd also offer up no explanation as to whereabouts the last sixteen, eighteen, twenty hours, which, in turn, never seemed to bother my grandmother. In many ways they shared a simple routine, even if their own respective routines seemed to be at odds with the routine of the 'house.' For instance, each day at six o'clock my grandmother would serve up a dinner for my grandfather, regardless of whether he was there to eat it or not. "He knows what time I serve it up," she always said, as if this were justification for her maintaining of the routine – most evenings my grandfather would find the dinner sat on the stove – dished up on an earthenware plate, balanced upon a boiling pan long since void of any water. Most nights the dinner was rock hard. "The peas are a little overcooked," he would say, without the slightest hint of irony.

"They were soft when I served them," my grandmother would retort.

"They sound like the odd couple," Stephen Knight said.

"Oh, they were certainly that," I laughed affectionately. "To say there relationship was strange would be an understatement."

Their house, too, was strange: a four-storey Victorian affair, which, by the 1960s, had seen much better days. In years gone by it had obviously been the home of someone wealthy or, in my grandfather's words, "well-to-do." In the basement - it was here that my grandparents spent the majority of their time - there had once been servant's quarters: there was still evidence of a collection of chords and bells that summoned those from 'below stairs.'

On Summer days I would spend hours charging back and forth through my grandparent's house – in through the garden door, navigating my way through the kitchen scullery, down the passage and up the stairs leading to the first floor, through the front and rear parlours, out through the French doors and then down an old wrought iron staircase which led to the garden. Hours were wiled away in this manner: my grandmother always allowed me complete access to the house; the nooks and crannies; the wardrobes and cupboards filled with treasure: a banjo, a drum, a gasmask, an old tin army hat, my grandfather's ARP Warden's helmet. These I used as props, especially during war games when the wrought iron staircase became the German headquarters, a cavalry fort – General Custer's last stand – a castle, a boat, the hill at Little Big Horn - charging up and down the garden shaping my fist and thumb into a bugle – da da da da da da da da da da da da da!

Above me in the second floor window there would usually be a rustling of net curtain. Behind them would be sat my Aunt Nell, always sat on the same chair as if on sentry duty. She was my great grandmother's 'lady companion.' They lived in the house also. Aunt Nell though, was not our real aunt, but rather a neighbour from years ago. Like my great grandmother, she'd lost her husband during the Great War. Later though, during the Second World War, when Nell's house was bombed, my great grandmother had demanded my grandfather "Go and fetch her," and she'd remained with the family ever since.

At the time, I never thought it anything out of the ordinary – these two women, these women without men - sharing the second floor of the house. I never thought it strange that they shared the same large double bed. In fact, as far as I was concerned, they simply shared a bed the same way *Morecombe and Wise* shared a bed on the television.

On the first floor of the house stood two double rooms - separated by wooden concertina doors - which usually remained completely void of life, although it was tastefully furnished, in that parlour-type manner, in preparation for the rare occasion it was used to entertain pre or post wedding guests or mourners to a family funeral. At one end of the room there was a three-piece suite, a bookcase full of books that no one had ever read, and a large glass cabinet with *Babycham* glasses and family heirlooms: china statues and the like; the sort of stuff you'd end up disappointed with the value of should you ever be foolish enough to present them to an expert on the *Antiques Roadshow*. In the other room there were a further two bookcases with similar amounts of unread books, a collection of family photographs in frames, and an upright piano: each Saturday night my grandfather, always the entrepreneur, rented this to the local pub. Other than that it stood idle: my grandmother played by ear, despite the deafness, although she was rarely witnessed. Occasionally, I would hear her play: on the rare occasions she entered the room to give it a cursory once-over with the duster. As soon as I'd hear the opening strains - Bach or Chopin or a medley of Mrs Mills' *Frothy Pub Songs* – I'd creep upstairs and sit myself down on the top step, never quite sure if she was really playing or whether she'd simply turned on the gramophone. Every now and then though, the piano would fall silent. "Is that you, Neil?" my grandmother would call out demanding to know. For a few moments

I'd hold my breath, shuffling down a couple of steps, trying not to make a sound. "*Neil*?" And then a few moments later, satisfied that no one was listening, the playing would start again, and I'd shuffle back up the stairs again, resting my head on the banister, listening as my grandmother performed a rousing rendition of *Ode to Joy* or *Pennies from Heaven*. At the songs finale my grandmother would pull down the lid and give it a final flick of the duster. This would be my cue to dash back downstairs undetected.

At one end of the parlour there was a large bay window overlooking the road, which was always disguised by heavy net curtains and large wooden shutters. At the other end of the room stood the set of French doors, which, on summer days would be flung open allowing the house a rare airing: even now I can envisage how the merest hint of the sun's rays would produce rainbow clouds of dust particles, which you could almost sweep a hand through: according to my dad, my grandmother "Never bothered with the housework, save for an occasional waltz back and forth with the carpet-sweeper." By contrast, for the last thirty years or so she'd been the 'woman that does' for the Chairman of the Shell Oil Company: four o'clock each morning she'd walk from her home at the Borough to The Strand, before going at the boardroom table and the Chairman's desk with a dry cloth and the beeswax. "Never mind cleaning for the head of Shell," my dad would laugh, "you could write your name in the dust on that sideboard."

The sideboard to which my dad referred had once been the protagonist for domestic strife between my grandparents: my grandmother had seen it in the showroom window of a shop at Waterloo, and had demanded my grandfather purchase it for the house. At the time, it had been a really expensive piece of furniture, and my grandfather, always a careful man - *careful* rather than mean – had been reluctant to make such an outlay. My grandmother though, had persisted. "We can get it on the never-never," she had suggested.

My grandfather naturally, was aghast at the idea: according to him "I'm more concerned with putting food on the table, never mind buying luxury items of furniture we don't need."

"But we can get it over fifty-two weeks" she countered. "I'll even pay for it myself, if I have to."

"Beat . . ." he said sternly, hoping this would be an end to the matter, "you can't *eat* a sideboard:" over the years this became a saying used whenever anyone in the family was contemplating buying stuff on credit.

For the next few months my grandmother brooded over the sideboard, often making mention of his unwillingness to buy it for her, until one day it suddenly appeared – it turns out my granddad had found a few months extra work and had purchased it cash: my grandmother never asked for anything else after that.

As a child the sideboard always held such wonder for me, with its two large cupboards and its six drawers either side. These would be filled to the brim with treasure: a velvet type glasses case which contained half a dozen glass eyes (my great grandmother's - she was blind in one eye), batteries, pens, paper, Shell desk diaries, transistor radios, torches, playing cards, dominoes, a cribbage set, a very old bicycle lamp. The latter was used for navigating your way to the outside loo. On winter nights I'd be terrified to pay a visit: it was always pitch black and freezing; there were spider's webs in all four corners, spiders the size of my tiny fist, and the moon would always cast weird shadows through the four-inch gap beneath the door. "I don't want to go out there," I'd plead.

My grandfather though, wouldn't hear of it. "Just put the radio on," he'd say, handing me the bicycle lamp and giving me a gentle shove up the garden path, "You'll have a bit of company then," he'd laugh.

Inside the toilet, alongside a toilet roll on a piece of string or the occasional cut-up-square's of last week's newspaper, there was a transistor radio hanging on a hook – for some strange reason my grandfather had transistor radios strategically placed in every room in the house. Whenever I slept over I'd see him get into bed in his long-john's and his thermal undergarment, and I'd spy him reaching for the transistor and firing up the dial. "There's a po under the bed if you need it," he'd say, before returning his attentions to the static-filled airwaves, frantically searching for signs of nocturnal life or Malcolm Muggeridge, who, as he was always telling me, was "a most interesting man."

"Malcolm Muggeridge?" Stephen Knight.

"Yeah, my grandfather had a lot of respect for Malcolm Muggeridge."

"And why was that?"

"I have no idea. Initially, I suppose, they had that same left-leaning when it came to politics, although my grandfather was not particularly religious, and certainly not religious in the way Muggeridge became in later life. Besides, my grandfather died long before I had any interest in writing, and so the subject of his fascination was never really broached."

"It seems a strange thing to mention," Stephen said.

It was sometime during the 1960s, probably during the summer of 1969, when my mother was pregnant with my brother, and I'd spent a lot of the summer holidays holed up at my grandparent's house.

On this particular day, my grandfather had driven me out to the country to pick blackberries – hundreds of the things, which my mother and grandmother would bake into blackberry and apple pies. On the way back to my grandparent's house, we stopped to fill up at a petrol station just around the corner from where he lived.

As soon as my grandfather was out of the car I'd always scoot across from the passenger seat into the driver's seat, and pretend to drive. Suddenly through the rearview mirror I caught a glimpse of my grandfather engaged in conversation with another man of similar years to himself. At the time I really wasn't taking too much notice: I was playing cops and robbers.

I got the car up into second gear.

The conversation between the two men continued.

I got the car up into third.

The conversation continued.

I was in fourth gear now, bearing down on the car in front of me.

Still the conversation continued.

I fired my cowboy gun out of the window.

Just then the driver's door was yanked open, and my grandfather gave me a gentle shove over towards the passenger seat once more, and then got into the driver's seat and engaged his key with the ignition. Before he put the car into first gear, he rolled down the window and the man who he'd been talking to approached the car and shook my grandfather's hand. He wished my grandfather a good day, and then lent down, smiled, and then gave me a little wave. I smiled and waved back.

It was only as we pulled up outside my grandparent's house that my grandfather gave me a little wink. "Malcolm Muggeridge," he declared proudly. I was already out of the car though, charging down the stairs that led to the basement entrance. "A most interesting man," he said to no one in particular.

Stephen Knight sat back in his chair, putting his hand behind his head, mulling over the story. "It really was him then?"

"My grandfather said it was, yes," I said.

"You believed him then?"

"What's not to believe?" I laughed. "Besides, years later I saw that same man on the television . . . he was debating the sacrilegious nature of *The Life of Brian* with John Cleese and Michael Palin."

"I remember that," Stephen laughed.

"It was the same man from the petrol station; that same man my grandfather had been talking to. Besides, whenever he came on the television, or his picture appeared in a magazine or in the newspapers, my grandfather would always point him out to me. "Malcolm Muggeridge, remember?" he'd always say.

"I'm still not sure why you used the encounter with Muggeridge in this particular piece, though?"

"I'm not sure, although I think it had something to do with *The Dead*."

"*The Dead*?"

"Yeah, James Joyce, from the reading list."

"I'm not sure I follow."

"Well, in *The Dead*, most of it concerns the Christmas party at the home of the Morkan sisters . . . Joyce has you believe that the main crux of the story is about this.

"Only, it's not about the party at all. In fact, the party is merely a prompt; a device Joyce uses, a preparatory scene, an elaborate plan to ensnare the reader – before his true intentions for *The Dead* can at last begin to be revealed. In fact, it's only later that we discover it's actually a trap.

"Throughout the text Joyce offers up tiny misleading clues: Gabriel's frosty encounter with the maid, Lily, or his exchange of words with Miss Ivors; the Morkan's trepidation over the arrival of Freddie Malins."

"I'm still not sure what that's got to do with you mentioning Malcolm Muggeridge in your piece?" Stephen says, still somewhat confused.

"For me, Malcolm Muggeridge is the prompt." I say, although I'm not sure that I'm making a clear enough explanation – I'm not quite sure whether this was really my intention when I was writing the piece or if this is something I've just realised during the tutorial. "In *The Dead*, Joyce used the story of the party as a ruse. In reality though, the story is actually about the death, many years previous, of a young man, Michael Furey, who, is not actually mentioned until the last page.

"For me, Muggeridge is the party, the young man that dies, my grandfather."

"I always thought *The Dead* to be somewhat doom-laden?" Stephen said. "The piece you've written, although it concerns the death of your grandfather, is certainly not that."

"No, but it's certainly melancholic, which was what I was really looking for'" I said. "That part in *The Dead* when Gabriel is standing in the hallway, and we can hear the singing from the room above. As a child I couldn't help but be mesmerised by the manner with which my grandmother played the piano, in that empty room, whenever she suspected she was alone . . . songs of melancholy and lament."

"The other's you've written about in your piece: your grandmother, your great grandmother, your aunt?" Stephen asked, although it was clear he already knew the answer.

"All gone now: my great grandmother, she died when I was just a young boy. She was a lovely old girl, despite the rather scary glass eye. My aunt that never was, Aunt Nell, she ended up in a mental asylum following my great grandmother's death – marching up and down the corridors, not knowing what day of the week it was. My grandmother too, she died about seven years after my grandfather. Ironically, in the months leading up to his heart attack *she'd* been the one that had been ill. Once again, we'd all gathered around her bed, although she was at home at the time. I always remember in the middle of all the hand-wringing and the worrying on the part of my mum and her sister, my granddad came into the room, switched off the light and shined the magic lantern on my grandmother's pillow (this was an early version of a slide show projector). For the next thirty minutes we all sat laughing in hysterics as my grandfather shined images of the Seven Wonders of the World on the ceiling, the walls, on the bedspread, on my grandmother's face!"

"What?" Stephen asked, amazed.

"I told you they were weird," I laughed. "Even so, despite all I've said, all the things I've written about them, they were really actually quite devoted to each other. I don't know; maybe they were like most couples from that era, staying together through thick and thin?"

"Yes, perhaps that was it."

"That evening at the hospital, when the final visitor's bell rang, my grandfather made a real fuss of us all: kissing every one of us goodbye, sharing a last joke, hugging us all, messing up our hair. "I'll see you all tomorrow," he called after us, waving us all to the door. He was very convincing.

"My mother and her sister though, they lingered a little longer at his bedside: long enough for him to give them brief instructions. "Look after your mother," he told them. "Look after yourselves. Look in the downstairs cupboard, behind all the old newspapers." The next day they found a stack of old biscuit tins; each of them full to the brim with banknotes: fives, tens, twenties, and *fifties*. He never trusted banks. He never had a post office savings account. "There's enough money there to ensure that your mum has a comfortable life," he told the pair of them.

"You know I have to ask?"

"Oh, I don't know . . . forty thousand, fifty thousand, it could have been more. However much it was, it was a lot of money at the time."

"I'm sure."

"My grandmother never had to worry about money again, I know that much."

For the last few minutes of the tutorial the pair of us sat in silence, conscious of the next student waiting outside the door, Stephen re-reading a couple of paragraphs in my piece, perhaps looking for further clues as to my grandfather, Malcolm Muggeridge, *me*.

"Thanks, Stephen," I said, getting up out of the chair and gathering all my belongings together: my leather bag, my original copy of the tutorial piece, my large writing pad, my scarf.

Stephen smiled. "I always said you'd be much more comfortable as a life writer?" he said, as if to confirm to me what *he'd* suspected all along.

"Stephen, much of what I write is about the dead . . . life writing, fiction, it doesn't really make a lot of difference to me."

"And why do you think that is?"

"I'm not sure, but I think I've always been more comfortable amongst the dead."

Stephen smiled again. "See you next week," I said heading for the door.

My grandfather died in the early hours of the next morning (Wednesday 13th February 1985). No one from the family was at his bedside: one of the nurses was kind enough to remain behind at the end of her shift in order to explain how she had noticed him raise his head from the pillow, how he'd let out a tiny gasp, and how then he'd fallen back into permanent sleep.

"I'm sure he didn't suffer," she had told my mother and my aunt.

The next morning the rest of us returned to the hospital, where we found the pair of them waiting at the hospital entrance: they'd just been back to thank the nurses on the ward for looking after my grandfather during his all too brief stay.

Earlier that morning they'd spent thirty minutes sat with the lifeless body of their father in the hospital mortuary.

Just then my dad turned up, and then my brother, and my uncle: I remember how everybody hugged each other, and we all said how sad it was. I also remember my aunt holding a large carrier bag, with PROPERTY OF GUYS' HOSPITAL printed on it, and how it took me a few minutes to realise that it contained my grandfather's belongings: his jacket and trousers, his well-worn shoes, his flat cap. *A whole life in that bag*, I thought.

On the way back to the multi-storey car park we bumped into the Irish comedian, Dave Allen. We all stood aside to let him pass, and he smiled and told us "Thanks." I always thought he would have liked this story: *The Dead*, Malcolm Muggeridge, my grandfather, *his life*; driving himself to the hospital with a heart attack, and then his belongings driven home again in a carrier bag marked property of Guy's Hospital.

This University 'Lark'

Every Wednesday evening, since I've been doing the degree, I sit in my dad's front room and deliver a report - the books I'm reading, the piece I'm working on, my latest tutorial or workshop. It seems odd talking about this sort of stuff with him. Before this we used to talk about work, football, politics, industrial relations, the state of the country, the state of my garden. We'd talk a lot about the family – it was always my favourite topic of conversation. We still talk about these things. But now we talk about 'Creative and Life Writing' also.

"They get you to read books," I tell him.

"Hold on," he interrupts me. He doesn't want me to say anything just yet: he needs to get himself comfortable. He disappears into the kitchen and returns with two teas.

"Okay, so they get you to read books?"

"Yeah, loads of books," I tell him. "There's a recommended reading list sixty books long."

"What sort of books?"

"I don't know, *books*. Classic books, proper literature, short stories, fiction, non-fiction, poetry, all sorts of stuff."

"I'm not sure I've ever really understood poetry," he says, honestly.

"Me neither."

"Okay, so what happens then? What happens once you've read all these books?"

"I'm not sure. I think I'm meant to deconstruct them."

"What, tear them up?" he laughs.

"If only," I laugh back. "No, I think I'm meant to break them down, work out how they've been written, the style, the content, the narrative, dialogue, that sort of thing."

"And why's that then?"

"I don't know. I think it's supposed to make me a better writer."

"And *has* it?"

Funeral Two – James Bradley

Sunday 23rd November 1997

There is no bell, so I'm forced to rattle the letterbox - not too loud just in case someone hears. "They wouldn't have gone out," I say, more statement than question, to which Sharon shrugs - part reply, part confirmation. The reason I know they wouldn't have gone out is that the last time they *did* the pair of them managed to get lost - perhaps my grandmother's Alzheimer's was finally starting to rub off on my granddad.

"They should have been wearing a sign," my dad had said at the time. "If found please return to . . ."

"They should have dropped pebbles," I'd replied. "They should've attached a piece of string to the door handle, unravelling it as they went, and then winding it back up again in aid of their return." We'd all laughed, even though the laughter really only served to mask the apprehension we felt at them losing themselves again on further ventures out - for three hours they'd walked up and down the local parade of shops, took a short bus ride, did a bit of shopping, before turning one corner too many. In the end they were forced to give themselves up to the law, walking into the local police station and declaring, "It's a fair cop, guv. We'll both come quietly."

I knock again, gently, although the long foreboding corridor prompts an echo loud enough to wake the dead. Still there's no sign of life from within. I raise the letterbox and peek through. The tiny passage still looks unfamiliar to me, although there is the faintest of smells – childhood, cooking, cabbage soup, Mr Sheen and vacuum clean - they'd only been living there for three months or so.

"They wouldn't have gone out, would they?" I say again.

"I wouldn't have thought so," Sharon confirms.

I knock again, reluctant to leave, reluctant to accept 'no answer' for an answer, reluctant to accept a wasted journey. I knock again, as if further knocking will make a blind bit of difference, as if it will suddenly prompt a shuffling of slippered feet on the new carpet.

It was different with their other flat – you rang the bell - they had an intercom then, regardless of the fact that they never quite got to grips with it. "Yes?" my granddad would demand, as if addressing a hawker or a door-to-door salesman.

"It's Neil." I'd say, pressing my ear against the speaker.

"Push the door, Neil," he'd shout in accompaniment to a pressing of the buzzer. Instructions given, he'd then come out onto the landing, shouting down the stairs, "Are you in? Are you in?"

"Yes," I'd shout back.

My grandmother was even worse. She never did manage to fathom the intercom system. Instead, she'd usually just stick her head out of the window, letting all the cold air in, before declaring, "*Hello?*" in a voice that suggested that she never entertained visitors at this hour of the day, regardless of what that hour *was*.

Today though, is different: we're already inside the block, managing to bypass the intercom routine on account of the door being left open. "They should shut the door behind them," Sharon declares. "These are vulnerable people, they don't want strangers and drug addicts and all sorts gaining access. Your granddad's an old man; he can't defend himself."

She's right, although I can't help smiling at the absurdity of that particular statement. A few years back my grandparent's were on their way back from a shopping trip to Lewisham, and some bloke on the bus had turned on the pair of them, calling my Nan a "Murderer."

"What's up with you, pal?" my granddad had demanded to know.

"That coat," he'd said, pointing to the fur coat my grandmother was wearing - God knows what fur it was. My granddad had bought it for her from some 'bloke at work' years back: the smell of mothball's alone would have rendered it lifeless.

"What's that?" my granddad growled, completely confused as to the bloke's jibe regarding some *poor, defenceless animal*. He thinks the man is talking about my grandmother! He genuinely hasn't got a clue. He still thinks it's 1957. What the hell does he know about public opinion regarding the fur trade? What the hell does he know about animal rights? "We had enough trouble looking after ourselves," *he'd* have claimed. The bloke on the bus though, he couldn't care less about any of these things.

He's not about to let the matter drop. He doesn't care whether or not my grandmother knows what day of the week this actually is, or that my granddad, most days, is usually as confused as she is. *He's* got an audience. *He's* standing up at the back of the bus, his four-zone travelcard affording him the moral high ground. "Murderer!" he screams.

"You want to get yourself some medical attention, mate," my granddad retorted, before delivering a perfectly weighted haymaking punch.

I knock again. "They *must* have gone out," I say, even though I still can't believe this to be the case.

"Perhaps they've nipped out for milk?" Sharon said.

Other than the 'nipping out' part, this would make perfect sense, especially judging by the amount of milk they manage to consume each week, "They'd be better off with their own cow!" my dad had joked.

I knock again.

Knock, knock.

Who's there?

No one.

I check my watch. It's nearly one o'clock. Sharon checks *her* watch. My weekend son, Jack, is still covered in mud from his football match; he looks tired, and it's obvious he just wants to go home. "We'll give it another five minutes," I attempt reassuring him, "and then we'll go."

Jack nods; giving me one of those 'no problem' looks. Even so, I'm conscious of the fact that he's not seen his grandparent's for a good couple of weeks – none of us have – so it's important to me that he sees them, that he maintains contact with my side of the family. I rub his head in thanks, all the while feeling those usual pangs of regret over the fact that he's constantly being driven back and forth in the direction of yet another family visitation right. My grandparent's loved seeing him though, and, as I'm always pointing out to him, they won't be around forever.

"She'll probably want to measure me again," Jack said, reading my thoughts, raising his eyebrows comically. Each time we visit my grandmother makes him stand up against her, back to back, so that she can measure his height against hers: she did the same thing to me when I was little, or until I outgrew her. And when we leave she'll open up the window and shout after us, "See you later alligator . . ."

"In a while crocodile," we'd call back with the obligatory reply.

I used to love saying that to her, although Jack now seems embarrassed by the whole process. "You're lucky she can still remember to do it," I would admonish him. But he's just a kid, what does he know?

The last time we visited my grandmother gave him a bag full of copper coins, "There's about a hundred pounds in there," she'd said excitedly.

Jack was obviously made up, until we got back to my parent's house and he counted up all the money on a tin tray. "Two pound, eighty seven pence," he'd said.

I knock again – it was getting ridiculous now.

Suddenly there was the sound of a door being unlocked, a chain being unchained, a squeaking of hinges, and the door being opened mere inches to reveal an unfamiliar face.

I'm confused. The door to my grandparent's flat remains firmly closed: it's the door opposite that's open, revealing an elderly man of similar years to my grandfather. "Are you looking for the gentleman that lives there?" he asks.

"Yes, mate. Have you seen him?"

"A couple of hours ago now," he says. "They took him away in an ambulance."

"*What?*"

"Greenwich Hospital, I would have thought."

"Cheers, mate," I say, although I'm already walking back down the corridor towards the exit.

Back in the car nobody says a word: none of us want to contemplate what might have happened to him. I turn over the ignition and the car starts first time – I usually have to coax it, pump the accelerator half a dozen times; jiggle the keys.

"I'm sure he's fine," Sharon says, although I can tell from her face she's not convinced.

I pull away from the kerb too quickly, struggling to remain calm; struggling to maintain complete control of the vehicle - the steering wheel, the gear shift, the air freshener – attempting to convince myself that the journey is no different to any other I've taken recently, save for the route being unfamiliar, and the fact that the radio/cd player remains mute: I don't want any driving music to accompany this particular journey, thank you very much – no soundtrack, no Clash, no Bowie, no Mott the Hoople; *no Elvis, Beatles or the Rolling Stones*. At a time like this you need to choose your music carefully, knowing that whatever song is chosen, whether *you* choose it or the radio station chooses on your behalf, will remain with you forever: I've always been like that. I've always worried about such things. Today's no different. If my granddad's dead I don't want Robbie Williams singing him on his way. I don't want Simply Red. I don't want ABBA or The Carpenters. A few years ago a friend of mine died: he was the same age as me – cancer. During the long night's wait at the hospital we were sat waiting in a family room – the radio was playing in the background. At the moment my friend passed away David Bowie's *Changes* suddenly came over the airwaves: I've always loved that song, but now it just reminds me of that moment – it doesn't remind me of my friend, just that terrible moment that he died.

"Do you know where you're going?" Sharon asks, pulling me back from the edge of a daydream.

"Of course, I do." I say, too sharply. For some peculiar reason I've always known instinctively in which direction to travel – it must have been all those years, as a kid, wearing those shoes with the compass in the heel. I could be driving down the Old Kent Road and would know, if I took the third exit at the Bricklayer's Arms roundabout, that Toronto, Ontario, was about three-thousand and sixty miles beyond the next set of traffic lights. I would know that if I were to keep going past the Drive-In *McDonald's* at Eltham I would eventually reach New York City; that I would eventually reach TRIBECA (Triangle Below Canal Street), De Niro's bar and Grill – chuck a right and I'd end up in Greenwich Village; head down the steps of the *Café Wha?* or the *Gaslight* and I'd catch a first glimpse of a young Robert Zimmerman singing Woody Guthrie songs of freedom.

Unfortunately, Greenwich Hospital is not in Greenwich Village. In fact, Greenwich Hospital is a million miles from the Greenwich Village of Bob Dylan and Simon and Garfunkel and the folk revival, the Greenwich Village of Peter, Paul and Mary, or Dave Van Ronk – Mayor of MacDougal Street. Pulling into the hospital car park it's clear that no spirit of the sixties remains here, save for the drug-addicted fallout. There are no sun children here; there is no sun machine coming down; there is no psychedelic trip on the Haight-Ashbury. What we find here is the death of the sixties – the Rolling Stones at Altamont, with Hell's Angels and violence and *Sympathy for the Devil*. What we find here is *Helter Skelter* and the Charles Manson Family. What we find here is Janis Joplin drinking herself into oblivion and Jimi Hendrix choking on his own vomit.

Even from a distance the hospital looks almost war torn – certainly ripe for demolition. Up close though, certainly having walked though the doors of the casualty department, you suddenly see where it all went wrong: there's certainly no sign of the bright-eyed optimism of Wilson's Labour Government; there's certainly no sign of Twiggy or The Beatles or Michael Caine or Terence Stamp. Walking through the automatic doors it's like walking into what a British hospital drama *should* look like: there are no Shakespearian actors playing the roles of football hooligans or RADA song and dance men playing drug-addicted low-life: the casualty department at Greenwich Hospital is pure authenticity. The dried blood on the vinyl flooring is real, not supplied by the prop's department - despite a half-attempted once over with a dirty mop - it's obviously been there weeks. Honestly; I'm scared to touch anything just in case I catch MRSA or one of the many social diseases on offer takes hold of me, and I suddenly become abusive – looking wide-eyed and spaced – or I suddenly start talking an aggressive form of gibberish, or suddenly start bumming fags from people or demanding seventy pence so I can get a cab to another hospital with better service.

"Can I help you?" the put-upon receptionist asks, although she barely raises her head above a reception desk that looks as if it's been built in protection of marauding malingerers.

"I'm looking for a patient: James Bradley?" I said. "I think he may have been brought in this morning."

"Was he on foot?"

"No, an ambulance, I think."

She checks her records. "Just wait there," she says, before disappearing through a set of rubberised doors to the right of the reception desk.

Sharon puts her arm around Jack, and then reaches out her other hand to caress my cheek with the back of her fingers. I feign a smile.

Over by the drinks machine a man is shouting – to himself, to someone else – no one's really sure. On the other side of the waiting room a youngish man and woman are trawling between the chairs demanding money with menaces. The woman has a dirty blanket around her shoulders, and the man has a cut above his eye, there is blood on his training shoe and he has a large piss stain on his jeans: both are holding cans of lager.

On a white board on the wall behind the reception desk someone has written a declaration: THE CURRENT WAITING TIME TO SEE A DOCTOR IS FOUR HOURS.

"This place is terrible," Sharon says, shuddering at the splatter of blood that trails across the floor beneath our feet. "Don't *ever* bring me here," she demands of me, "No matter how unwell I am!"

A few moments later the receptionist returns. "Mr Bradley was here," she said, matter of fact like. "But he's gone."

"Oh, right."

"The sister will be out to talk to you in a moment," she said.

"He must have gone to my dad's," I say.

Sharon nods, but continues to maintain a look of uncertainty.

The sister is a West Indian woman of about fifty, with a shock of white hair and old-fashioned glasses. She introduces herself to us in one of those sing-song Caribbean voices like she's in church or somewhere, before leading us through the rubberised doors the receptionist went through a few minutes earlier. Away from the lunacy of the reception area, this room appears much calmer: it's a crash room by the looks of it, or at least from what I can glean from my limited experience of watching *Casualty* on the television. The sister walks across the room and picks up a clipboard; she checks the details, before returning to where we are standing just inside the doors. "James Bradley," she says, "Passed away at eleven-fifty."

"*What?*"

"James Bradley," she repeats the information. "Passed away at . . ."

"What are you talking about?"

Sharon grabs my arm. Jack looks uncertain: he's far too young for this crap. He starts to cry. "Heart failure," the sister offers, as if that's supposed to make sense.

"What are you saying?" I stammer. "Are you telling me he's *gone?*"

"I thought you knew?" the sister said, only now looking up from the clipboard. "The receptionist . . ."

"The receptionist told me he was gone."

"Well, yes . . ."

"I thought she meant; he's gone. I thought she meant; he's gone home. I didn't think she meant; he's *gone*."

"I'm really sorry," the sister said. "I just assumed . . ."

"You just assumed *what*?"

"I thought you knew?"

"He's gone," I say to Sharon. She has her arm around Jack. He's crying. She's crying. I cry.

"I thought you knew," the sister says the words over and over.

"Where is he?" I demand.

"Where's who?" she says

"Are you winding me up? James Bradley; passed away at eleven-fifty?"

"He's in the hospital mortuary."

"I want to see him."

"But he's . . ."

"I *want* to see him!"

Thirty minutes later we're still waiting: we've been taken to a family room. The walls could do with a new coat of paint and Van Gogh's *Sunflowers* hangs at a crooked angle. A young nurse had earlier brought us tea, which was served in green NHS Cups and saucers. Everyone was being very sympathetic.

Despite the early afternoon hour, I check my watch: my granddad's dead, but still Jack has to be delivered back at five o'clock on the dot. She, his mother that is, will cause a fuss if he's not there: not even a death in the family can breach a family court access order. "Do you want me to drop Jack home," Sharon says, knowing how anxious I get.

"No," I say, too sharply. "There's still plenty of time."

Just then the door to the family room opens and a chap pokes his head around the door, "Mr Bradley?"

"Yes."

"We're ready for you now," he says.

I kiss Sharon, and I kiss Jack, and then follow the chap along a corridor and then through a set of double doors, which lead out to the underground car park. "It's not too far," the chap says, his only attempt at breaching the silence between us.

Over in the corner of the car park there's a white painted building, which looks like a car park attendant's office. *This* can't be the place, surely, I think. As if reading my mind though, the chap points in that same direction, leading me across the last section of tarmac. Reaching the building he stands aside and beckons for me to enter. Inside the room is bare, save for a low coffee table and a collection of soft chairs not too dissimilar from those in the family room; a potted plant sits in the corner, a couple of paintings or prints hang on the wall, and there is a large square window of glass with a drawn venetian blind.

Upon entry I'm immediately greeted by another chap, this one in a white half-coat, which reminds me of a steward on a cruise liner. He in turn beckons me towards another door to the right of the covered window, which he opens and bids me entry. "Take as much time as you need," he says. Tentatively, I take a few steps into the room: just enough to allow the chap to pull the door closed behind me without hitting the backs of my shoes. In front of me my granddad lays on a sort of plinth, his head on a pillow, his body covered by a long white sheet. I edge closer and can already see specks of congealed blood around his nose and his mouth. There is a gash on his head and a cut on the bridge of his nose. On closer inspection I can see the indentations from his glasses, which, without them, makes his nose seem even more Romanesque: my granddad had one of those noses slightly on the outskirts of Rome.

I've never seen a dead body before. At least, not in this sense: I've never been left alone in a room with a dead body before. I'm still not quite sure what the protocol is. Should I just stand here? Am I meant to talk to him? Am I allowed to touch him? How long should I stay in the room for - the chap in the white half-coat told me to take all the time I needed, but was he just saying that to be polite?

I edge closer. I use the outside of my fingers to touch my granddad's cheek. It's stone cold. I lean forward trying to get a better look at him, at the gash on his head, at the cut on the bridge of his nose, wondering how he got them? Was he attacked? Did my Nan hit him over the head with a frying pan? Did he fall over and hit his head on something? The whole thing was a mystery to me.

I run my hand across his Kirk Douglas hair, and swear blind that I feel it growing. I shudder and then I cry. I kiss his head: it seems an unnatural thing to do.

I stay in the room for about fifteen minutes: not too short, but long enough to make a point following my demands that I be allowed to see him. I suddenly feel like a grown-up.

The chap that guided to me to my granddad's bedside is the same one that guides me back again – back through the underground car park, back through the double doors, back along the corridor, back to the family room;

the family suddenly smaller by a unit of one. I give him a tenner - my granddad would have tipped him, and my dad would have tipped him - it seemed like the right thing to do.

Back in the room I don't bother sitting down again. "Come on; let's go," I say.

"Do you think we should let them know we're leaving?" Sharon says.

"You are joking?"

Around twenty minutes later we arrive back at my parents house. I call out to my dad – he's upstairs, or out walking the dog – I get no reply. Going through to the dining room, I see my mother in the kitchen. "We tried to phone you," she says by way of explanation, "but you'd already left." My mother's face looks drawn.

"We've just come from the hospital," I say. "They let me see him."

"Your dad went round there this morning," she says. "He was with him when it happened."

"Where's Nan?" I ask, and my mother points to the living room. I creep up and take a peak through the glass doors that divide that room from the dining room. My Nan is sat on the sofa. She looks lost.

My grandparents had lived in their flat at the Borough (between the Elephant and Castle and London Bridge) for fifty years; made up they were, happy as Larry, having long since discovered their own new Jerusalem, their very own Shangri-La, their very own version of *The Enchanted Cottage*. In the last few years though, my granddad had started complaining about the four flights of stairs, the pains in his chest, his breathlessness. My grandmother, too, was well into the grip of Alzheimer's by that stage, despite my granddad's claims as to her mere forgetfulness.

My dad had approached the council, and had managed to secure a move for the pair of them to a sheltered accommodation property a mere five-minute drive away from him. It was all meant to be so perfect.

I shake my head at the bitter irony of it all, but just then the front door bell rings and I'm immediately set on edge – the whole household is. Through the lace curtains I can just make out the outline of a car. I open the door with the familiar dread. Jack's mum stands there. "Jack, your mum's here," I say. Immediately, he appears at my side, his coat on, his overnight bag slung over his shoulder. I see him off with a hug and a kiss, "Behave your self at school," I tell him.

"Yes dad."

"You were really brave today."

"Yes dad."

"I was really proud of you."

"Yes dad."

"I'll see you next week."

"Yes dad."

A few moments later the car pulls away from the kerb fast enough for poll position in a Formula One Grand Prix. I wave from the doorstep, but Jack's not really looking, and soon the car's long gone. I close the door, and curse the day. I curse the relationship I have with his mother. Why does it always have to become so poisonous?

In the kitchen my mother continues with her preparations for Sunday lunch. Sharon is out in the garden talking to her own mother on the phone, explaining what's happened. In the living room my grandmother is still sat on the sofa: she plays with the buttons on her cardigan;

occasionally she wrings her hands. I enter the room and join her on the sofa. "You okay, nan?" I say.

"Is that you, Jimmy?" she says: my dad's Jimmy, not me. She's like that most of the time now – confused. I know she's my grandmother, but she must have driven my granddad mad. "Isn't it about time we had another cup of tea Jim?" she'd always be asking.

"You've just had a cup of tea," he'd retort. "Look; it's there on the table."

"I can't drink that; it's stone cold."

Dutifully, my granddad would shuffle off to the kitchen, before going through yet another tea-making routine in accompaniment to the radio: deep down I think he liked these moments, the escape from the insanity of the living room - whenever we visited he would always disappear into the kitchen. He made the best cup of tea in the world; only it took him twenty-five minutes to produce it.

"Gawd knows what he's doing in there," my dad would always laugh. "I mean; how long's it take to make a cup of tea?" I realise now though, that the tea-making routine was just an excuse, that this was actually my granddad's escape from my grandmother's disease, his little bit of respite from her inane list of scripted questions.

"Isn't it about time we had another cup of tea, Jim?"

"I've just made you a cup of tea. Look; it's there on the table."

"I'm not drinking that, it's stone cold."

It was comical to watch though, this vaudeville routine of theirs. They were like a couple of music hall stars who'd been together for sixty years, still bickering, yet still as devoted to each other as the day they first met. But now he'd gone, and the act was at an end.

My grandmother, of course, sat on the sofa in my parent's house, is none the wiser. In reality, her *reality*, she's actually sat at home, in her flat at the Borough. "Your dad's taking a long time with that tea," she says, rubbing her hands together like a child in anticipation of some treat. She reaches out and takes my hand in hers: she now thinks I'm my dad; over the next few months and years the generations will be shunted upwards, until one day we'll all become strangers to her. "Your dad's late tonight," she says again. "I don't know what could have kept him."

"He's gone," I say softly, not really wanting her to hear me.

"He's never normally this late," she says.

"Nan, he's gone."

"He's probably doing overtime," my Nan says: according to her, he was always doing overtime, despite the fact that he'd been retired for nearly twenty years.

"Nan, he's *gone*!"

"He's gone?" she repeats my words, grabbing my hand and gripping it tightly. She has these gnarled, bony fingers – a combination of old age and arthritis. "My Jim's *gone*?" she says, the full weight of the words bringing her to tears, crying into my arms like a young girl that's fallen down and hurt her knee. For the briefest moment I'm frozen in terror, not knowing what to do, until suddenly my mother enters the room and takes charge of the situation, pulling my grandmother towards her and rocking her in her arms.

At that moment it's difficult to watch – the tragedy of it all.

Outside, Sharon watches through the glass door, crying, and I'm just standing there, my feet frozen to the carpet. It's the most tragic thing I've ever seen.

When she eventually stops, my mother wipes her eyes with a lace handkerchief and kisses her on the forehead. My grandmother kisses my mother's hand in return. We all stay frozen in silence. Two minutes later though, it's as if she's suddenly forgotten the reason for her tears; forgetting the terrible news we'll soon need to repeat. "Jim's taking his time with that tea," she says.

The Brass Angel (Novel Extract)

Tutorial Submission – Stephen Knight

Detective Sergeant Dave Langdon extended his hand for Sergeant Harrison to shake. 'Hello, Sarg,' he said: he always called him "Sarg," even after all these years.

'Hello Dave,' Harrison smiled. 'You're looking well,' even though they both knew that this was a lie, that Langdon looked anything but well.

'You too,' Langdon said, still somewhat self-conscious in his former sergeant's company, acutely aware that this was the one man that he'd never been able to fool. 'How long has it been, a year?'

'More like two.'

'Has it really been that long?' Langdon said, knowing that it had been, knowing that it felt more like ten.

'I heard about Jan?' Harrison said, knowing that he needed to broach the subject, deciding to get it out of the way from the outset.

'What are you gonna' do?' Langdon shrugged. 'You know she's married again?'

'Christ, I'm sorry, Dave. I didn't even know that you'd gotten divorced?'

'Just a few months back funnily enough, she married a civvie, works in computers, lives down in Southampton, seems happy enough.' Langdon reeled off the information as if he were reading from a police note-book, laying out the facts, concise and to the point.

'It wasn't your fault Dave, you do realise that?'

'Of course it was my fault,' Langdon said honestly. 'You know what I was like back then?'

'It's the job that's all, you can't beat it,' Harrison said regretfully. 'It demands too much of us sometimes.'

'Maybe.'

'Christ, if I had a pound for every copper that got divorced over the years.'

'What about Laura though?' Langdon asked bitterly. 'Can I blame that on the job?'

'Leave off Dave, you can't take the blame for that, not even the job's to blame for that one.'

'No?' Langdon was not convinced. 'That's not what Jan thinks.'

'She's just upset that's all,' Harrison smiled a benevolent smile. 'She needed something to blame and the job, *you*, they suited her purpose, that's all.'

'Yeah, but it was still a copper that killed her, that killed Laura, a copper that knocked *her* down?'

'Of course it wasn't, it was just some arsehole that's all, that was just the job he did. If he'd been a doctor or a bricklayer you wouldn't even mention it.'

The door to the café opened then, bringing with it a cold wind that passed between them.

'He didn't even do eight months, can you believe that?' Landgon said bitterly. 'Three times over the limit, and he doesn't even do eight months.'

'Yeah, I know,' Harrison said, well used to the ludicrous nature of the law, as angry as Dave on that score. 'But then that was the courts, that wasn't the police service.'

'I hate them all most days, the courts, the force, the CPS, the fucking probation service, none of them deliver any justice to anyone.'

'Come on Dave, you wanted revenge, you didn't want justice?' Harrison said, well remembering the night all those years back that Langdon had phoned him in a rage, threatening to kill the drunken policeman that had taken his daughter, had taken his wife, taken his marriage. And who could blame him? Even so, Sergeant Harrison knew that Langdon was really not like that, despite the bluff, the bravado, the natural rage. Harrison knew better than anyone that Langdon was a pretty sensitive sort of bloke on the quiet, away from the job; knew that he was a copper that genuinely cared about the victims, even about the perpetrators in most cases; a well read man that understood the reasons behind crime and punishment and cruelty, even if he'd made a macho attempt over the years at preventing such crime and cruelty, going in hard, always using brutish force first and tact second, secretly hating the methods that he was forced to use, that all coppers were forced to use when brutal needs must. Hence the reason Sergeant Harrison was confident that Langdon would never attempt seeking revenge on the man that had taken his daughter's life, more concerned that Langdon would simply attempt taking revenge on himself, one day in the not too distant future perhaps, finally succumbing to that terrible police disease of suicide, choosing to take his own life as if penance for his broken marriage and for his broken daughter.

For a few moments the pair sat in silence, the café continuing to splutter coffee and conversation, the café chaos continuing all around them as they sat in bonded reflection amongst the spilt sugar, their cups of tea as yet untouched.

Looking out through the window now Harrison noted a few of the more hardy customers enjoying a tea and a smoke in the fresh air, considering the cold weather, extremely fresh air, the café offering al fresco dining, in order to get around the smoking ban.

Observing the honorary society of puffers now, Harrison couldn't help but smile at the absurd nature of it, wondering what aliens would make of it all, these people huddling together on street corners, to the left and right of office buildings, in the snow sometimes. 'I'm glad I gave it up when I did,' he said motioning the smokers, yet he remembered reading recently that smoker's were amongst the most sociable of groups, despite the public ostracising, especially in the workplace where the nicotine addicted are known to form wide-reaching networking contacts simply by virtue of the fact that nicotine addiction does not discriminate between managers and workers, doctors and dustmen. Funnily enough, this observation was similar to the one his late wife, Lizzie, a hospital matron, had always made regarding the faster recovery times of smokers following surgery, with all but the truly infirm smoker eager to get out of bed and nip off the ward in search of a very quick post-anaesthetic puff.

'I need your help Dave?' Sergeant Harrison said suddenly. 'I need a favour?'

'Yeah, of course, anything, you know that?' Langdon said, relieved to have moved away from the subject of grief and disappointment and revenge, despite the fact that it rarely left him completely, laying just beneath the surface, ready to spout any time during the long days and sleepless nights.

'I need you to look up some information for me?'

'On?' Langdon said, ignoring the fact that it was illegal, trusting his former sergeant implacably, certain that he would never ask unless he had a genuinely good reason for doing so.

'A missing person,' Harrison said, slipping the photograph across the table.

'Which one am I looking at?' Langdon asked, picking up the photograph and immediately recognising the man sitting opposite, sat there between two other men, one a little older and a young lad, middle twenties perhaps.

'The young lad, he's been missing for a few months now, completely disappeared, and I mean completely,' Harrison said sadly.

'Any ideas?' Langdon asked, thinking that there was something about the younger man that seemed familiar somehow, something about the eyes.

'I don't know, taken by aliens or something,' Harrison shook his head. 'Left no trail whatsoever.'

Even though he didn't say it, it troubled Langdon to see his old sergeant at a loss with this, knowing that he was a problem solver, a practical man that always had an answer. 'So what is he, to you, I mean?'

'A nephew of sorts.'

'He looks familiar?'

'He should do, his face was splashed across all of the newspapers once.'

'Oh, yeah?' Langdon said surprised. 'When was this?'

'Years back, you probably wouldn't remember.'

'Try me?' Langdon said intrigued.

'It was about twenty years ago, when you were still a wooden top at the old station...'

'Wait a minute, this isn't the circus boy?'

Sergeant Harrison was amazed that Langdon would remember, not the events of that night, no one could have forgotten those, but rather the fact that he should still remember Jimmy, that he should recognise him after all of these years.

'This is him now,' Harrison pointed to the photograph. 'Well, almost, that picture was taken a couple of years back.'

'And this bloke,' Langdon said, pointing to Charlie. 'Is this the boy's grandfather?'

'Yeah, Charlie,' Harrison smiled. 'I'm not sure anyone knew, but following the accident, I helped him get custody of the boy, it was a long old process.'

'And you kept in contact?'

'He became my best friend; they both did, the boy, like a nephew to me, a son almost.'

'Christ, do you know I still think about that night from time to time,' Langdon said.

'I think everyone does,' Harrison replied, shaking his head at the thought of it.

'I was only a young copper then. Even so, I thought I'd seen it all, you know how it is, thought I'd seen everything this job had to offer, always thought that life couldn't get any more weird, any more surreal, any more...'

'Any more *tragic*?' Harrison smiled sadly.

'Exactly,' Langdon said. 'Even today, I still find it hard to believe, that poor little sod, that lost little kid, turning up at the police station like that.' He picked up the picture and studied the image more closely. 'I remember hearing it out over the radio and all of us rushing back to the station, blue lights and sirens going ten to the dozen, and you being mad with all of us,'

Langdon laughed. 'Even though, you were just as amazed as everybody else, just as gobsmacked.'

'It's funny, but I was never surprised after that,' Harrison said. 'I just knew that the job would never throw up anything like it again . . . his mum and dad killed like that.'

'When I first heard it I thought it was a joke . . . that someone was playing some prank on one of the wooden tops,' Langdon laughed almost nervously. 'You know the sort of stuff we used to get up to?'

'Don't remind me,' Harrison said, shaking his head as if in admonishment of a schoolboy, secretly finding it amusing, experienced enough to know that such pranks were necessary in terms of bonding, in terms of releasing the pressure gage on a fraught job - Harrison had often been forced into explaining away that gallows humour to each new station commander, the fact that a police station needed humour, no matter how black.

'It was just so bizarre.'

'Bizarre doesn't even help describe it, doesn't even dent it.' Harrison agreed.

For a few minutes the pair sat in silence thinking about that night, those strange events, both of them feeling old.

Just then though, the silence was broken by Langdon's phone ringing, accompanied by a strange vibrating little dance across the table. 'Sorry,' Langdon said, 'I really need to take this, immediately getting up and slipping outside to hold his conversation away from prying ears and eyes.

A young girl approached the table collecting the cups and giving the surface a cursory wipe with a cloth.

'Two more, please,' Harrison signalled her, holding up two fingers.

Looking around he noted that the décor had not changed. Years ago, when he'd still been on the force, this café had been a favourite haunt of his, away from the police canteen, the front desk and the back office, the café, in stark contrast serving up daily doses of the real world, plus two slices of toast, sat there amongst thieves and builders, office workers and transients, all of them attempting escape from their respective rat races for the odd-thirty minutes or so, tea and sympathy and page three tits, Tony Blackburn, god help us, adding background noise, as if the café really needed any more background noise, the froffee-coffee machine providing all that and more in crazed percolation, hissing out hot water over the cries of customers demanding full English breakfast.

Occasionally, Antonio the café owner, sadly long gone, his son Antony overseeing the family goldmine now, would treat everyone to an opera, clearing the corner table and placing down one of those old flip-top record players, selecting from a pile of old long playing records the soundtrack from his homeland, the great Caruso and others belting out the likes of *Recondita armonia* from Tosca or *Recitar!...Vesti la giubba* from Pagliaccio. On those all too brief occasions a wonderful serenity would fall upon the café, even the froffee-coffee machine seemingly tempering its noise during those few precious minutes when the air would be filled with some opera that no one, other than Antonio and his staff, would understand the words to, yet which transcended the lives of all those bearing witness, piercing their inner thoughts, Antonio's tears bringing forth comfort, respite even, from the outside world, the final few bars, the well-played scratches, sadly bringing them all crashing back to earthly reality.

Upon conclusion the entire café would be silent, builders in hardhats and bankers in bespoke pinstripe, mesmerized by the sheer wonder of it; not quite sure what they'd just heard, just been witness to, yet grateful for having shared Antonio's brief escape to Italian shores.

Looking around the café now Sergeant Harrison noted how that same table, that one that held the record player, was instead in occupation, four young men in suits, from the local bank or building society by the looks of them, Harrison lip-reading their animated discussion regarding the merits of a new cashier, her physique, her ample bust; each of them secretly wondering no doubt as to the best way of broaching with her the subject of drinks, cinema, sex, romance, marriage, joint account and cheap mortgage.

When old man Antonio had died his son, Antony, had set about making subtle changes to the business, that corner table, for instance, being cleared of the record player and operatic debris, wiped clean with a damp cloth in pursuit of seating an extra four behinds upon newly purchased chairs.

Looking at him now, Harrison noted that Antony was almost the spitting image of his father, in feature if not weight, that same shock of grey hair, that Roman nose, that sing-song ability to hold four conversations at once, yet still find time to deliver tea, cappuccino in most cases these days, shaken milks or a fried egg sandwich.

When Sergeant Harrison had first arrived Antony had brought the café's proceedings to a complete halt, bringing all to order with a piercing whistle, removing the apron, as his father had always done, slipping from behind the counter and greeting him with a bear hug, followed by two macho kisses on either cheek.

The Brass Angel (Novel Extract)

In the old days Sergeant Harrison had been a real friend to his father, offering kindness and company and the occasional protection from, well, *protection* - some new kid on the block occasionally turning up on the doorstep demanding money with menaces. Not that Antonio ever needed protection, whether serious or otherwise, Sergeant Harrison acknowledging the fact that you couldn't run any form of Italian eating establishment without some form of friendship with those in the Anglo-Italian underworld, experienced enough to know that Antonio was probably indebted to some particular Italian family or that. Even so, as a policeman, as a friend, certainly in years gone by, he had sometimes been called upon to remove a rowdy group of teenagers or would-be gangster, usually with a cuff around the head or the occasional threat of police brutality. Much more than that though, Antony knew that Sergeant Harrison had shown unflinching loyalty to the family over the years, especially during his mother's long illness and resultant passing and his father's resultant long battle with grief, those all too brief moments of operatic wonder suddenly all the more poignant, his father's tears all the more painful.

When Antonio had died suddenly, some fifteen years ago now, it had been Sergeant Harrison that had helped with the arrangements for the funeral, as he had done when his mother had died, helping the family in the only way he could, as a policeman, dealing with all of the mundane stuff, cutting through the red tape, performing the simple practicalities with the air of a man well used to seeing people in grief, at their most vulnerable. As such Sergeant Harrison had rarely bought a cup of tea or paid for a breakfast, accepting the gratuity in kind, the only such gratuity he'd ever accepted during his years on the force, content in the knowledge that he was beyond reproach, beyond the corruption that had tainted many of his colleagues over the years, especially back during the so-called good old days.

Purveying the café now, it was hard not to remember those good old days, a fact suddenly confirmed by the first strains of that old British Airways theme, *The Flower Duet*, turned up to the maximum volume in his honour, Antony winking at him, pointing to the slick hi-fi system upon the wall, Sergeant Harrison bowing his head in mock gratitude.

'The record player's gone,' Antony said, dramatically, standing behind the counter like some famous operatic impresario. 'The music though, it lives on!'

Throughout the aria Antony, despite going about his café business, kept a close eye on Sergeant Harrison, their glances occasionally meeting, a shared smile between the beauty of the voices and the chaos of the custom, the words finally fading as before, the café immediately coming back to full life with the sudden appearance of Detective Sergeant Dave Langdon, Antony greeting him in the same fashion with bear hugs and kisses, before leading him to Sergeant Harrison's table.

Sergeant Harrison could still hear that music, could still hear Antonio's booming tenor voice. He smiled at the thought of it. What memories.

'Something funny?' Langdon said, returning to his seat.

'I was just thinking about the old days,' Harrison said, smiling again.

'You know, I saw him that night that circus boy?' Langdon said, he'd always referred to him as 'that circus boy.' He took a casual sip of tea. 'I'm not sure you knew that?'

'I didn't,' Harrison said surprised.

'I remember you going spare,' Langdon laughed. 'Claiming that there wasn't a single patrol car on the streets or a bobby on the beat, that it was unprofessional, ordering us all back out again. And, of course, we all scampered away again, although not before I'd managed to sneak a peak at him, instantly regretting that I ever had.'

'Oh yeah, why's that?'

'I don't know, something about the eyes I think,' Langdon said, picking up the photograph again and studying Jimmy's image. 'Something haunting.'

'Young Jimmy certainly had those,' Harrison agreed.

'I've never told anyone this,' Langdon said embarrassed, 'but I cried that night, you know, having seen him, I don't know why, it broke my heart I think, the perverse nature of it.'

'It was certainly tragic, I'll give you that'

'No, it was more than that,' Langdon suddenly became animated. 'Much more than that . . . I don't know . . . like you were saying earlier, we're used to tragedy in the job, tragedy at home, me with my Laura and you with your Lizzie . . . but this was different, this was tragedy at its most perverse, at its most sickening, what happened to that little boy...'

'That's why I need you to find him for me, need you to find him quickly?'

'What's going on, Sarg, what's happened?'

'It's the boy's granddad,' Harrison pointed to the photograph once more. 'He's dying.'

'Shit,' Langdon said, not really knowing what else to say.

'I don't think he's going to last.'

'So, what happened then, between the pair of them, they have some sort of falling out or something?'

'No, nothing like that,' Harrison said. 'I'm telling you Dave, you couldn't find two people more devoted to each other than these two. I mean it, nowhere. Believe me, you hear people going on about family values, politicians and policemen, in the newspapers and on the telly, no one can you give you the definitive answer, what it means, most of them talking rubbish half the time. Yet these two, this luckless old man and his daydreaming grandson they're the living embodiment, they *are* the family, and there's no one knows the value of it better than them.'

'Christ, Sarg, I've never heard you talk like this before, I've never heard you being so passionate about anything.'

'Dave, I'm getting old and I've seen it all, *everything*, but I've never seen anything like these two. All those years as a copper I never saw anything quite like what happened that night, the pair of them coming to the station like that.

For a few minutes the two men sat is if under a spell, with only the froffee-coffee machine sufficient enough to bring them both back to reality, both back to the reason they were sat there amongst the spilt sugar and those discarded tea cups. 'Look, I know at the time there were plenty of jokes floating around the station…'

'Come on Sarg,' Langdon attempted explaining it away.

'Dave, don't get me wrong, I understand it, that search for humour, I know it's one of those things that helps coppers get through it, a way of coping with the sick things you see on this job, I understand that....'

'It's just our way Sarg, policemen, it's how we cope...

'Dave, I'm not knocking it, you're missing the point, son,' Harrison said. 'I couldn't give a toss about the jokes. What I do care about though, is that boy and that old man,' he pointed to the images in the picture. 'It just wasn't right what happened to that boy. That's why I need to find him. If it's the last thing I do, I owe them Dave, the pair of them for letting me be witness to the events of that night, I owe them for letting me into their family, for allowing me an insight into their tragic little family unit, and I owe them for giving me back my humanity, can you understand that?'

'Yeah, of course I can,' Langdon nodded. 'Christ, Sarg, let's find him, let's see if we can't put them back together before the old man calls it a day?'

'Thanks Dave, I appreciate this, you don't know how much I appreciate this,' Harrison patted Langdon's hand, smiling, knowing that he'd made the right choice in calling this particular policeman, knowing that he'd made the right choice when it came to asking him for help.

'Leave off Sarg, they'll think we're a couple of poofs,' Langdon said laughing, but then suddenly turning serious. 'Besides, it should be me thanking you.'

'Alright, so where do we start?' Harrison asked, all business now.

'You've done the missing persons stuff I assume?'

'Yeah, I met the lad's girlfriend at the nick. She turned up on the same day as me to report him missing.'

'Doesn't she have any idea where he is?'

'Get this, the poor cow had only been his girlfriend for one day!'

'What?'

'In fact, she'd only found out his surname the day before she went to the nick.'

'So it wasn't serious then?'

'No, that's just it,' Harrison said. 'You can't believe how serious it actually is.'

'I'm not sure that I understand?'

'Look, it's a long story, Dave, and it really doesn't matter now, not at this moment in time. In fact, none of it matters, none of it will make sense until we find him, until we find Jimmy.'

'Okay, so what's his full name, his date of birth, I'm going to need all of that?'

Sergeant Harrison produced a piece of paper and passed it across the table to him, 'It's all there,' he said. 'Everything you need to know about him: where he worked, what little family ties there are, national insurance number, everything.'

'So what are you thinking?' Langdon asked.

'I'm not sure. Obviously there are things I don't want to think about...'

'Alright, but I've got to ask, did you come to me because it was me, or did you come to me because of the body squad?'

'A bit of both I think, although the strong possibility of him being dead has been at the back of my mind for some time now. He's not a suicide though, if that's what you're thinking, he's not really anything, other than a devoted grandson and someone that's a bit lovelorn that's all.'

'Okay, I'll see what I can come up with, put the word out to a few pals of mine,' Langdon said, folding the piece of paper and putting it in his pocket. 'Anything else you can give me other than that?'

'Like I've always said, like I always tried to teach you, look in the most unusual places, but . . .'

'But don't forget the most obvious ones?' Langdon smiled, remembering the lectures that Harrison was always giving to the young coppers, knowing that the Sergeant would have already made a good fist of investigating the boy's disappearance on his own, not really requiring police resources, resourceful enough to figure most things out for himself. Hence the reason, Langdon realised now, that his old sergeant was obviously desperate for help.

'Exactly,' Harrison said. 'Don't ignore the obvious, check all the John Doe's first."

'Of course.'

'Dave, I need a result on this one, and I need it fast?'

'How long do you think he's got, the old man, I mean?'

'Who knows,' Harrison said sadly. 'Although I fear it's going be sooner rather than later.'

'Alright, I'll get a couple of the lads on it straight away, Eddie Carson, you remember him?' Harrison remembered Carson all too well. He didn't like him, although he trusted Langdon's judgement enough to let it go. 'There's also a young kid, Steve Malcolm, a university graduate, he'll be full of enthusiasm.

'I appreciate this Dave, truly I do.'

'Yeah, I know,' Langdon said. 'Besides, I owe you.'

'Not on this one you don't,' Harrison said sadly. 'Just do it because you're a good copper that's all. Believe me Dave, if you can find the boy, if you can get him to that hospital bed before the old man dies, it'll be the best police work you'll ever do.'

Writing Seminar – Tobias Hill/ Tutorial - Stephen Knight

Stephen Knight's view of my novel has not changed.

"It still reads like an airport novel," he says dismissively. "It's still full of cliché, and it needs further re-writes."

"Any suggestions?" I ask, although I'm no longer sure that I really want to hear the answer.

"These characters in your story," Stephen smiles. "I think they're all based on you?"

"What?"

"The character in the previous chapter . . . Jimmy . . . I think it's you?"

"But he's dead," I laugh.

"Oh, I realised that," he laughed. "But it's still you."

"I'm not sure why you'd say that?"

"Have you ever considered life writing?" he asks.

"Yeah, of course," I say, although I'm still a little guarded, not quite sure where this is leading. "You've read some of it, remember?"

"Ah, but those were comedic pieces."

"I like writing comedic pieces," I say. "I've always liked using comedy."

"Look, there's nothing wrong with using comedy in your work, but I've noticed how there always seem to be a reluctance on your part to take things seriously; to write things seriously," his eyes are burning into me, and

I want to look away, to get up, to escape the confines of his claustrophobic office. "I've read your life writing pieces, and they're much more vivid, even if you use a lot of humour to mask a more serious tone."

"So what about the novel?"

"Just carry on with it. Keep re-writing. Keep editing. You'll get there in the end."

"You're not saying I should abandon it then?"

"No, of course not. It's just that I think you're far better suited to the life writing genre, that's all. I really think there's a story, in there, somewhere, that you really want to tell . . . that you really *need* to tell."

As usual I depart his office even more confused than when I entered: I'm never quite sure whether he's giving me good advice or bad. Is he suggesting I abandon the novel? By telling me to go away and re-write it; is he really saying, go away and write something else?

I look at my watch. It's almost two o'clock, and I need to get across the road – hopefully grab a coffee on the way – there's a writing seminar at two.

During the first term of the second year we're required to attend a series of guest seminars. These are delivered by a varied collection of writers – most of them unknown to me – including poets, novelists, playwrights, actors, theatre directors. Amongst those that deliver a seminar is the poet and novelist Tobias Hill.

According to his biography:

Tobias Hill *was born London, England, on 30 March 1970. He read English at Sussex University and spent two years teaching in Japan.*

He is the author of a collection of poetry Year of the Dog (1995). Midnight in the City of Clocks (1996), influenced by his experiences living in Japan, and Zoo (1998), which coincided with his tenure as Poet in Residence at London Zoo as part of the Poetry Places scheme administered by the Poetry Society. He is also the author of an acclaimed collection of short stories, Skin (1997), which won the PEN/Macmillan Silver Pen Award.

Adaptations of his poetry and short stories have been broadcast on BBC Radio 4. He has also worked as a rock critic for the Sunday Telegraph and as the poetry editor of the Richmond Review. His fiction includes the novels Underground (1999), The Love of Stones (2001) and The Cryptographer. His latest novel is The Hidden (2009).

His seminar is delivered quietly, without fuss, almost as if he's embarrassed standing before us – *what do I know about writing that could possibly be of any help to you guys?* He's wrong.

'There's no such thing as the perfect novel," he suddenly declares. "I like reading airport novels. I love reading what the literary critics describe as *rubbish*."

He'd like my novel.

He claims that his own novel, *The Hidden*, took five years to write, and even then he took time out to deliver a collection of poems - *Nocturne in Chrome and Sunset Yellow* – a year's worth of poetic observation regarding living in London.

During the seminar he talks about his particular area of London, Cricklewood, and notes how it seems to have no form of identity. This seems somewhat strange, at least to me, as I'd always thought of it as an Irish area. By chance he reads about a demolished dance hall on Cricklewood Broadway, *Ashton's*, which immediately has my ears pricking up: his description of the dance hall is one of suburban disco, with drunken young girls, and even drunker young men, spilling out onto the vast pavement; of sporadic fights breaking out on the dance floor and in the taxi rank outside.

My first Christmas Eve with Sharon I went to Ashton's, which was an old haunt of hers - it was a terrible place. Earlier in the evening we went to a pub, the Welsh Harp, which was just as bad: at the time I remember thinking amidst the crush to get served, *when is a polite time to leave? How soon can I make my excuses, and declare my goodbyes?* I remember saying to Sharon, "We need to leave this place, *now!*" Inside the atmosphere was grim, ugly almost. There was a tension which threatened to spill over and spoil that Christmas and every Christmas yet to come: we later hear that a mass brawl took place and that someone's Christmas was ruined by a long custodial sentence, another by way of a seven-inch blade.

Ashton's is even worse though; an Irish dance hall from years ago: an Irish stronghold – the next generation or two – The Dubliners replaced by disco. Circling the hall is a balcony allowing unrestricted views of the dance floor below. It is here that I spend the entire evening: never letting go of the handrail in case I should topple over and end up in a heap on the sprung boards that vibrate beneath the stomping feet below.

From the balcony I spot Sharon, happily dancing with her friends, and I can't help but wonder just how long this relationship can last? How could I explain to her that I hated it there? How could I explain to her that I hated being that side of the river (north)? How could I explain to her that I hated everything about that place?

Between fights and sporadic mayhem – when blood is spilt and honour is rarely satisfied – girls dance around their handbags, as their mother's may once have done, whilst young men, with cheekbones like their father's, swarm to the bar like an incoming tidal sea crashing against a pebbled beach. Even beneath the mirror ball – despite Tobias Hill's attempts at capturing Ashton's demolition – there's no poetry to be had here. There's certainly no romance to be found here.

After the seminar I mention to him the fact that during my courting days I once went to Ashton's. "Oh, wow," he says. "Was it how I described it?"

"Worse," I say. I explain to him the Irish connection - he seemed to have no idea. I explain the fact that for years Ashton's, along with the Galtymore Dance Hall, acted as if border to an emerald isle that stretched from Cricklewood Broadway, through Shoot Up Hill, and came to a drunken halt at *The National Ballroom*, in Kilburn High Road.

Tobias is really easy to talk to – I feel immediately at ease in his company, talking about writing, about his work, about mine. We talk some more about Ashton's: he seems fascinated by my description of it, but is pleased that it was everything he imagined it would be. "I only wish I'd gotten to go there," he says.

"You only wish that, you don't really mean it," I laugh.

"And yet, despite that night, despite your description of it, you still married your wife?"

"Absolutely," I said. "Just seeing her dance beneath the mirror ball was enough for me."

"I'm glad," he said.

I mention how much I enjoyed his seminar, as well as the fact that Stephen Knight described my fictional literary attempts as an 'airport novel!' He offers a sympathetic laugh. "Do you think Dan Brown worries about such criticism?"

If only I'd had Tobias Hill's number on me during that tutorial with Stephen Knight, I could have called him - *Hi Tobias, I have a bit of a situation here*, I'd say. *I need you to get here now. I need you to defend my (un) literary honour.*

"It's fine as a first draft," Stephen Knight repeats his familiar mantra, "but you need to go away and re-write it."

I need Tobias Hill with me now; I need him to be my representative, my advocate, my agent, my literary counsel. I need Tobias Hill to engage Stephen Knight in literary conversation; I need them to debate the merits of an airport novel; I need them to become so engrossed with their respective arguments that they simply do not see me retiring to a point of safety; that they simply do not see me escaping the room with my tail between my legs.

Surveying Stephen's room I realise it's probably not big enough for a Harry Hill type *fight*; there's far too much order for fisticuffs. Besides what could the pair of them do?

Stephen and Tobias circle the room, sizing each other up. Stephen will make the first move; lunging at Tobias' chest with a rolled-up copy of James Joyce's *The Dubliners*; Tobias will counter with Graham Greene's

Brighton Rock; Stephen will be left with a Pinkie brown type scar upon his face

'It's fine as a first draft,' Stephen Knight says bringing me back to reality.

'Thanks,' I say; once again I have neither the heart nor the nerve to tell him that the piece has been written and re-written over and over again.

'But you need to go away and re-write it.'

'Okay,' I say, leaving his office deflated, not quite sure whether I've just been given some really good advice or yet another damn good kicking.

Writer's Block

The only cure for 'writer's block' is to *write* – sound advice indeed, even if a little simplistic. Most writers at some time or another have experienced writer's block – unable to progress any further with the next word (the first word often), the next line, paragraph or chapter. Writer's block however, is not necessarily the same thing as a writer losing confidence or faith in their craft: in my case, even the most constructive of criticisms were enough to send me scurrying towards bed, pulling up the covers in a hopeless attempt at warding off the dark clouds gathering above.

In terms of the novel it was already complete – in my head, at least – with any criticism of it, those parts of it written and presented, whether constructive or not, not really a major problem. Of course I knew it needed major re-writes. No, for me, the content, the structure, the exposition, was never really a problem, especially in terms of writer's block. My problem was I simply couldn't finish. In my head, the story was finished – the life stories of the characters I'd created were as familiar to me as those of my own family and friends: as far as a I was concerned these characters had long since been brought to life (or death, to be more precise), with absolutely no chance of me discarding them now, whether through re-writes or the 'fat-trimming' process.

The more I ploughed on though, the more I struggled with the advice I'd been given: the harsh criticism, especially from Stephen Knight, whose accusations regarding it being little more than an airport novel, haunting me, even now: in his heart of hearts I'm sure he believed I was tough enough – man enough – to take the criticism; never once realising how truly crushed I was.

Whether he was like this with other students I've no idea: one or two I've had conversations with since have hinted towards, what they described as, his 'tough love' approach. In my case though, perhaps because of my background, the persona I projected – I think many people saw me as some sort of cockney wide-boy, some Sid James like character, who'd slipped in under the radar – Stephen Knight obviously thought I was more than tough enough to take his criticism, like some grizzled prize fighter, taking it on the chin, licking my wounds in private, before bravely returning to the ring in anticipation of yet another beating. The truth was though, I'm sure unbeknown to Stephen, I was as frail and as fragile as every other student on the course: I was suffering the same doubts – constantly questioning my abilities – constantly worrying that this was going to end the same way as everything else I'd tried – that thing my dad called the 'five minute wonder!'

Just why I took to writing I have no real idea. I'd never wanted to 'write' before, and there was certainly no one in the family or amongst my wide circle of friends that had ever committed anything 'literary' to paper. Shortly after my thirtieth birthday though, I just picked up a pen and started to 'write.'

At the time I remember having insisted on 'no celebrations whatsoever!' Besides, what was there to celebrate? A divorce? A sudden bout of ill health? The first irrevocable fractures in the relationship with my young son? Instead, I found myself retreating to my small flat on Camberwell Green, pretty much ending all contact with those closest to me. In fact, far from feeling that life was starting over again – what with my new accommodation and the first faltering steps with Sharon – I was suddenly of the opinion that my life was ending, not starting. Indeed, within a few short weeks my relationship with Sharon ended – my decision, not hers – as I struggled to deal with the recent past.

What made me start writing? What made me suddenly pick up a pen and frantically put it to paper? Even now, I'm not quite sure - there was no sudden moment of realisation, and there was certainly no epiphany. In all honesty, that first moment I took a pen to paper I think, subconsciously at least, I was actually considering a 'note' – a few lines in an attempt at explaining away the despair I felt, the helplessness of my situation, not really seeing any real end in sight other than an inevitable return to the middle of Blackfriars Bridge. Instead though, I started writing about 'snow' of all things - my first memories of snow, my memories of that tiny garden in Ruby Street. In fact, within a few short hours I'd filled up dozens of pages regarding my parent's first real 'home' of their own, which, despite its temporary nature, would become a place spoken about with such affection - a place where they, where *we*, as a family, seemed so happy.

Why I wrote what I did, again, I have no idea, although it soon became clear to me that I was writing it for them, my parents: at the time, it was the only thing that really made any real sense to me – that tiny house always so full of love and happiness.

Whilst I wrote, in secret mostly, my mother, also in secret, was writing to Sharon: assuring her as to just how much the whole family loved her, how she knew *I* loved her; how she knew I was lost somehow – had always been lost – how she prayed that I'd one day find my way back to all of them, to Sharon and to her, yet smart enough to realise I needed the time and space to work it all out for myself. Even so, I knew she worried – I knew they both worried – that I'd never solve the problem of over-thinking every little thing; over-worrying about every minor detail of my life, over-worrying about my death, worrying that I'd never be able to explain away the things that constantly drove me to distraction. But then that was my mother all over.

I remember when I first declared to everyone my intentions to become a 'writer' my mother just smiled – a genuine smile – perhaps hoping that at long last I'd finally found something that I liked doing; something she hoped would make me happy. "That's nice," she'd said at the time, acknowledgement enough to make me invest in a word processor, even though I could barely afford to pay my bills. My dad, on the other hand, was pretty scathing of the suggestion, although I've always put this down to the fact that he was still pretty unhappy with me for getting divorced, abandoning my son, running away from everything, and burying my head in the first few chapters of a memoir that finally comes to life (writing) here in this book.

"Writing?" *he'd* said at the time. "It's not really a proper job, is it?" For him it was all about going to 'work,' and putting bread on the table, and paying the gas bill. It's funny, but I think he thought writing was somehow 'dishonest.'

Not that I realised it at the time, I finally came to understand (as a result of writing about my parents, for my parent, at least with them in mind) that they were actually just two heads of the same coin. They both worried about me, I know, but they both came at it from different angles: my mother always viewed me as this Peter Pan type character, refusing to grow up. Not that she considered that a negative quality. She always described me as a "dreamer," yet she always said it with that same smile, as though that were a good thing to be.

"Yeah, he's a dreamer all right," my dad would counter though: for him 'dreaming' was the same as 'writing,' it had no place in the real world.

In his Afterword, reflecting upon his memoir (*And When Did You Last See Your Father?*) Blake Morrison describes the writing process as a respite to his father's terminal illness and eventual death. In stark contrast, when my mother died, my literary output was non-existent; there *were* no stories to tell, or so I thought, other than a recording of sombre facts and memories of a day that everyone was trying desperately to forget.

Despite suffering writer's block, following the death of his father, Blake Morrison attempted capturing childhood memories, which he would later combine with journal extracts written during his father's illness: whether he intended them for publication or not, in just fifty-one weeks his memoir was finished.

If only I could write like that. If only I could conjure up such stories of my past. If only my life had been more interesting. In actual fact, during the three week vigil leading to my mother's death - even if I didn't realise it at the time - a life story was actually told, in snippet form, not just the life of my mother, but of a family struggling to establish itself in the modern world, desperately searching for a New Jerusalem.

In the years that followed my mother's death I became fascinated with the subject, morbidly so, wanting to talk about it all the time, constantly wanting to relive the agony of it. During that time I discovered that I'd been most happy amongst the dead, amongst memories of those that had passed away - their presence in my life, and the small part I played in theirs – vivid memories that I could almost reach out and touch.

Every week I would visit my mother's grave, take fresh flowers, until it became a place of respite, the place where I felt most comfortable. Like Morrison, I too became a death bore; even going as far as to start writing other people's eulogies, family members, friends, strangers eventually; attending their funerals and read-ing from the pulpit their life stories, the circumstances surrounding their deaths.

Almost as if by way of research, I suddenly found myself studying people's emotions, observing their grieving process. Within my own family the process was diverse; my dad, naturally, was crushed, constantly seek-ing solace in the past, constantly revisiting places that he and my mother had visited in the hope that it might bring him comfort (I'm not sure that it ever did). My brothers by stark contrast were strangely normal, although my eldest brother adopted a mean streak, made all the worse by alcohol; his method of dealing with grief was to flit between silence and rage, angrier at the world than he'd ever appeared before. My younger brother though, who was so strong at the time of my mother's death, was the only one that appeared to remain normal, keeping his grief to his self, never showing any sign of emotion whatsoever. Sharon meanwhile pretty much kept her own counsel, her emotions delicately skirting around mine, ignoring the elephant and the heavy signs emanating from my corner of the room. Even so, she constantly encouraged me to write, seeing that as my only means of escape from the void into which I'd fallen.

"What can I write?" I'd demand of her.

"Write about anything. Write about your mum?"

That was impossible of course; unlike Morrison, that would never do. I came from a family and a background, which simply didn't talk about *those* things. During my mother's illness no one ever mentioned the word "cancer;" my grandmother's Alzheimer's was simply put down to forgetfulness, so there was no way I could write about that - at least up until now. In fact, the story that Blake Morrison took a mere fifty-one weeks to achieve – he's even written an accompanying book since (*Things My Mother Never Told Me*) - took me almost ten years to even consider, let alone attempt committing to paper.

The Telephone Call

Tutorial/Accredited Assignment Submission

When the telephone rang the first time I wasn't actually at my desk, although those past few weeks I'd usually been within earshot of its annoying ring. The woman I share the Taxation Department with – it sounds important, but it's not – lifts the receiver, and in best telephone voice declares, "Taxation Department." After a brief moment she shakes her head in my direction and carries on with her conversation: some clerk of chambers probably, chasing up his barrister's Legal Aid fees, the whole thing a bloody racket as far as I could glean from the job.

The Crown Court at Southwark was set back on the southern side of the Thames embankment, midway between London Bridge and Tower Bridge, a stone's throw from the HMS Belfast. To the right was Hay's Galleria and to the left English Grounds: back then it was a massive bombsite of land, but would later be transformed into the home of the London Assembly.

Some fifteen months earlier, I'd actually been summoned to the court to perform jury service, which lasted about three weeks: at the time I was unemployed following redundancy from the HMSO (Her Majesty's Stationery Office) at Vauxhall.

For some reason most people seem reluctant to do jury service, although I was quite looking forward to it: I imagined myself playing the part of Tony Hancock in a half hour episode entitled, *The Twelve Angry Men*. Besides, it would get me out of the flat for a couple of weeks – away from *Richard and Judy*, and *Fifteen-To-One*, away from the continental quilt and an another afternoon nap that would usually stretch way into the early evening.

The jury service itself was pretty uneventful: I only did the one trial; an open and shut case, which none of us could agree a verdict on.

Of course, knowing what I know now, cynically appraised, the whole thing seems like a big charade - *Bring on the dancing jurors*, they'd cry - every defendant guilty, the juror's the only people not able to grasp that fact.

In between the trial – you can't believe how much waiting around jurors do, sat outside court rooms whilst barristers and judges argue points of law and golf handicaps – I would often chat to the court usher. Like me, he'd been made redundant, in his case from British Gas: in the years previous hundreds of thousands of people had lost their jobs, especially from the privatised utility companies – all of them falling victim to Maggie's boom before the inevitable bust.

"There's a load of us here," he said. "A bloke from British Telecom, another from the Electricity Board, we've even got a couple of fella's that worked in the bank." He told me that there were always jobs there and that, if I was interested, he'd give me the contact details of whom to ring, see what's on offer, that sort of thing.

About a week later I sent a letter, CV, etc., explaining that I'd been on jury service and that I was looking for work. A few days pass when I get a phone call: a chap from the Court wonders if I wouldn't mind coming in for a chat - it was all pretty informal. Indeed, when I turn up for the interview I find it's that same informal approach: I met these two managers, we sit on comfy chairs, both of them seem really nice, a job's offered, as simple as that really. At the conclusion we get chatting, one of them asks me about where I live, where my parents live. "Eltham," I say; it turns out that he knows the area pretty well.

"Do you know the big roundabout?" he asks.

"Do you know Westmount Road?" I counter.

"Yes, I know that really well."

"Do you know St. Luke's Church?"

"Yes."

A couple of years previous there had been a really bad car crash on Westmount Road; six teenagers crashed on the brow of the hill, the car caught fire, and they all died. This was one of those nights when everyone came out of their houses; drawn by the flashing blue lights, the build up of traffic; neighbours, *neighbours* you rarely talk to under normal circumstances, all milling around in dressing gowns - for a few hours that old spirit of the Blitz returned to a semi-suburban street. A few days later a rushed memorial service was held at St. Luke's Church, the whole community coming together in a shocked vigil of remembrance.

Most mornings on my way to work - a new job these days, a new place of employ – I pass that spot where the accident happened; that traffic-calmed stretch of the road. Today there's a plaque cemented into the pavement, the names of those young people transcribed upon it, and a tree festooned with teddy bears, and birthday cards, and ribbons, and forget-me-nots:

Vicki Raynham (18)
Miriam Tickner (18)
Daniel Garwood (17)
Mark Higgins (17)
Stewart Innes (17)
Daniel Jones (20)

By chance, a couple of the lads have plots up near where my Mum's buried now, the graves well visited, well attended to. On the anniversary of the accident, birthdays, Christmas, special occasions, all of their friends put in an appearance, clean the headstones and change the flowers, drink a few beers and generally pay respects - on those days I'm always lifted by the sight of them, all of them having grown a little older, their friends staying the same age they always were.

As I pass by that spot it's hard not to think about that interview, hard not to think about the unwitting things I said that day.

"Do you know the big roundabout?" he asks.

"Do you know Westmount Road?" I counter.

"Yes, I know that really well."

"Do you know St. Luke's Church?"

"Yes."

A few months into the job a colleague mentions the fact that the manager, the one I'd had the interview with, had lost his daughter in a road traffic accident. *What?*

It turns out *his* daughter was driving that night - a Mini Metro, whether that's important or not – those six friends weighing down the car, the petrol tank scraping the tarmac and sparking flames upon the road.

I'm not sure how long I let it pass now – too long, I know that much - that guilty secret; the fact that I knew about his daughter, that I'd stumbled upon the truth - *I was really sorry about your daughter, you know; that day at the interview, the things I said, I just didn't know, I just never realised*: I think it was probably about the same time that my mother first became ill. Even so, he smiles and nods his head as if to confirm that he understands – *how would you know?* More than that though, perhaps he realises that we're about to share some bizarre spirit of bereaved kindredship - only I haven't received my telephone call in the middle of the night, or in the middle of the working day.

Curiously, when the telephone does ring, I'm actually taken by surprise, as if I weren't expecting it, "Taxation Department." For the briefest moment I forget. For the briefest moment I actually manage to live a normal, mundane life.

"Is that you, Neil?"

The office is open plan, allowing hearing access to every one-sided telephone conversation; every gripe, every piece of office gossip. The section where I work contained four desks that intertwined like honeycomb – two for *Taxation*, one for *Pre-Trial*, and the other for *After-Trial* – casually divided by photographs of loved-ones, potted plants, lever-arch files and a small sign declaring: *You don't have to be mad to work here, but it helps* - humourless office humour, David Brent not quite yet envisaged, but not too far from the awful truth.

Upon receipt of the telephone call the woman I share the department with, she's worked there years, gets up and busies herself discretely with the filing cabinets and a watering of the office plants: these are the things that you remember, the tiny things you appreciate at some later date. We'd worked together then for some time and were well used to each other's little idiosyncrasies. Each day around four o'clock she'd leave with a flurry, eager to get home to her husband: they'd been married for thirty-odd years, and yet she still claimed excitement at the prospect of walking through the front door and seeing his face.

Most days she'd give me the latest excerpt from her life story: her daughter's on-off relationships; her daughter worked for MI5, and so I was always asking if she got a discount on flat-pack furniture - she never got the joke.

Most lunchtimes she would have her head stuck in a glossy holiday brochure; she was "going on a cruise in the summer," she'd tell me, and was planning to have her bedroom redecorated – yellow, as I recall.

The bloke opposite, Paul, is equally discrete, hiding himself behind a massive pile of court files. He's only doing the job in the absence of the regular woman, who's off enjoying two weeks in Spain: she's another one that's been there years; the one that always dons the novelty Christmas hat come the festive season, the one that always has one too many glasses of sherry, the one that always ends up showing everyone her big knickers. By contrast, Paul is a quiet sort of chap; rebellious like me, in a spirit-of-punk type way, but far more subtle with it. He claimed that industrial relations were all about mind over matter, although in his case I think it was more mind over *mantra* - he held loosely based Buddhist beliefs, along with a touch of *Feng Shui*, witchcraft and a smattering of Catholicism. Most summers he packed himself off to a monastic retreat, from which he'd come back looking completely exhausted. Wherever he worked in the building - he was always covering other people's jobs - he would always bring with him a collection of plants, which he claimed, with the right care and attention, would give out energy signals, although, as far as I could make out, the plants seemed to be sapping energy from *him*.

One morning on my way to work I saw him standing along the Thames embankment. His eyes were closed, deep in mediation, and in his outstretched hand he held a piece of string from which dangled a large crystal.

"Morning," I said loudly as I passed by.

"*Neil?*"

I'm surprised to hear my dad's voice at the other end of the line: he never rings me at work – he worries that he'll 'get me into trouble.' Even so, I'm distracted somewhat by the woman to my right who, even then, at that precise moment in time, was going through her usual routine: most days she screeched at the top of her voice. Today though, perhaps because of the telephone call, it appears worse, as does she, as if escaped from her cage, wings flapping; an annoying bird in full flight.

Someone's upset her probably, looked at her the wrong way.

Just why she acts the way she does, I still have no idea. Even now she's twittering, making these manic hand gestures in order to attract people's attention.

"Can you keep the noise down please?" I say, attempting to maintain an air of politeness, although I feel like Jack Nicholson in *One Flew Over the Cuckoo's Nest.*

Sadly this request has no effect whatsoever, and so I attempt signalling with my free hand, Peter Kay style, the fact that I'm on the telephone. She though, seems to mistake the gesture for some form of mating ritual, *no billing and cooing for her if you don't mind*, quickly looking away as if in cementation of her disinterest.

"Forfucksake, I might as well bang my head on the desk for all the good it will do me," I growl. "Can't you see; I'm on the *phone?*"

Observing her now across the desk, it's as if I've suddenly made a clockwise movement with the dimmer switch inside her head.

"Did you hear what *he* said?" she suddenly demands of no one in particular. "Did you hear what *he* said?" By now it's like a mantra. "Did you hear the way *he* talked to me?"

"I'm sorry, Dad," I say into the mouthpiece. "It's a little noisy this end."

Already I can see her leaving her chair and rushing headlong towards the desk of the office manager - looking to make a formal complaint probably. As usual, he placates her; following her down the corridor to the women's toilet, where he will stand, embarrassed, on one side of the door whilst she sobs on the other.

Elsewhere in the office there is sudden movement; out the corner of my eye, I can see half a dozen members of staff (remaining seated) making crocodile movements towards each other, their chair wheels gliding excitedly across static-proof carpet tiles, eager to know just *what* it is I've done to upset her.

"Are you still there, Neil?"

My mum and dad were meant to be in Bournemouth. Today though, is Friday, and they're already home: they weren't due home until Monday at the earliest.

The plan had been to take one last look at the old place; to take one last stroll along the front; to take one last stroll upon the pier; to take one last stroll along the East Cliff; to take one last stroll along the *prom, prom, prom*. Now though, they're home again, their trip to Bournemouth cut short – no stick of rock, no bawdy seaside postcard, no wishes that we were there.

"We're home," he says.

"How's mum?"

"She's gone to bed."

"Do you want me to come home?" For the briefest of moments there's a deafening silence at the other end of the line, "Dad?"

"There's no need to rush," he says.

"Let me sort some stuff out here and I'll get the train."

Once again his end of the line goes quiet: he's not replaced the receiver. I know he's still there though, hiding at the other end of the coil.

It had started off as back pain, "Your mum's been suffering back pain," is how my dad had described it. Only it wasn't back pain as I knew it; it wasn't the sort of back pain that postmen suffered from; it wasn't the sort of back pain brought about by too much heavy lifting; it wasn't the sort of back pain that entitled you two weeks off work and a golden certificate from the doctor. This was a deceitful sort of pack pain – a back pain that hid a multitude of nature's sin.

"We've been to the hospital," my dad said. "Your mum's had a scan."

This was the sort of back pain that started with a visit to the doctor and ended eight months later with your dad making a phone call to you in the middle of the working day.

"I have to go." I say to the woman I share the job with. She's nice. She just nods. She doesn't need an explanation. "I'm not sure when I'll be back."

Slipping from the building with little fuss, and the best wishes of those within earshot, I make my way quickly along Battlebridge Lane and through the lower side arches of Hay's Galleria. As I reach the main internal courtyard I'm immediately hit by the warm sun beaming through the high glass ceiling; the sunlight raining down upon the curved black girders and the cleaned stone power-washed of its past. Despite the architectural splendour, this is but a tourist eye view of London: it's far more Richard Rogers than it ever was Charles Dickens, with its smattering of *faux* market stalls spaced like the numbers on a clock face around the galleria's water feature.

Outside *Balls Brothers* (the local wine bar) a large group of city traders mill around with their Cabernets and their Chablis. Whether it's the hour of the day I have no idea, although they seem louder than usual. Some of them have removed their jackets and ties, like ordinary people. Some play *Petanque* (French Boules), scuffing their welted leather shoes upon the gravel: an ill-thought-through Parisian street scene in the heart of a cosmetic London Town. Under normal circumstances I hate these people with their garish braces and their cufflinks and their swept-back hair. Today though, for some peculiar reason, their presence sparks nostalgia in me – so much so that I almost feel regret as I quickly pass through the galleria behind, take the escalators leading up into London Bridge Station two at a time, and make a mad dash up the tunnelled incline towards platform four.

By chance, luck, karma, an Eltham train stands at the platform: who knows; perhaps the driver knew I needed to make my connection; knew that I couldn't afford to wait another thirty minutes for the next one. For a few minutes past the time of departure the train stands idle allowing ample time for me to step aboard and for the doors to close seamlessly behind me.

Moving through the compartment, with far too many empty seats to choose from, the train suddenly jolts – the rear carriages concertina their way to the front – and I slump into a seat on the left hand side, still breathing heavily from the dash up the incline toward the platform.

As the train leaves the station behind I'm lulled by the gentle rocking motion, that nostalgic feeling I felt in Hays Galleria not quite yet dissipated.

Out the window on my right is Guy's Hospital, on the left English Grounds and Tower Bridge Approach. Snaking its way towards Bermondsey the train picks up speed somewhat, past wharves and warehouses not quite yet embraced by regeneration, not quite envisaged as loft-style apartments.

It was some twenty-odd years ago now that my mum and dad first made this journey; went off in search of their New Jerusalem, carrying with them a bundle of photocopied homes for sale; travelling to the outskirts of London with some regret over the fact that they were finally contemplating an escape from Southwark, the borough of their birth.

Around me my fellow passengers, my fellow escapees, those attempting a head start to weekend happiness, feign interest with the passing urban landscape. They obviously don't realise my connection to the buildings and landmarks that we pass. They probably don't know the things I know. They probably don't realise the minutia of trivia that floats around inside my head.

They probably don't realise that, in 1852, at London Bridge Station a gentleman by the name of W. H. Smith opened one of his first bookstalls.

They probably don't realise that my Granddad Jim once took a train from Brighton to London Bridge having already suffered a heart attack on the East Sussex coast.

They probably don't realise that when a doctor at Guy's Hospital questioned him as to why he had not gone straight to a hospital in Brighton he replied that, "I just thought it would be too far for people to come and visit me!"

They probably don't realise that Guy's Tower, the tall building that dwarves the hospital grounds over to our right, when viewed from the platforms at London Bridge, looks like a big dog.

They probably don't realise that I was born in Guy's Hospital, on the fourteenth of June 1962.

They probably don't realise that I share a birthday with the late American actor, Sam Wanamaker.

They probably don't realise that Sam Wanamaker came to England in 1950 having been blacklisted by the House Un-American Activities Committee during the McCarthy witch-hunts.

They probably don't realise that, over to our right, my Granddad Joe once lived in the same house as the fictionalised Little Dorrit.

They probably don't realise that, during the Blitz, when my Granddad Joe's house was bombed he found an empty Victorian house near Borough High Street, took a crowbar to the front door, and lived there for the next fifty years.

They probably don't realise that the New Globe Theatre, on London's Southbank, was the brainchild of Sam Wanamaker.

They probably don't realise that during Sam Wanamaker's twenty-year campaign to have the Globe Theatre built he was my Granddad Joe's neighbour.

They probably don't realise that the father of the first girl I kissed, despite my not remembering *her* name, operated Tower Bridge - that he actually pulled the lever that made the bridge go up and down.

They probably don't realise that if you stand in the middle of Tower Bridge, with one foot on the south side and the other on the north, you will experience the sensation of a mini-earthquake whenever traffic passes by on either side.

They probably don't realise that, as the train rattles through Spa Road Junction, there was once a station here (Spa Road Station), or that the line we travel on was the first purpose-built railway into any capital city in the world.

They probably don't realise that the railway was built by four hundred English and Irish labourers.

They probably don't realise that, despite building the railway together, away from work, the English and the Irish hated each other with a passion, and would often fight.

They probably don't realise that, in an attempt to stop drunken clashes between the rival nationalities, the labourer's were encamped on separate sites, hence the name *English Grounds* given to the large expanse of land that would soon disappear beneath Ken Livingstone's blueprint for regeneration.

They probably don't realise that the song, *The Red Flag*, by Jim Connell, was penned during a journey between Charing Cross and New Cross Stations, on that very railway line, in the midst of the Great Strike.

They probably don't realise that every May Day my dad would take an unpaid leave of absence from work (annually risking the sack): it *was a protest,* he claimed, *a show of solidarity* - this was years before it was made an official bank holiday.

They probably don't realise that the enormous derelict building on our left was once the home of Peek Freans Biscuit Factory.

They probably don't realise that my mother worked there on the Christmas pudding production line.

They probably don't realise that Bermondsey was unofficially named 'Biscuit Town' as a result of the factories presence in the area.

They probably don't realise that on summer days, with the chimney's burning, the air was filled with the glorious aroma of custard cream biscuits.

They probably don't realise that Sharon collects friends in the same way that I collect photographs of tragic British comics.

They probably don't realise that most days, when I wake, I contemplate, for the first few seconds of each new day, a suicidal end to my life.

They probably don't realise any of this stuff.

They probably don't realise that my family once lived in the shadows cast by the enormous Old Kent Road Gasworks over to our right.

They probably don't realise that we lived in a prefabricated house, which had arrived on the back of a lorry.

They probably don't realise that in the 1960s an unexploded German bomb was found in the grounds of the gasworks.

They probably don't realise that the people that lived nearby were never evacuated during its dismantling process.

They probably don't realise that the army ordered everyone to stay inside their homes, open all doors and windows in deflection of the blast, and to lay face down on the floor with our hands covering our ears.

They probably don't realise that my dad had thought this a ridiculous idea because. "If the bomb goes off, it'll take half of bleedin' Southwark with it," he'd said at the time.

They probably don't realise that those tiny little houses were made from asbestos.

They probably don't realise that my mother has returned from Bournemouth in order to die.

They probably don't realise that, at this precise moment in time, she lies sleeping in a room, which she has tastefully decorated with that very thought in mind.

Tutorial with Maura Dooley

As usual, I'm nervous. It's the first time I've presented to Maura - Blake Morrison has taken a term-long sabbatical to finish his latest book – and I'm wondering just what she'll make of this latest submission: deeply personal, as it happens, which has never sat too well with me. With fiction you can hide the truth behind layered scenes of fantasy. You can 'fudge' the truth; you can show yourself in better light, you can avoid all forms of personal heartache. "It's wonderful," she says, though.

"Thanks," I say, blushing, although I'm not quite sure whether she's referring to the piece in general - the writing, the description, the dialogue - or the actual subject matter.

"Obviously, there are things you need to improve on."

Here we go, I think. "Of course," I say.

"One of your biggest problems is that you tend to over-egg the pudding."

"I know, I know," I hold my hands up in submission. It's the usual criticism of my work.

"You never seem to know what to leave out," she frowns.

"You should see me packing a case for my holiday!"

She laughs. She always gets my sense of humour. What she really means though, is that I tend to throw everything into a piece of writing. Perhaps it's an insecurity thing, I don't know, but sometimes I feel like one of those a sit-com writers looking for a joke every thirty seconds or whatever the statistic is - never knowing when to stop.

Last term I had a similar conversation, and received similar criticism from Blake Morrison. He though, came at it from a completely different angle, all business, taking his pencil and dividing the piece up into four or five different sections. "Your problem is wanting to tell the whole story at once," he'd said. "Now, if it was me," he motioned the different sections that he'd highlighted, "this would be one book, this another." It was fascinating seeing how his mind worked - offering me an insight into writing as a 'profession,' rather than just self-confession. "There are three to four books here at least," he'd smiled.

"You mention this part about you feeling suicidal?" Maura jolts me back to reality.

"Yes," I say, sheepishly.

"You write about how unhappy you feel sometimes?"

"Most of the time, actually."

"Well, this piece reads as if you've suddenly decided to share all of these innermost thoughts, and now you're forced to . . ."

"To confess everything, I know, I know."

"Yes, to put it all in this one piece."

"Like primal screaming or something, or a stream of consciousness?"

"You've only just boarded the train."

"I know."

"You haven't even reached New Cross Station."

"I know, I know."

Maura's great. She 'gets' me. In fact, I think she knew all along, even during our very first meeting, what it meant to me. I think she realised from the very beginning the enormity of what it was I was trying to do - that the things I'd written in the past were merely a build up to me delivering this particular piece. I think she also knew that it was her duty to tear this particular piece to shreds by way of constructive criticism. Only she doesn't, not really. For the most part she has nothing but praise, and I leave her office feeling ten feet tall.

"It's a wonderful start," she says again, just before I reach the door.

The Email

From: Maura Dooley

To: Neil Bradley

Email Subject: Following on from tutorial

"I truly believe that there are certain people to whom or through whom the territory, the place, the past speaks . . . Just as it seems possible to me that a street or dwelling can materially affect the character and behaviour of the people who dwell in them, is it no also possible that within this city (London) and within in its culture are patterns of sensibility or patterns of response which have persisted from the thirteenth and fourteenth centuries and perhaps even beyond?"

'Cultists Go Round in Circles,' Barry Hugill, The Observer, Sunday, 28 August 1994

Neil, that quotation is from an interview with Peter Ackroyd. I'm sure you'll know his work but if not, you should look him up. Also, Iain Sinclair. The others I mentioned are Arthur Morrison 'A Child of the Jago' and 'Mean Streets, and many others,' and Henry Mayhew, 'London Labour and London Poor.' Both 19th

Century writers, the library should have their work. All of them have basic stuff on Wikipedia to give you an idea of whether or not they'd be useful. Mayhew may sound dry but, believe me, he is fascinating.

It's a great project. Good luck with it!
All the best,
Maura

Trainspotting

At New Cross Station the train stops almost grudgingly: the station, along with the streets that surround it, appear grim, even with the sun shining down on its deserted platforms - for most commuters the station passes in a blur, serving only to signal the close proximity to the city or an escape route *from* it.

The area itself has always seemed confusing: Bohemian some might describe it – those that flitter around the entrance to Goldsmiths College, the bright young things, the liberals, the radicals, the artisans, the artistic, the academic, the work shy. Despite this description though, it actually boasts (or, at least, boasted) one of the biggest Irish communities in South London, even if there's little evidence of that same community today, save for the interior of the Marquis of Granby public house (John Kelly's bar), which sits on one corner of the New Cross triangle – a one-way system that disrupts the traffic on its way through that particular part of South London. Tentative entry through its doors reveals a *Life on Mars* like time-warp, the punters a mixture of Irish labourer, their numbers shrinking with every new arrival from Eastern Europe, youngish locals scattered around the pool table, and a smattering of staff and students from Goldsmiths – authenticating the process with endless pints of Guinness and drooping roll-ups.

It was here that the Bonzo Dog Doo-Dah Band were formed, amidst constant traffic noise, two of the fiercest barmaids you're ever likely to encounter *anywhere*, an Irish jukebox, and nicotine patterns stains that crept up the bar and across the ceiling, and will linger long after the introduction of any nationwide smoking ban.

Today the train stands at New Cross for twenty seconds at most, hissing its doors closed in rejection and quickly moving on through St. John's Station (trains rarely stop there), Lewisham, Blackheath and then Kidbrooke, with its sprawling housing estate (long since targeted for demolition) – it was here they filmed Gary Oldman's semi-autobiographical film *Nil By Mouth*.

Leaving Kidbrooke Station behind, seemingly as fast as possible, the train suddenly runs parallel to the A2, which links London with Canterbury and the south coast of Kent. On its approach to Eltham the railway line arcs, sweeping the train left across the motorway. Back in 1972, on this very spot, a train crashed: a seaside special returning from Margate following a beano (a thing of the past). At around nine-thirty in the evening the excursion hit that particular arc in the railway line and violently derailed, resulting in five passengers being killed, including the driver, along with a further 126 passengers being injured: an investigation found that the train had been travelling at three times the recommended speed, whilst a post-mortem revealed that the train driver had been drinking heavily.

Today thankfully, the train takes the bend at a far more leisurely pace, and as it leans gently left the horizon reveals the prominent rising outline of Oxleas Wood at Shooters Hill, where, above the tree-line, one can just make out the flag and turrets of Serverndroog Castle - a recent nomination for the BBC's *Restoration* prize. This was built in memory (folly) of the seafarer Sir William James, director of the East India Company: these days the castle has been vandalised and stands derelict.

During the early 1990's Oxleas Wood became the scene of a general election battleground, with Neil Kinnock flying in by helicopter for a Mexican standoff with Peter Bottomley, the Northern Ireland Minister. This followed government plans to route a major cross-capital link road through the middle of a woodland which had stood undisturbed for some eight thousand years, and came during the last weeks of an election campaign which Kinnock finally looked as though he had a chance of winning – at least up until Rupert Murdoch decided that this was not to be. That day I stood up at the top of Oxleas Woods watching as Kinnock shook hands with people, thinking that there appeared a genuine optimism following two terms of being beaten down under the Thatcher government.

The battle for Oxleas Wood was eventually won and lost (depending on your viewpoint) in the European Parliament, although Kinnock's own battle ended following his disastrous evangelical pre-election performance at Sheffield... *Well, alright, alright, alright, alright* . . .

On the night of the General Election I witnessed Kinnock's post-election speech: stood on the steps of the Labour Party HQ in Walworth Road his summation of Britain under Thatcher chillingly depressing.

As the train approaches Eltham Station the foreground suddenly reveals a large open expanse of greenery: Eltham

Pleasance, a horticultural gem, barely visited by the majority of the local populace (other than by those with spray cans). Through the trees, behind the high brick wall, beyond the secret garden, and the goldfish pond, one can just make out the Tudor Barn. This was built in the 16th century by the biographer and Parliamentarian William Roper, who lived there with his wife, Margaret, daughter of Sir Thomas More – *A Man for All Seasons*.

At the end of the 18th century the Tudor Barn, renamed Well Hall House, became home to the Bland Family, Bohemians, Hubert Bland and Edith Nesbit. As socialists, and followers of William Morris, the pair often produced joint left-wing pamphlets under the name *Fabian Bland*, in memory of their son who died during routine surgery at the age of fifteen.

Across the road from Eltham Pleasance is a Co-operative supermarket. Cars pull up at all hours of the day and night, people dashing in and out for milk, newspapers, cigarettes and lottery tickets.

It was in the mid-1800s that the Rochdale Pioneers established the *Rochdale Principles* on which the Co-operative Movement was built.

Next door to the supermarket is a Co-operative Funeral Home. My mother's neighbour, Denise, works there part-time.

Whilst at school my brother stole a copy of Shakespeare's *Macbeth*. I took it from his shelf and secretly read it. I didn't understand it.

Hubert Bland and Edith Nesbit were also the founder members of the Fabian Society, a forerunner of the modern day Labour Party.

Whilst at school my brother stole a copy of Anthony Burgess' *A Clockwork Orange*. I took it from his shelf and secretly read it. I'm not sure I understood it.

Although a prolific writer on socialism, Edith Nesbit (writing under the name *E. Nesbit*) is best remembered, as a children's author, with arguably her most famous work, *The Railway Children*, written whilst living in Well Hall House.

When I was younger my mother took me to see a film adaptation of *The Railway Children* at the ABC Cinema in the Old Kent Road. Secretly, I loved it. Secretly, I loved Jenny Agutter. After that, I gave up on reading, and watched only films.

The station sign reads *Eltham* – the *Royal* part of the title non-existent, other than in the tourist literature: Royal Eltham, home of Henry VIII and his Plantagenet Eltham Palace. The Tudors though, they preferred the Palace at Greenwich, abandoning Eltham Palace, which eventually fell into disrepair following the chaos of the English Civil War.

In the 1930's, Eltham Palace became home to the philanthropic pairing of Sir Stephen and Lady Virginia Courtauld, who rebuilt the great hall and transformed the palace into an art deco master residency, which is now managed by English Heritage. Again, few of the locals are even aware of its existence, let alone being able to boast visitation rights.

Stepping from the train I turn left towards the exit and make the long walk from the front carriage back along the platform. Ahead of me commuters walk a collective steady pace towards the stairs. I, on the other hand, hang back, lingering on the platform long enough to watch the train's departure: I think about Edith Nesbit, about *The Railway Children*, about Jenny Agutter - the first girl, if only in celluloid form, that I saw naked - running headlong towards the end of the platform, embracing her absent father as he emerges from the steam. "Daddy, my daddy." She cries, and I'm in love again, in love with Jenny Agutter

Today there's no steam – electric current removes the train from view in relative silence. *Mother, my mother*, I think as I head towards the steps that lead down to the empty ticket hall.

Exiting the station I cross the giant expanse of commuter car park - at this time of day it's still pretty full. Midway down the car park there's a pedestrian bridge that leads across the A2, the distant roar of cars audible above the boundary wall, whilst to the left there's a foot tunnel that leads under the railway line.

Passing through tunnel I notice the graffiti that plays cat and mouse splatters with the council's anti-graffiti van. Most days the council repaint the walls and make right the graffiti vandals wrong, only for the vandals to return a few hours later - re-spraying on blank brick canvas. As usual I curse their actions, including those of the well-meaning council: I dread to think how much it costs, these men constantly painting the Forth Bridge or the Eiffel Tower or that meaningless tunnel beneath the railway line. It would be cheaper, surely, to put up a camera or carry out a police surveillance operation for a few nights - try and catch them in the act? If I had my way I'd spray the little fuckers with the tools of their trade, cover their faces in shades of azure and apricot, brilliant orange or burnt umber: anything but this stupid game. Who knows; perhaps it's because I'm feeling old, feeling angry, feeling tired - perhaps it's because I'm taking a journey that I don't really want to take - that the vandalism bothers me so much. Perhaps it's the futility of their actions, the futility of life, the futility of work, the futility of chemotherapy.

Emerging on the other side of the tunnel into bright sunlight I'm struck by the semi-urban, secret garden type nature of the place. Crossing the road I pass a young girl, late teens, early twenties (I've never been good with ages), casually smoking cannabis. As we pass by one another we're both lost in a fog of Class 'C' smoke. I shake my head, but can't quite decide just which one of us it makes the more paranoid.

From here to my parent's house it's pretty much wall-to-wall housing amidst generous smatterings of greenery. A century ago most of the land was purchased by a Scottish Parliamentarian, Archibald Cameron Corbett, who immediately declared the land Presbyterian, which meant that no public houses, off-licenses or betting shops could be built there, and which only adds to the curious nature of the place: in many ways Eltham is filled with contradiction. Falling just inside the capital on the London and Kent border, it's not quite urban, not quite suburban – there's a mixture of pleasant streets – with its middle and working classes, so interwoven that many can't remember what they were originally. Even so the area remains rich in both history and trivia.

Across the road from the entrance to Eltham Palace is the former home of the singer Kate Bush. The giant gates to her house declare *Wuthering Heights*.

Radio, stage, film and television comedian, Frankie Howerd, lived in Eltham – *'ere no missus, titter-ye-not!*

Before leaving for stardom in Hollywood, Eltham was home to Bob Hope, along with his brother, the film and television producer, Jack Hope.

Boy George was born in Eltham, along with Jude Law, who began his career at the Bob Hope Theatre.

Eric Liddell, who won the 400 Metres gold medal at the 1924 Olympic Games, attended Eltham College – his life story formed the basis of the film *Chariots of Fire*.

Deputy Labour Leader, Dennis Healey, lived in the Eltham 'Hutments,' which were built to house workers of the Royal Arsenal at Woolwich.

A short walk from Eltham Station you can find the former home of Herbert Morrison, grandfather of former Cabinet Minister, Peter Mandelson, and one of the pioneer leaders of the Labour Party. During the Second World War an air raid shelter, the *Morrison Shelter*, was named after him.

The first indigenous Australian, Yemmerrawanyea, to ever set foot in Britain, died and is buried in a church graveyard in Eltham.

In 1993 the reputation of Eltham was tarnished, and the area brought to national attention, following the racist murder of black British teenager, Stephen Lawrence.

Under normal circumstances the walk from Eltham Station to my parents home is a pleasant one, which winds its way along streets decorated with FOR SALE signs: welcome to the neighbourhood – welcome to the postcode lottery and the rubbish collection rota, and the permit parking. Along one particular stretch two or three of the houses have the same lights, the same giant plant pots sat either side of similar coloured front doors – keeping up with the Jones' turned into an unimaginative art form.

My parent's house has changed over the years – pebble-dash wall covering skimmed with plaster and carefully concealed beneath liberal coats of yellowish exterior house paint. The front garden has disappeared too – replaced with a drive, the end result of a subsidence insurance claim. At the time, between the giant cracks in the wall and the redecoration process, there had been a massive trench from pavement to front door – with occupants and visitors forced to navigate their way to the doorbell via three long planks of wood. There was also once a great tree, which my dad took a saw to, a tree which, during one hot summer, very nearly defeated him, a tree which he hacked away at, a tree which refused to buckle or in any way surrender its prominent position amidst the greenery.

One day, under a bright yellow tennis ball sun, my dad was there, chopping and sawing and cursing (he never swore). A chain saw would have done the trick. But oh no, he was using the tools of his trade - the tools of someone *else's* trade in actual fact; a saw which he bought as an apprentice, a chisel, and a hammer too – all to no avail. For all the good it did him, he would have been better off taking a fiddle bow to the saw, giving us a tune, a waltz, a sad lament. Still he kept sawing away though, undeterred, the tree refusing to budge.

My parent's house was located on a very narrow stretch of the old A2, which, until the relief road brought… well…*relief*, was clogged most hours of the day and night, with traffic running between Dover and London, and then back again in the opposite direction. This meant that every time the traffic lights turned red along that particular little stretch a procession of cars, buses, coaches and lorries would grind to a halt outside the house.

Most days my dad barely noticed the hiss of air breaks or the constant revving of engines. This particular day though, with that tennis ball sun beaming down on his thick head of hair, he hears nothing; he was deaf in his left ear anyway, so he could only hear on his right side at the best of times. Today though, he's in Buster Keaton mode – oblivious to the traffic, oblivious to the coach full of people opposite, oblivious to the fact that you should *never* lean your ladder against the same tree branch which you are about to saw through.

Before the lights turn green again, my dad was up on the deck, along with the ladder, the tree branch - the occupants of the coach just catching sight of my dad's paint-splattered work shoes protruding over the garden wall.

Tutorial with Blake Morrison

When I arrive for my tutorial with Blake Morrison I find he's not in his office – he emailed his 'I may be late' apologies in advance – so I'm forced to linger in the corridor outside his door. Through the small square of glass I can see inside his ordered space that acts as home whenever he's on campus: the book covers in frames, theatre posters, family photographs (I assume), the odd postcard – an ordered writer, with an ordered office, an ordered biog, and an ordered haircut.

Blake Morrison (from his web page) was born in Skipton, Yorkshire, and educated at Nottingham University, McMaster University and University College, London. After working for the Times Literary Supplement, he went on to become literary editor of both The Observer and the Independent on Sunday before becoming a full-time writer in 1995.

A Fellow of the Royal Society of Literature, and former Chair of the Poetry Book Society and Vice-Chair of PEN, Blake has written fiction, poetry, journalism, literary criticism and libretti, as well as adapting plays for the stage. His best-known works are probably his two memoirs, "And When Did You Last See Your Father?" and "Things My Mother Never Told Me."

Since 2003, Blake has been Professor of Creative and Life Writing at Goldsmiths College. He lives in south London, with his wife and three children.

At the moment I'm midway through his novel: *South of the River*, in reference to South London, which has always appeared somewhat cut-off from the rest of the capital: the title is a play on words, black cab-driver talk – *I never go south of the river*. In fact, most Londoners, one suspects, would probably like to see it cast adrift, despite acknowledgment of its Tate Modern, the Globe Theatre, the London Eye, Aquarium, and London Assembly, the Saatchi Gallery, the National Theatre, the Royal Festival Hall. But then all of those are in touching distance of a bridge, an escape route to the other side.

I'm reserving judgement on the book until I've read it, yet I can imagine Blake grinning to himself as he jotted down the working title – *South of the River*. I imagine Blake being proud of the fact that he, too, lived south of the river, that he, too, could boast such an adopted piece of southern geographical residency: Blackheath, south of the river. Of course, most native South Londoners wouldn't actually class Blackheath as being "South of the River." For most it's considered a sort of enclave, a tiny principality - an area of South London that could just as easily be lifted up and planted down somewhere else like Hampstead or Holland Park, Richmond or Kew.

On his arrival at the office I mention to Blake how shortly after moving from Camberwell to Eltham someone asking whether I'd experienced "Blackheath Relief" yet.

"Blackheath Relief?" he asked, turning the key in the lock and bidding me welcome.

"Yeah, that's when you drive through South London, up Blackheath Hill, and then you suddenly feel relieved!" Whenever we've met he's always allowed me time to go through my little vaudeville routine with him. "Of course, when you drive down the hill in the opposite direction you end up with a touch of the *Deptford Despairs*!"

South of the river - native South Londoners call it "Souf London," whilst comedian's and radio pundits call it "Sarf Londaaan" – I don't know why it bothers me so much.

"You don't mind if I eat my sandwich?" Blake says.

"No, of course not."

A few nights previous I'd watched the DVD of *And When Did You Last See Your Father?* - starring Colin Firth as Morrison and Jim Broadbent as his father. It was different from the book - not quite as intimate. All the same, it's a pretty good film in that *typically British* type way.

Sitting opposite him now it seems odd to me: it seemed odd sitting opposite him having read the book, but this is different. Now I'm sitting opposite Colin Firth, to all intents and purposes, and in my mind Blake Morrison will forever mourn at the bedside of Jim Broadbent – it's just the way my mind works; the weird scenarios that play themselves out in my head. Besides, Blake already thinks I'm a lunatic as a result of the last time I sat in his office. On that occasion there was a giant sized mock-up of his book (*And When Did You Last See Your Father?*), which was leant up against the wall. For some reason, upon seeing it (you couldn't really miss it), I went into a kind of Kenneth Williams mode, commenting in a high-pitched voice, "Oooh, that's nice?"

At the time he seemed somewhat taken aback, claiming shyly that it had been a gift from his publisher. Of course, now I was in that mode the character seemed to take over, "Colin Firth, eh?" I said, in a sort of *nudge, nudge, wink, wink* type way.

"Yes," he said embarrassed.

"It'd be a nightmare reading that on the train, though?" I motioned the giant book.

"It's not real," Blake said, deadpan.

"Oh, right," I say. "Of course, when they film my book I'm hoping to get Charlie Drake to play me."

"Charlie Drake?"

"Yeah, you know, the Worker, *hello my darlings*."

"I think you'll find he's dead."

Silence.

Blake Morrison picks up my submission piece and waves it in front of me. "I'm a little confused," he said. "It reads as if I should be aware of a previous chapter?"

"Aren't you?" I say.

"No."

"It was meant as a follow-up piece to the one I submitted to Maura (Dooley)."

"Ah."

"I thought you might have seen it?"

Blake shakes his head.

"It was submitted as part of my last assignment."

"I see," he says, picking up the bundle of papers again.

"Perhaps I should have written some kind of introduction?"

"It really doesn't matter," he attempts reassurance, although I think he senses it bothers me. "This is a life-writing piece, I'm assuming?"

"Yes."

"What happened to the novel?"

"Don't even go there . . ."

He sits waiting for a further explanation as to why I've suddenly shifted my attentions to life writing. None is forthcoming. "Okay . . . well there's certainly enough here for us to work with." He reads through the first half of the first page again, re-familiarising himself with the piece. "Do you want to explain it?"

"It's about a train journey," I say, which is pretty bloody obvious, whether he knew what was coming or not. "It was a train journey I took . . ." I falter, not quite knowing what to say next, suddenly feeling very tearful – not quite sure where this has come from. "It was a train journey I took when my mother was dying . . . this was the start of her dying . . . a few weeks before she died."

"I see," he said. "And have you written any more?"

"No," I say, far too quickly.

"And why's that?

"I'm struggling, if you want to know the truth."

"Struggling, how?"

"Just struggling, that's all."

"Struggling to tell the story?"

"Yes," I say, honestly. "The piece I submitted to Maura was about getting a phone call from my dad at work telling me to come home . . . I was at work, and he rang me at the office . . . he'd never ring me at work usually."

"Your mother was dying?"

"Cancer," I said. "All over. It took about nine months from start to finish."

"I'm sorry."

"The thing is, I read your book . . ."

"*My* book?"

"*And When Did You Last See Your Father?*"

"Ah." Blake nods his understanding, the nod of a man who knows exactly what it was I went through, although I man that seemed to suffer none of the problems I did, the problems I continue to suffer with regards committing a record of it to paper. "And have you tried writing about his subject previously?"

"Yes . . . I've tried at least."

For the remainder of the tutorial we talk about my parents, about his parents, about his reason for writing the book, along with the follow up (*Things My Mother Never Told Me*). I begin telling him about how I'd been struggling with the novel, how I'd got bogged down with it, the advice I'd received during the tutorials and workshops not really helping, how they'd only served to confuse me more.

"And this new piece?" he asks.

"I'm not quite sure what this is either," I say honestly. "I mean; I know *what* it is. I know what is I'm trying to write, in my head at least."

"It's a tribute piece?"

"Exactly," I say, hoping that he can make more sense of it than me. "Only I'm not suite sure who it's a tribute to."

"It'll work itself out," he reassures me.

Author's Note: Be careful when using colloquialisms in your writing.

Blake questions me over the 'Beano' reference. "Are you talking about the comic?'

"No," I laugh.

"I'm not sure I understood that bit."

I recently saw some footage of George Harrison talking about The Beatles *Magical Mystery Tour* film, which he claims was based on a 'beano,' when all the factories in Liverpool shut down for the day and everyone went off to the coast on a 'works outing' – a massive piss-up to all intents and purposes. "It's a jolly-boys outing, a trip to the seaside, a work's outing," I attempt explaining, although I don't suppose Blake has ever been on a beano. "It's probably a working class thing, something that only happened in factories."

He nods his understanding, "You said though, they're a thing of the past?"

"Yeah, I'm not sure anyone goes on beano's anymore. It's all stag dos and hen weekends now, and even then they're opting for places like Dublin or Eastern Europe or some such place," I say regretfully. "I don't think anyone bothers going to Southend or Margate anymore."

For Blake, of course, at least according to his book, it was trips across the Yorkshire Dales with his father or days out at Fountain's Abbey, skiing holidays in the Alps, driving his father's car across some deserted stretch of beach up north somewhere.

"It's a shame though," I say. "For me they were always Davey Crockett moments."

"Davey Crockett?"

"Beano's," I smile at the thought of it. "Yeah, whenever my dad went on a beano, I always ended up with a Davey Crockett hat!"

Returning home late at night, pissed probably, his one day during a full year, he'd creep into my bedroom, stagger more like, and place a Davey Crockett hat down at the end of the bed. The next day I'd wear it to school.

"A Davey Crockett moment." Blake smiles at that.

Funeral Three – Doreen Margaret Bradley

Friday 8th May 1998

There has always been something weird about engaging a key with a lock to a home you no longer live in. The key's the same. The lock's the same. It's the same door; there's the same familiar click as the lock is released and the door opens inwards. This house though, despite its familiarity, is not my home. Not any more.

Closing the front door silently behind me, there is an empty silence, as if no one's home. I know this not to be the case though.

Along the passage and up the stairs a collection of pictures line the walls: LABOUR WIN LANDSLIDE VICTORY (a photographic reproduction of the front page of the London Evening Standard, virtually a year to the day), there are wedding photographs of my two brothers, Lloyd and Jason, standing awkwardly alongside their respective better halves, there's a photograph of Sharon and myself - looking a lot younger than we are now – taken at my parents' ruby wedding anniversary party, there's a group photograph of all the family (on the rare occasion we all got together) taken in the back garden a few summers back, there's a picture of my mum and dad at a freemasons festival.

Since my last visit a short week back nothing appears to have changed, even if know that everything has changed, knowing that there will be no going back – no *getting* back – from this tragic moment in time.

In the dining room the large oval table has been cleared of this morning's post-opening, junk-mail-discarding, ritual. In the centre of the table is a vase containing freshly-cut flowers. These though, are no real indication of a special occasion, a get-well-soon, a birthday or anniversary: my dad has bought my mother flowers every single week since they first got married (I marvel at his discipline). *He* sits in the living room. From my secret vantage point in the dinging room I can see him through the glass doors that divide the two rooms. He looks lost. He's sitting on the sofa, normally reserved for guests (for Sharon and I, the only two people that can really lay claim to regular visitation rights). He sits motionless, as though there's nothing for him left to do. The Daily Telegraph's been discarded. Everywhere has been dusted, the carpet's vacuumed: none of it really needing doing since the last time, just before they took themselves off to Bournemouth on Tuesday.

For a few moments I linger in the shadows of the dining room, not wanting to break the spell he's under – not wanting to disturb his staring off into familiar space. There's no sign of my mother, no sound of her presence in the house.

I clear my throat theatrically, but my dad's deafness (he's deaf on his left side) prevents an acknowledgement of my arrival. In the end I'm forced to drop my keys on the table, careful not to leave a scratch on the polished grain. Immediately he springs to attention, looks for things to tidy, but finds no relief.

"Dad," I say.

"Neil," is all he can muster in return. Usually we go through this small talk routine about work and the weather and politics. Today, instead, he heads straight to the kitchen and fills the kettle.

"How's mum?" I ask.

"She's upstairs," he says, although I can't work out whether I've just fallen victim to his deafness or a dose of misinformation.

"I'll just pop up and see her."

"She's in your room now," he says, shaking his head, before turning his back on me and doing a Tommy Cooper routine with the teacups. I linger for a few moments watching his hustle and bustle: keeping himself busy, that's the key.

Of course, I already know what's prompted this 'moving of bedrooms.' I'm not that naïve, even if I don't really want to hear the truth of the matter. A few months back, when my mother was still relatively healthy, appearance-wise at least, there'd been a little flurry of activity. The room to which my dad refers – my old room - was suddenly treated to new wallpaper, a new coat of paint on the window frames, a couple of framed photographs hung on the wall, a small bedside cabinet and a table lamp, my mother's doing. In many ways I think she is just trying to protect my dad from the heartache of dying in the bed they've shared throughout their married life: I think she worries that, if what's about to happen *happens*, he won't be able to sleep in that same bed anymore, that he won't be able sleep in that same room anymore, that he won't be able to *sleep*.

During the build up to this event – it was 'an event' the way I saw it – my mother seems to have gone about her business with a quiet dignity: preparing herself for the end, getting her affairs in order. Yet all of this was done in secret – secrecy reigned supreme in her house. Firstly there was that secret back pain, and that secret appointment at the doctor, followed by that secret hospital appointment. Then there was that secret scan, and that secret diagnosis. Secrets though, despite revelation at some later stage, can only ever prompt further secrets. And so my mother found herself living out that secret moment of her life in, well, *secret*. As a family of sons, and daughter-in-laws – my dad was privy to the secret of course – we'd remained blissfully unaware of the machinations until we, too, had part of that same secret revealed to us. We were aware of my mother's treatment, of course, even if we never quite got to grips with what that 'treatment' actually entailed. We were aware of the fact that she was undergoing treatment, although even this was undertaken in relative secrecy. We were aware of the appointment dates, the times of those appointments, the venues for her treatment, yet were equally aware of the fact that, for a long period, her appearance remained unchanged. Today though, following that telephone call, and following that unwanted journey home, the full extent of that secret is about to be revealed to me.

I climb the stairs slowly, lingering in the tiny hall at the top of the staircase, where the sun bathes me in rays of sunny dust particles, which fall from the skylight. I take a deep breath, attempting to slow my rabbit-like heartbeat. I attempt figuring out what my opening words to my mother will be.

Through the crack in the door I can just make out her, now, tiny frame beneath the quilt – she lies still. She's not sleeping. But she doesn't move either. I clear my throat theatrically again, as I'd done to little success with my dad a few minutes earlier, and make a big production of easing the bedroom door open further.

"You alright, mum?" I say in a sing-song voice, entering the room, kissing her, and then taking up a seat on one of the two chairs that have recently been added to the sparse furnishing. "How was Bournemouth?"

"I couldn't eat the food," she smiles.

On the bed at her feet is a large black metal box – the sort of thing you keep important papers and documents in.

"What's that?" I ask, more by way of prompting conversation than really wanting to know the answer.

My mother smiles leaning forward and lifting the lid of the box. "My whole life is in here," she says. Inside I can see it's filled to the top with papers, photographs; pieces of jewellery. Delving in amongst the lucky dip she plucks out a *Co-operative* brochure, which she leafs through until she's found the page she's looking for. "This is the headstone I've chosen," she says, proffering me the brochure. I can't say anything. I'm choked. I lean down and inspect my shoes. I didn't expect it to happen as quickly as this. "Brown marble granite," she says proudly - you'd think she was talking about a new car or a three-piece-suite. My eyes well and a giant tear falls on to the toecap of my right shoe. I'm not *prepared* for it to happen as quickly as this. "It was expensive. But worth every penny." Another tear falls, and then another: I promised myself I wouldn't cry, not today; there are weeks left for that, I hope. "The top is covered with marble chippings," *I carry one with me now wherever I go,* "and there's plenty of room for flowers." By now the tears are bouncing off the toecaps of both shoes like Jolson's *April Showers*. "I love flowers," my mother said.

"I'm really sorry, mum," I say, not because I'm crying, but because of what's happened to her - what's *happening* to her - what's about to happen to her. I lean forward in the chair and touch the quilt on her bed, and she gently touches my hair, and I cry even more.

She draws me in. "Everything's going to be alright," she says. I don't believe her. But still I allow myself to be drawn into the lie - I allow myself to believe, if only for the next few moments, that none of this stuff is really happening. For the next I-don't-know-how-long I keep my face buried in the quilt and she rubs my head as though she would a small boy on a hot summer's day.

"You alright, mum?" Looking up I suddenly notice my brother, Lloyd, standing in the doorway: I don't know how long he's been there, or how much he's seen or heard. He enters the room and kisses her, and I wipe away the tears from my eyes with my knuckle, attempting to pull myself back together thinking *if I'm like this now how will I be at the end?* Ten minutes later my younger brother, Jason, arrives, looking uncertain, followed by my dad bringing up the rear with a tray of teas. We all take up positions in the tiny bedroom. No one speaks. From downstairs in the living room we hear the chimes of the clock on the mantelpiece.

And so it begins.

Saturday 9th May 1998

All about the practicalities now – sorting out who comes when, who will do what. None of us are quite sure of the timescale – we've not been given the exact date. It's happening all the same though. I can tell this by the way my mother's dressed: it's late in the morning and she's still wearing a nightdress. She seems relaxed though, as if a great burden's been lifted from her shoulders (transferred on to all of ours). Her bed has been made again and so she sits on top of the covers. Her toenails are painted blood red. "I've always had nice feet," she says. "Elegant." Sharon and I nod. "It's because I've always bought good shoes, even when I couldn't afford them."

"I love the colour of that nail polish," Sharon says. She's so like my mother. She's so good, so nice, so incredibly beautiful. She has this long dark hair and milky-white skin; she maintains a naturalistic look, with little to no makeup - Irish blood/first generation English Rose. My mother has high hopes for her and has always considered her a daughter: she knows that she came to my rescue following my divorce; she knows that she came to me on the rebound and that she stayed with me (forever). I think she wanted to see the pair of us married. I think she really hoped it would happen. But, like a fool, I kept resisting. It's too late now, though, surely? I've left it too late. I've left it *all* too late.

"It's important to look after your feet," my mother says, almost absentmindedly. "It's so important that you buy good shoes." I feel like I should be taking notes – writing something down about looking after my feet and buying good shoes - as though my mother were giving me life lessons. I suddenly feel the tears welling up in me again. But I won't cry. Not in front of her. I promised myself I wouldn't do that again, even if I don't really know how this can be achieved.

"The garden's looking lovely," Sharon says.

My mother smiles – pride on her face. "It always looks best this time of the year." All three of us look out of the window – the net curtain is pulled back to reveal an explosion of her colourful handiwork over the years. "It took so long to get it like that," my mother said, the slightest hint of regret in her voice. She brings her knees up to her chest and rests her folded arms upon them. At that moment she reminds me of the Edward Hopper painting, *Morning Sun,* its lone woman, typically ghost-like, as with all of Hopper's paintings, sat atop a bed, daydreaming, looking towards an open window. I snatch a glance in my mother's direction. I feel like a voyeur, spying on her through a blown curtain.

"This afternoon, I can cut the grass, if you like?" I offer, more in an attempt at moving the conversation on. *It's not going to be like this, is it?* I think. *We're not going to have to make agonising small talk from now until . . .*

"I've had a lovely life," my mother says.

"I'll go down and cut it now," I announce, "before it gets too hot."

Downstairs Jason and Lloyd have arrived – sharing a meaningless conversation with my dad: the weather, football, some outrageous story they've just heard on the news. "Mum wants me to cut the grass," I lie, walking straight past them and heading out the back door into the garden, not quite sure anymore just where I fit amongst the women or the men in the family.

Closing the door behind me, I walk up the garden path, the overhanging lavender brushing my jeans, and on through the ivy-clad arch, still amazed at the way the ivy, so thick, is the only thing holding up the rotting trellis-work frame that hides beneath it. On the other side of the arch there is a smaller, more ordered, garden with apple trees and low-growing shrubs and a bricked circle where my mother hides the washing line from the neighbours. Beyond that is a large wooden shed, which lists slightly to the right, and beyond that a greenhouse where my mother spent hours filling tiny pots with wet earth and cuttings snipped from the gardens of the stately homes of England – "They'll never miss a few cuttings," she'd always smile.

I fumble the key into the padlock that guards the shed door – there's nothing worth stealing inside: a couple of rusting bicycles, two worn out sun-loungers, and a lawn-mower. As I turn the key I worry that the lock will snap: it's rusted from the rain and a lack of oil, and so I'm forced to apply far too much pressure than it really deserves before it springs open with a loud 'click.' Forcing open the door and stepping inside I'm immediately struck by the hot, almost claustrophobic, nature of its confines. Even so, I'm comforted by the solitude it offers, the almost melancholy nature of it – this and the fact that no one can see me from the house, which is an added bonus at this moment in time.

Moving aside the sun-loungers I pull at the lawn-mower, which seems reluctant to want to come outside and play. I pull at it again, and again, finally yanking it from the corner, although not before the bicycles topple over and a jar containing screws, nuts and bolts falls from a shelf and smashes on the shed floor. I curse, attempting to clear up the mess, cutting my finger, before dumping all of the contents, broken glass, nails, screws into an old terracotta plant pot – *I'll sort it all out later*, I lie to myself.

For the next hour or so I attempt creating isometric lines with the lawnmower, pushing and pulling the thing up and down the small stretch of lawn – I have the turf at Wembley Stadium or the centre court at Wimbledon in mind.

"Just mow the grass," my mother had said earlier. "Every couple of weeks in the summer . . . during the winter everything else will pretty much take care of itself, save for the occasional pruning." Midway through though, I suddenly lose heart; I'm suddenly struck by the feeling that perhaps I shouldn't be doing this. This was my mother's job. This is *still* my mother's job.

Upstairs in the bedroom my mother smiles, "He'll never be able to keep it up," she says to Sharon, shaking her head.

"Your mum says, you're just making it more difficult for yourself," Sharon calls from the open window. I ignore her, ploughing on until there's not a single blade of grass left to cut. Throughout the process, I can see them lip-synching, the pair of them plotting - Sharon and my mother – more secrets.

That night on the way home in the car I question Sharon over what has been said in the privacy of my mother's bedroom.

"It's private," she replied.

I felt somewhat slighted – I hated secrets. But then that was just my mother's way. I know what she's like. I know that all the people who come to visit over the next week will be treated to the same – life lessons. I know she'll have different things to say to different people; things she'll have to say to all of them, and some things she'll say to them alone. "She's like the Godfather," I laugh. "She's like Don Corleone, dishing out instructions on the day of his daughter's wedding."

"She just cares about everyone," Sharon said, "that's all."

"Okay, I know I shouldn't ask, but am I going to get *whacked*?"

"Oh, you," she says, slapping my shoulder playfully. "What are you like?"

"Is Luca Brozzi going to dump my body in the Hudson River?" All the while I've got one eye on the traffic light, my hand resting on the vibrating gear stick, and as I watch the light she watches me. "No, seriously," I say, attempting to avoid her gaze, "am I going to be sleeping with the fishes?"

Sharon smiles, bringing her hand to rest on top of mine. Just then though the lights change from red to green. I pull the gear stick down into second and then up into third, and Sharon's hand falls away from mine.

Sunday 10th May 1998

Dad cooks Sunday lunch. Everyone's there – it's like Christmas. My mother overseas the preparation of the potatoes and the gravy and the vegetables, "No parsnips for Neil," she says. "He never eats parsnips."

My dad, I can tell, is all hot and bothered. But he pulls it off with minimal fuss. Everyone sits around the table. Everyone chats. Every thing is blissfully mundane. My mother plays with her food - puts on a 'show' of eating - but rarely brings a fork to her mouth. It's like the last supper, although I'm still not sure just who it is that's being betrayed.

Monday 11th May 1998

I ring work – tell them I won't be coming back for a while. I speak to Georgina, the woman I share the

Taxation Department with. "Everyone sends their best," she says.

"Tell everyone thanks," I say. "I'll give you a ring . . . you know . . . when . . ."

Tuesday 12th May 1998

We're back in my mother's room again – Sharon and I – it's our turn to spend an hour sitting on the two chairs. My mother spends the majority of her time upstairs now, only coming downstairs to use the toilet or to make little forages into the garden. Occasionally, she drifts off, falls asleep sitting up: sometimes it only lasts seconds, other times it runs into a few minutes. When she opens her eyes again she smiles, pleased, I think, to see we're still there: it's been two minutes at most.

Prompted by something – a memory or brief dream – my mother delves into the metal box at the end of the bed and produces a bundle of old, black and white, photographs, which she fans out on the quilt, "I'm not sure how old I am in that one," she says, pointing to a particular picture of herself in much younger days. Sharon reaches for the picture and spends a few moments studying the image, "I loved the way people dressed back then," she says, handing me the photograph and immediately reaching for another. I recognise the staircase in the picture – it's the one that led down into the garden at my maternal grandparents' ramshackle old house (the one on the front cover of this book). In the picture my mother strikes a pose, mimicking some film star from yesteryear, although she looks far too self-conscious to carry it off: this just makes the pose seem all the more innocent, the photograph all the more sadder.

"I wish I'd had my teeth done," my mother suddenly says. The pair of us don't offer up any reply, although it bothers me that she should mention it: my mother has a slight overbite, which has lately become exaggerated as the skin pulls tighter across her cheek bones. Even so, there's never been any hint of vanity with her.

"Look at your dad in this one," Sharon says, holding up another picture: this one shows my dad proudly sat astride a racing bike, drop down handlebars, taken in the street outside the same house as in the previous photograph.

"The *size* of him," I laugh. In the picture he's really chubby - his hair's greased back, although not quite a Teddy Boy. "That must have been my granddad's cooking!" A strange phenomenon in my family was the fact that many of the, perceived, female roles were carried out by the men: we all cooked, we all did, still do, the ironing. My Granddad Jim certainly always seemed to do the cooking, conjuring up these giant dinners with a famine's worth of potatoes on each plate – butter on the marrow, butter on the cabbage. Everything would be covered in salt. This he would pour straight onto the tablecloth to form a mini salt mountain, which he'd then run a knife through, before sprinkling the salt with a flourish, the way a conductor commands an orchestra with an extravagantly waved baton.

"Look at this one," Sharon says, passing me a photograph depicting a birthday party - my mother's. She's in the centre of the picture with pigtails and a party hat. I'm not quite sure, nor is she, what age she is. In amongst the party guests sits my dad, still chubby, but a younger, boyish version: he sports a broken arm in plaster and a sling.

"I didn't even like him," my mother said. "He was always pulling my pigtails."

"A sure sign of love," Sharon laughs, resting her hand on my leg.

"I thought he was flash," my mother says, laughing too.

"I think it's so nice," Sharon says, "the pair of you knowing each other all those years, living in that same street." I worry that she's going to cry. "Staying together all this time . . ."

Just then I wondered whether or not I'd find that - this thing the pair of them had, this bond – but then suddenly realised that I'd already found it with Sharon, suddenly knowing that it had been staring me in the face for all along. I should have gotten married. I realise that now. We should *get* married. I should do it for my mother, before it's too late, grant her that peace of mind. But then I have these notions, these sparks; these impulsive feelings towards things I should do now, at this very moment in time. These impulses though, they just as quickly fade.

Another photograph, this time of my mother singing in the choir - at the Royal Albert Hall or the Royal Festival or Westminster Central Methodist Hall? Before I can ask another photograph's pushed in my direction. This one shows my Granddad Joe, in that same garden from previous photos, sitting in a deck chair in-between lines of washing, with skinny folded arms hidden beneath rolled-up shirtsleeves. "He had everything in that garden," my mother said, "chickens, goats, vegetable patches, an old Lambretta Scooter. Years later he *buried* that in the garden, along with all the old family pets."

"I wish I'd met him," Sharon says genuinely.

"He was a wonderful man," my mother said. "He was a wonderful father," by which, I think she meant that my grandmother probably wasn't.

My dad arrives mid-conversation, carrying a tray of teas as usual, "He was certainly a character, old Joe, I'll give him that much," he says, smiling, shaking his head at the thought of him.

"He was always turning a coin somewhere," my mother said, "selling home-made toffee apples on the doorstep, constructing these strange-looking bicycles and renting them out by the hour. He rented his piano to the local pub," she smiled. "Every Saturday evening all the regulars would turn up to collect it, and then they'd wheel it off down the road, before returning it to us after the Sunday lunchtime sing-song."

"He was never home," my dad said, laughing now. "Off with his other family probably."

"He was so hard working. So caring," my mother said, ignoring my dad's remark. "He was always working, all hours of the day and night, selling programmes at the Lord Mayor's Show; always looking for work whether it was the Festival of Britain, the Queen's Silver Jubilee or the Ideal Home Exhibition."

"One year he came home from the Ideal Home Exhibition carrying this giant cardboard box," my dad laughs. "He walked into the living room and placed the box on the floor. He had this massive grin on his face."

"What was in it?" Sharon asked.

"Chicks."

"*Chicks*?"

"Yes. Baby chickens," my dad said. "Hundreds of them."

"How wonderful," Sharon says, her face lighting up like a child's.

"He said they were going cheap!" We all laugh, but the joke goes over Sharon's head.

"Chicks," she said again in wonder

"You should have seen it," my dad continued. "There were hundreds of these baby chicks running around the living room. He had to sit up all night, trying to keep them warm with a bar fire and a light bulb."

"Wow," Sharon exclaimed. "But what happened to them?'

"Well," my dad said wryly. "Once they all grew up, he wrung their necks and we ate them all!"

We all burst into laughter again, even my mother, although Sharon sits crushed, looking like an eight-year old who'd just lost her first rabbit. I squeeze her hand. My dad sits on the edge of my mother's bed and she gentle rubs the back of his neck. I smile, amazed at how easily this has now turned into routine; amazed by the very normalcy of it all. In real life these would be snatched moments, all of us too busy with our own lives, with work, with television, with consumerism, with foreign holidays, with football. Now though, I realise how precious these moments really are; realising, all too late, that I should have been preserving them as if they were photographs – hidden treasure – in a black metal box. I want to cry, but can't help but smile at the joy of this moment.

Sharon passes me another photograph – my dad dressed in a three-piece suit, outside the flats at Bankside during their courting days.

"I remember dancing with him at the Festival of Britain," my mother motions the photograph. "He was a good dancer." She rubs the back of my dad's hand.

"Did you hear that?" Sharon says, poking me in the ribs playfully.

I ignore her. I never dance.

"Every Sunday evening, during our courting days, we'd go over to Soho to have a 'shilling coffee.' We didn't have a lot of money," my mother says. "That was our one luxury. We'd walk from the Borough, along Bankside, over Waterloo Bridge, up through Covent Garden . . ."

I imagine the pair of them, in the glow of love, young, the whole world in front of them, like Terrance Stamp and Julie Christie in that song - Terry and Julie escaping over the river where they feel safe and sound, just stopping long enough to gaze on Waterloo Sunset.

Wednesday 13th May 1998

My mother asks for the Vicar to be summoned. We're all stunned. We're socialists, we don't need God. We need a cure - some miracle. God's not going to supply that, whether we believe in Him or not. Besides, it's gone too far now - the disease has taken too firm a grip: my mother has already accepted that fact. She smiles, "I need you to go to the Vicarage and fetch Father John," she says. "He's always seemed like a nice man. He was really good when those teenagers were killed in that car."

"I'll go." I say.

He has to go though, my dad; make his peace with God, even if I know he secretly hates Him. He's always been respectful like that – keeping his faith between himself and the God he doesn't believe in.

Father John came in the afternoon. There's no way he could be described as a 'trendy vicar,' with his longish grey-blond hair, beard and glasses, although he's typically Church of England - I've often seen him walking around Eltham in a long black cloak like Peter Cushing in his *Hammer Horror* days.

On arrival at the house he was very business-like: my mother introduced him to everyone, "This is my daughter-in-law," she says. Sharon, I can tell, is overjoyed, I could see it on her face; my mother smiles at her, at the little white lie she's just told.

"Would you like tea?" my dad asked.

"Not for the moment, thank you," he replied. "I think I should talk to Doreen first."

A few moments later my mother and Father John go upstairs to her room, closing the door behind them. The rest of us take up seats in the living room. Occasionally, someone glances up at the ceiling – he stayed up there for nearly an hour – none of us knew what was going on – more secrets.

"She has nothing to confess to *him*, surely?" I said.

"She's probably just planning the funeral service," Sharon says.

This made sense. My mother was big on that sort of thing. "I want lots of flowers," she had said a few nights earlier. "I want a service in the church. I want everyone to walk in the road from the house to the church." She wanted to stop the traffic for a few minutes: for years cars and lorries and buses had thundered back and forth past the house. "They can wait for me for a change." Throughout her wish list come the day of the funeral we all sit passive. Occasionally we nod, feign smiles, laugh out loud, although none of us really want to hear any of it. "I want Barbara Streisand's *Evergreen*," she continued. My dad had worried about whether we'd be able to have our own music – he wasn't sure what the rules were. My mother though, was adamant. "If Princess Diana can have Elton John singing in Westminster Abbey, then I'm sure I can have Barbara Streisand singing in St. Luke's," she'd said.

When Father John returns back downstairs he walks straight into the living room and takes up a seat in my mother's armchair, "I think I'll have that tea now," he said.

Immediately there is an almighty scramble as my brothers and I, the wives and the sister-in-laws, all jump up from the sofa and the dining room chairs: none of us really eager to make the tea, yet none of us really wanting to be left in the room with the Vicar. In the end it's settled by my dad, "I'll make it," he said. "You talk to Father John."

For a few moments we all sat there squirming in the uncomfortable silence, whilst Father John gets up and walks around the room studying the photographs and the oddments. "A remarkable woman, your mother," he says, picking up a framed photograph from the nest of tables and studying the image of my parents (in younger days). "I don't think I've ever met anyone quite like her."

"She's been really strong," I said.

"That's because she's at peace with her life, with her death, at peace with her friends and her family, and with God."

"I'm not sure any of us believe in God," I said. "Not anymore."

"Your mother does."

"We're socialists."

"Ah," Father John said, sitting back down in the chair as though it suddenly all made sense to him. "I should have realised."

A few moments later my dad brought in a tray of teas and handed Father John a bone china cup and saucer (we all have mugs). Father John thanks him, but my dad doesn't stay in the room: we all sat listening as he goes upstairs to where my mother lays in her bed. "He's really upset," Jason said.

"Of course he is," Father John smiled. "He's obviously had a wonderful life with your mother."

For the next hour or so we just talked, about the family, about my parents; everyone chipping in with their own little story; everyone becoming more animated with each new reminiscence. Throughout, Father John has the cup and saucer perched upon his clenched fist – precariously balanced - chatting happily about the funeral, and my mother's wishes come the big day. For the longest time none of us can take our eyes off the cup and saucer: we're all convinced that it will topple and that tea will spill on my mother's carpet. After he'd left, we all commented upon it, saying how strange it was, the way he held it like that.

Later that day, in the early evening I think, my mother called us up to her room. She said she wanted to convey her wishes regarding the funeral. "Father John will say most of it," she says. "There'll be Barbara Streisand," she smiles at my dad, "and a hymn, *I vow to thee my country*, and you can all choose some other music if you want to." Already my mind's wandering, thinking about the music *I'd* choose were it my funeral. "Neil, I want you to deliver the eulogy."

"Yes, mum," I say dutifully.

"It can't be like that last funeral," my mother suddenly says, referring to my Granddad Jim's funeral. "No one should go like that."

We all nodded, the memory of that cold day – the day he died, the build up to it, the funeral especially - despite the weather turning warmer now, still vivid in everyone's mind. On that day there'd been a light dusting of snow and the temperature had dropped to below freezing. It had been so cold that we'd been unable to get into the chapel: the cemetery superintendent had to come with a kettle-full of boiling water, which he poured over the padlock securing the chapel doors. It had been so cold that one wondered just how the gravedigger's had managed to dig through the frozen earth to form the grave.

When the priest eventually deigned to put in an appearance, he'd demanded eighty pounds before the funeral could be performed – those were the first words out of his mouth, "Have you got my eighty pounds," he'd said. He didn't even smile.

Upon his demand for money, my dad had handed over the envelope without question. Standing behind him though, my brother and I could barely control our rage, "I can throw you down the hole, if you like," Lloyd had growled.

"Oh well," the priest had said, ignoring him by way of selective deafness. "Shall we get this over with?"

Inside it seemed even colder. The chapel was freezing - *stone cold amidst the cold stone*. Varying members of the family sat shivering in the pews; shivering at the cold, shivering at the cold words of the priest as they fell uncaring from his lips; the insincerity floating upwards towards the rafters, lost amidst the rotting wood and the cold slate that grants bare protection from the elements: his words were meaningless, his performance on the alter steps indifferent – certainly not eighty quid's worth.

Dearly beloved . . . the family, ever respectful, allows the priest to go through the motions . . . *we are gathered here today* . . . has he got the right speech one wondered . . . *in order to celebrate the life of our brother, James -* his name was Jim, it wasn't James, despite the bogus claims of the certificates in relation to his birth, death and marriage.

Out the corner of my eye I spied our friends and relations studying my mother out the corner of *theirs.* Everyone knew what she was thinking – everyone *thought* they knew - *That'll be me soon,* she'll be thinking. I'm sure they were half right. That evening – everyone having gone home, the best china cups and saucers dripping foam on the draining board, my dad having dropped my grandmother back to the nursing home – my mother declared her intentions, "I don't want a service like that," she'd said. "I want a proper service in a church."

The room falls silent. None of us really know what to say. It was like that bit at the end of *The Deer Hunter* when everyone's sitting around the kitchen table too embarrassed to talk.

Thursday 14ᵗʰ May 1998

The Memorial Hospital sits hidden midway up Shooters Hill. Driving up the winding path through a long line of overhanging trees it appears more like one of those hospitals you see on *Heartbeat* – some cottage hospital – only on a slightly larger scale.

Parking the car in the small deserted car park I get out and follow a confusing array of signs and arrows, which eventually point me in the direction of a tiny brick built lean-to with a sign over the door declaring: SUPPLIES OFFICE. Inside three men, dressed like hospital porters, sit watching a small black and white television. I clear my throat. All three men look up, somewhat surprised, as though they seldom receive visitors. "Can I help you, mate?" the porter closest to me says, in a breezy voice.

"I've come to pick up a commode," I say, almost a whisper, almost too embarrassed to make such a demand.

"Have you got your authorisation form?"

"I've got this," I say, holding up the A5 chitty that the doctor had given me that morning.

"That'll do," the porter says, snatching the form out of my hands not even bothering to look at it. "Follow me."

I follow him out of the office and we walk back across the car park, past my car, and into another building, the doors flung open, like a large storeroom. "Take what you want," he said dismissively. Inside there were piles of stuff I couldn't quite comprehend – a mountain of commodes, and orthopaedic devices, and the sort of thing Thora Herd used to advertise on the television in the afternoons or in the back of the Sunday supplements. I took a few tentative steps forward. It reminded me of those images of concentration camps – mountains of suitcases and shoes and miniature wooden legs. "I haven't got all day," the porter suddenly prompts. "You said you wanted a commode?"

"Yes."

"Take that one," he says, pointing to the one closest to me. "They're all clean."

I grab the contraption – a black metal frame on wheels, with a plastic toilet seat and an off-white translucent bowl – and pull it towards me.

"Sign here," the porter says, thrusting a clipboard and pen at me. He surely can't think I'd want to steal this? I sign in the region where his finger points to and he tears off a top copy and hands it to me, "Enjoy," he says.

I quickly wheel the commode back to the car, hoping that no one sees me. The stupid thing though, won't fit into the boot of the car so I spend the next ten minutes adjusting the seats and trying to force it through the passenger door.

Of course, having driven back to my parent's home, my view impaired by the monstrosity in the back seat, it's the same push me, pull me, process – *it went in, so it must come out again, surely?* Cursing - I swear blind it's grown during the journey - I pull and tease the thing until I finally manage to manoeuvre it onto the pavement. Over my shoulder I notice my dad standing at the front door. I know what he's thinking: *She's not going to want to use that.* He's right. "I'm not using that," my mother says. "I'll use the toilet downstairs, like a normal person."

Throughout the last eight months it's the first time I've seen her angry. "What do you want me to do with it?" I say.

"Just put it in the back room, upstairs," my dad says.

I carry the commode upstairs, careful not to scrape the wallpaper and put it down next to a large doll's house, which my mother never got around to renovating.

I walk to the window and peer at my mother through the net curtain - she's down in the garden, shuffling up and down the path in her nightdress, examining the flowers and the plants. It's all about dignity really. There's something terribly undignified about dying.

Friday 15th May 1998

Everyone arrives this morning – most of them unannounced: family, friends, and well-wishers. In fact, there are so many people crammed into the living room and the dining room that my dad is forced to send me out to the *Co-op* to buy more teabags and tissues.

For some reason there is a party atmosphere – they remind me of excited, yet scared, children queuing up to see Father Christmas at Selfridges: everyone's talking ten to the dozen, everyone's attempting to be heard above everyone else; everyone drinking tea and the kettle at a permanent state of boiling point.

My Aunt Mary was one of the first to arrive (the one whose husband the police had mistaken for Ronnie Biggs). She gets a longer visit than most on account of the fact that she's always been like a surrogate mother to my dad; even now there's an enchanting bond between them. Whenever my dad visits her she always walks him to the bus stop afterwards, puts her arm through his; sends him on his way with a kiss, a lump of cheese, a few cans of *Guinness*. My dad's family was full to the brim with matriarchal figures, especially my Aunt Mary, who seemed to be the guiding voice in any discussion involving the family. Today though, she just looks broken - when she came back downstairs again, having visited with my mother, she struggled to maintain her emotions,

"I remember years ago, Doreen made me these curtains," she says. "Hand sewed they were. She was so . . ."

"Here you go, Mary," my dad says, sitting her at the table and putting a cup of tea in her hand.

"Not fair," she says. "My poor Doreen."

Others in the room nod their agreement. Not fair.

By eleven o'clock the house was so full with visitors that my mother was forced to rise from her sick bed and tentatively make her way downstairs - that way everyone could see her and she them. Entering the dining room, walking like a pencil drawing in a flicker book, some of the people in attendance actually gasp, whilst others immediately burst into floods of tears. Others, I thought were going to break into applause, although I'm not sure whether this was a result of them being shocked by her appearance or the fact that she'd even managed to navigate the staircase.

For the next few hours my mother held court. Looking around the room it struck me that this was how the funeral would be, save for the fact that no one had bothered dressing up for the occasion, or that the congregation would be short by a unit of one. Initially, everyone speaks in hushed tones as if eagerly awaiting that moment when the pressure gauge is released and the room be allowed to take on an air of informality.

Once again it is my Aunt Mary that started the ball rolling, despite her earlier tears, talking about the 'old days,' the family, my parents, their courtship, the war, rationing: everybody suddenly laughing.

For me, observing it all from the dining room, it seemed like a perfect moment: my mother, sat perched on the edge of the armchair cushion like a sparrow, was obviously in her element - centre of attention one moment, her illness completely forgotten the next. Even so, I couldn't help but smile bitterly at the cruel absurdity of it all - loving her more at that moment than I'd ever done before: loving the perfection with which she handled the situation; the way she put everyone at their ease; the way she made each and every one of those present feel important – important to her, important to us.

Two hours later she was back upstairs in bed: exhausted by the sheer effort of it all. Downstairs my dad was cursing under his breath, working the vacuum cleaner around the dining room, looking for signs of invisible dirt on the carpet, "She should have stayed in bed," he kept saying. "There was no need to get up." I know now that he's counting down the days – attempting to calculate just how much time she had left – worrying that those two hours of effort will actually reduce her life by four hours, six maybe. Deep down, he knows what she's like though. Most days, we don't even know how she summons the energy. Even now, with the days passing too quickly for any of our liking, she's busying herself, in between long bouts of exhausted sleep, with preparations – preparations for her death, the funeral ceremony, the family's responsibility to itself after she's gone. "I just wish she'd slow down," my dad said. "She's exhausted."

Saturday 16th May 1998

The wedding invitation (my cousin and his girlfriend) has been stuck to the side of the fridge, by way of a New York yellow taxi fridge magnet, for about the last four months now. It had been sent so early that I'd not really taken any real notice of the date. Sharon though, she remembers everything - jots everything down in a diary: birthdays, wedding anniversaries, family parties, christenings - she's so like my mother in that respect.

Plucking the invitation from the fridge door she waves it in my direction. "Do you know you've got your cousin's wedding coming up?" she'd said a couple of weeks back.

"When's that?" I say, still not too concerned: my mother was still undergoing treatment then, and had not yet announced her decision not to undergo further treatment should her latest bout be unsuccessful. Unbeknown to us of course the treatment was never meant to be successful: the chemotherapy was never intended as a cure, but rather a means of keeping my mother alive, allowing her enough time to get her 'affairs in order.'

"It's in a couple of Saturday's time," Sharon had said at the time.

"I'll have a word with Lloyd and Jason," I say dismissively, "find out what everyone's doing." By now though, none of us can even contemplate a family wedding, especially with my mother becoming more and more unwell as the week drags on. My dad though, he wouldn't hear of it.

"You all have to go," he'd said earlier in the week: this was an order rather than a suggestion. For him it was about duty to the family – the wider family - regardless of our own problems, regardless of my mother's condition. "You have to represent the family." He was always big on that sort of stuff.

Of course, when I was younger I always loved such occasions, especially those involving the family on my dad's side: everybody singing and dancing and telling these wonderful family stories; everyone drinking; my granddad singing; my Uncle Tim singing; my Uncle Alf singing rude songs; all the woman folk dancing and laughing and breaking into song.

The weather's nice – a good day for a wedding. I know my mother would have loved it, although I realise that her non-attendance will now be used as a measure of exactly how unwell she really is.

I don't attend the service: Sharon is in attendance, along with the rest of the family, although I slip into view just as the happy couple exit the church, and force myself to appear, as if a passing ghost, in the family group photo.

Later, at the reception, my immediate family sit on a big round table. The celebration is muted. During the speeches my cousin, the best man, asks everyone to raise their glasses to those that couldn't be with us today: everyone dutifully stands, glasses are raised. "To absent friends," all of the guests say in unison. It's only now that I notice people, other guests, looking and raising their glasses in the direction of our table. It's only now that I realise they're actually toasting my mother. It's only now that I realise my mother will probably die soon.

Towards the end of the evening my cousin corners me: on these occasions we'd normally rib each other over our respective football teams – most of the family supported Millwall, although years back him and his brother had opted for Charlton Athletic. Often we'd talk about the punk era, about Joe Strummer and The Clash or Paul Weller and The Jam. Today though, he struggles to say anything, other than to make a stammered attempt at telling me how sorry he was over my mother, before turning on his heels and quickly scurrying away from me. I shake my head. *It's not supposed to be like this*, I think.

When I return to the round table it's a similar story: Lloyd and Jason confirm the fact that they, too, had people approach them, telling them how sorry they were to hear the news about our mother. Even now people are looking over at us, trying not to make it too obvious: most seem frightened to come within a hundred yards of the table.

We all have to just get through it now – keep up the family appearance. We all want to bolt though, make our apologies – no last trips to the bar, no last family story, no last reluctant dance beneath the mirror ball with our better halves, no lingering beneath the harsh lights of the hall and the poor caretaker pleading with us to, "*Please* go home." Yet we're bound by my dad's words about us having to be there. And so we stay, dutifully seeing out the last few hours sat sullenly around our table. Occasionally, a guest, a family member, would take a guilty peak in our direction "Such a shame," I overhear my aunt say. "Their poor mother." Everybody nods. *Poor souls* the women think. *Poor sods*, from the men.

Sunday 17th May 1998

The house is doom-laden now. Each morning, following another sleepless night, we drive back to Eltham - there has been no phone call in the middle of the night – and we begin the process again: the waiting, the tea-drinking, the not-really-reading of the daily papers. No of us can bear it anymore. Nothing seems to be happening. Things are definitely slowing down though. Everyone seems aware of that fact. Upstairs my mother succumbs to long hours of exhausted sleep.

At midday Sharon and I take Jack to the Wimpy Bar at Eltham. Midway through the meal though, REM's *Everybody Hurts* plays over the radio. I immediately ask for the bill and we return home.

At ten-to-five Jack is sent upstairs to say goodbye to his grandmother: his mother will arrive at five o'clock sharp, and I know now that my mother will not last to see another fortnightly access visit. When the front door bell goes he comes down in floods of tears, "I want to come to the funeral," he says.

"Okay," I say, giving him a hug and a twenty pound note. "I'll have a word with your mother."

Later that evening Sharon and I sit with her again. "I used to love going to evening classes," she'd said out of the blue - each year she'd sign up for a course at the local education institute. She was always doing something: dressmaking, pottery, painting, upholstery; she made her own clothes and there were pieces of furniture scattered around the house that she'd lovingly restored.

Monday 18th May 1998

A Macmillan nurse and a doctor came today – a nice bloke with a beard – he was very polite. He didn't stay for tea; he stayed barely long enough to explain what happens next – nothing actually. 'It's very much a waiting game from here on out,' he said.

That morning the GP had written out a prescription, which I'd taken to the chemist to be filled. Upon handing over the prescription the chemist had come out from behind the counter and eyed me suspiciously, and then he'd made me wait whilst he made a telephone call. A few minutes later though, he came back and informed me that it shouldn't take too much longer: this time he seemed far friendlier - far more sympathetic.

Ten minutes or so later I returned home with a giant white paper bag, the contents of which I daren't even take a peak at; this I left at the foot of the stairs in anticipation of the doctor's arrival.

In the dining room the doctor and the Macmillan nurse offer no good news; I think my dad's waiting for a telephone call from the prison warden or someone, the state governor perhaps, or the senator, hoping to hear word of my mother's reprieve – some stay of execution. "It shouldn't be much longer now," the doctor informs us.

There follows an awful silence, as we both comprehend the words.

"I'll be back later," the Macmillan nurse says, 'make sure she's comfortable.'

My dad, finally defeated, holds out his hand for the doctor to shake, and then I follow suit. He shows the pair of them to the front door, and I retire to the kitchen, pushing the button on the kettle and preparing the cups. I hear the front door close and the sound of my dad's feet climbing the stairs. I turn the lock in the back door and gently slip into the garden. Out on the patio I pull up a wrought iron chair and sit down. For the merest seconds

I close my eyes, preserving the image like a camera; my mother had laid the patio herself, stone by stone, which she brought home two at a time in a shopping trolley from the local builder's yard. Over the years she'd transformed the garden in a labour of love, which saw it change completely from its original bog-standard appearance: she was always good like that. She had an eye for it, I suppose – an ability to change things, with an artistic flair and feminine sensibility. Behind me, up at the bedroom window, behind the net curtain, my parents lay on the bed together - a last cuddle and a last embrace.

Late Evening

The Macmillan nurse returns and heads straight upstairs to my mother's room. She spends a few hours with her, talking about what's to come, answering any questions she might have. She rubs cream into my mother's skin – stop her getting bedsores. Everything now seems to be moving apace.

When she finally comes back downstairs again she heads straight for the kitchen where my dad makes her a cup of coffee. This is the signal for everyone to go up: my brother Lloyd and his wife, Anne, my nephew, James, and nieces, Danielle and Terri-Anne, my brother, Jason and his wife, Lorna, and their son, Joshua: as the weeks have dragged on he's become noticeably more introvert, more shy – he's really young and has spent a lot of time in my mother's company over the last couple of years. And then finally it's our turn, Sharon and I, the whole process so painful.

On the bedside cabinet there's the paper bag, which I'd collected from the chemist earlier. There's also a new contraption: a little electronic box with flashing lights – this will drive the morphine.

"Goodnight, Doreen," Sharon says, kissing my mother, the embrace lasting just too long to prevent the start of fresh tears.

"Goodbye, Sharon," my mother replies, brushing away the tears from Sharon's cheek.

It's my turn now. "Goodnight, mum," I say. "I love you." I'm reluctant to leave now. I don't want this to be it. I don't want it to end like this.

"I'll see you in the morning," my mother says, reading my mind – still attempting reassurance.

"I'll see you tomorrow, mum," I kiss her again.

Just as I'm leaving she calls after me, "Neil?"

"Yes, mum?"

"You have the ending to your book now," she says.

Tutorial – Stephen Knight

Author's note: Funeral Three would eventually be submitted as my final portfolio for the course under the working title: DRINKING TEA

I've never seen Stephen Knight like this before. Usually when we meet for tutorials he's all business, offering up wave after wave of (mostly) constructive criticism. Today though, he seems almost jovial, asking how I am, making small talk. His whole demeanour seems weird to me.

This is the last tutorial we will have together – my final portfolio (Funeral Three/Drinking Tea) is due for submission in less than a month. However, he seems reluctant to talk about it – even now it sits there on his desk, untouched. Usually he'll pick it up, point to some passage I've written, before tossing it down on the desk dismissively. Today though, he barely looks at it.

Ten minutes pass in this fashion. Fifteen minutes. Still it's only small talk.

"So, what did you think of it?" I finally ask.

For a few moments he doesn't really say anything, other glance in *its* direction. Just then though, he lets out a sigh and declares, "I've not really got anything to say, if you want to know the truth."

Inside, I'm furious. Is that it? You've got nothing to say. "Stephen, for the last year and a half you've been giving me grief about my writing . . . giving me a good kicking, if *you* want to know the truth. Now though, when I need advice, when I need your opinion, you've got nothing to say to me?"

He smiles at that – my anger.

"I don't see what's so funny?" I say.

He smiles again. "The reason I've got nothing to say is because there's nothing *to* say."

"What?"

"It seems pretty perfect to me."

"What?"

"You've done it," he says. "You've achieved, pretty much, what you'd set out to do."

"What?"

"There's been a real shift in your writing."

"I worry about it being termed *misery-lit.*"

"It's not misery literature," he reassures me. I must have made a breakthrough, because he normally says *it's not literature!* "Misery literature's something completely different from what you're attempting to do." I sense a thawing in his approach; for the first time I think he's seeing what it is I'm attempting to do, seeing that I'm attempting to write something different, a proper thought piece – literature?

Since being on the course we've had this running battle, all be it a very calmed one, about what it is I should be doing, and what it is they're expecting from me, "Anyone can write a novel," he'd once scoffed. "It just depends on what sort of novel it is you're attempting to write."

He reads through a couple of pages again, "It's the same with a memoir," he says. "Anyone can write a memoir. Anyone can write about how crap their life has been. What you are attempting to do here is different, I can see that."

Having gone over old ground, I know how he understands my writing process; my need to get everything down on paper, writing in massive swathes, ignoring the editing process, ignoring the re-writes; normally he's demanding I go back to the very beginning, demanding I chop and change this bit or that – *completely lose that page, trim that paragraph, you don't need any of this!* As a poet of course this is probably the expected process; poetry demands twenty different versions of the same twenty lines, thirty sometimes. It's a laboured process that demands constant tiny changes. It's harder to do that with a novel though, or a memoir. It's hard to fine tune a hundred and twenty thousand words.

"So you really think this works?" I ask, nodding to the submission piece.

"Absolutely," he says. "Just carry on. Keep editing. Keep rewriting where possible. But, in your case, just get it down. Just keep going, no matter how long it becomes."

"Thanks I say."

For the next few minutes we sit in silence.

"Well," he says finally, "if there's not anything else you need from me?"

"No, thanks, Stephen," I say, standing up, gathering my belongings: my bag, my scarf, my notebook. "Thanks for everything."

"When my dad died, I never managed to get there in time," he suddenly blurts out. "I was on the motorway . . ."

"I had about nine months to get there," I smile bitterly.

"Good luck with it," Stephen says as I make to leave.

"Thanks, Stephen," I say again.

"I always knew you were a life writer!" he calls out just before I can close his door firmly behind me.

Funeral Three (Reprise)

This morning I drove back to Eltham on my own: Sharon had to work. Last night I didn't sleep at all, expecting the telephone to ring – even now I'm not sure whether I felt relief or not when the alarm clock signalled my rise: a quick cup of tea, a shower and shave; a grabbing of the car keys, and a cursory check that all the windows were locked.

Back over at my parent's house I find my dad and Lloyd sat talking in the living room. It's ironic. My brother's never really been one for visiting. Even when he did, especially years ago when he was first married, he'd cause an argument, say something out of turn – he was always full of demons. Now though, he's the one that gets to stay over; he's the one that gets to keep vigil with my dad through the night. It's typical of him – the eldest son – stepping up to the plate like that. He has all the traits of a man's man. Whenever we part he always attempts a bear hug, kissing me with an affection that has always caught me off guard. I always kissed my mother goodbye – the last few weeks I've kissed her goodbye as if in ritual – although I've never been that comfortable with my dad or my brothers. Not even a handshake. My dad's always been affectionate though, especially with my mother; always holding hands in public, buying her flowers every single week that they were together as man and wife. With others though, it has always been more in his actions and his deeds, rather than in the physical embrace: my dad's a practical man - completely grounded – shovelling out affection by the bucket load, only in letter form, a helping hand, money when people needed it, advice, friendship, a shoulder to cry on. Today he just looks helpless.

"How's mum?" I ask. Lloyd smiles, but my dad leaves the room, squeezing past me in the doorframe en route to the kitchen and another round of teas. It's only now that I hear the noise. "What's the hell's that?" I say. Lloyd doesn't answer though, other than to curse under his breath, glancing towards the ceiling, before picking up the newspaper and losing himself in the sports pages.

Of course, I already know what the noise is. I don't need Lloyd to tell me. My grandmother had made that same noise during *her* final hours: a rasping breath – a fight for breath – that was so desperate, so loud, it seemed to shake the house.

Jason arrives. He asks the same thing, "What's that noise?"

It's the morphine that does it. It's *that* which kills you in the end. It's been my mother's biggest fear these last few months – that sense of losing control. Yesterday evening there was this tragic-comic scene during which my mother attempted getting in and out of the bed all at the same time – acting as if forgetful, not quite sure as to what she wanted to do – *we* certainly had no idea what it was she was trying to do. My poor dad, standing over her, half helping her out of the bed, half helping her back into it, was completely distraught. Suddenly my mother rounded on him, "I knew this would happen," she said far too sharply, completely out of character, pushing my dad's hand away from hers.

At that moment I wanted to reach out to him, rest a hand on his shoulder and tell him it wasn't his fault; tell him that it was the morphine and my mother's scattered memories that had prompted her outburst. Only I didn't say anything, looking away in embarrassment, crushed in the same way that my dad now seemed crushed. My parents had never shared a cross word, certainly not in front of me, which seemed to make my mother's words all the more cutting; her dismissal of my dad more akin to a slap in the face. Even so, it was clear to me at that moment that this memory of my grandmother's last hours had haunted my mother, in the same way that this image, in years to come, would haunt me. "The same thing happened to my mum," my mother said, far softer – defeated now.

Early afternoon Jason and I sit helpless in the tiny bedroom – sat upright on the two dining room chairs as if in a private box at the opera - looking on passively at the tragedy being played out before us; the background music at odds with the performance: no *Tosca* or *Cavalleria Rusticana* – downstairs in the living room my dad, predictably perhaps, has chosen Tony Bennett to provide the soundtrack.

My mother's gone now - no longer with us. She still breaths, if you can call the horrific gasps for breath *breathing*. But the spirit of optimism has long since left her body; the spark in her eyes has gone, replaced with a dull ember — the morphine drip has seen to that. All that remain now are a collection of skeletal bones and a rasping body lying beneath bed sheets that have become too heavy for the legs, the elegant feet, and the painted toes they hide beneath. Now she lays staring at a patch on the ceiling.

There are moments that you share in life – with friends, loved ones, strangers sometimes – little moments in time that remain burnt into your memory. I remember the time Jason and I went to Wembley Stadium together to see David Bowie. I remember the night before his wedding – I was his Best Man. The pair of us never went out. There was no stag night. Instead, Jason cooked a pizza; we drank cups of tea and watched music videos on the television. The next day we drove to my parent's house. St. Luke's Church was just around the corner, and we made the short walk together, suitably dressed and buttonholed. Showered and shaved half hour before the ceremony, Jason discovered that he'd forgotten his socks, and was forced to wear a pair of mine even though his feet were twice my size: I mentioned it during the best man's speech, the fact that he'd been forced to cut the ends off them just to allow access to the toes – the joke went down like a led balloon.

I remember the night he showed me photographs of my son, Jack, following my divorce. I remember how one particular picture had prompted giant tears that dripped as if from a tap that requires a new washer, tears which bounced upon Jason's brown leather sofa - we fucked him up over the years, his mum and dad, I realise that now, with our grudges and our incessant playing out of kitchen-sink drama.

There are moments in life that you'll never forget – those units of time when the world halts and you're forced to observe some tragedy as if watching some slow motion car crash. I've no doubt, for Jason and I, *this* would be one of those moments. For nearly thirty minutes we sat there listening to my mother's desperate fight for breath. The pair of us never said anything – no conversation passed between us. Suddenly, not able to bare it any longer, I grasped my mother's hand, and brought my lips to her ear, whispering the only thing I could think of to say, "Let it go now, mum. Enough now."

For a few seconds the words seemed to spark something in her eyes, a glimmer of something perhaps, the merest hint of understanding. Suddenly her breathing slowed and her horrific gasping for breath dissipated just long enough to allow Tony Bennett's voice to scale the stairs.

"Get dad!" I blurted.

Immediately, Jason rose from the chair and rushed downstairs, leaving me alone in the room with my mother: I knew then that this was the last time we would be alone together, yet I couldn't think of anything to say, even though I felt that I should.

"I love you, mum."

I don't say anything.

"Don't go, mum."

I don't say anything.

"Come back to us, mum."

I don't say anything.

The opportunity passes.

Jason and Lloyd enter the tiny room, followed by my dad, who sits on the edge of my mother's bed, with Jason resuming his position in the chair and Lloyd standing behind him. I pass my mothers hand from mine to my dad's. The door is closed.

Once again my mother is gasping for breath. "Do you think this is it?" Lloyd asks. I've never known him to be uncertain before – he's usually so confident in his own opinion.

"It stopped for about ten, fifteen seconds," I said, worrying that no one would believe me. "Jason heard it too," I said, worrying that they'd all think I'd panicked.

My mother's breathing stopped again . . . five . . . ten . . . fifteen seconds, and then it started again. It stopped again . . . five . . . ten . . . fifteen . . . twenty . . . twenty-five.

My mother died a few moments later. Her breathing slowed to virtually nothing: my dad would comment later that he'd expected it to be like a film, with violins playing and my mother's final moments filmed in soft focus. Only death is not like that – it doesn't adhere to a film script. In its stead, as a last slap in the face, the disease played one last cruel joke on us – nature giving us the Kubrick–like treatment - her lungs filled with blood and then poured from her mouth. I was so shocked that I actually reeled back in my chair in an attempt at freeing myself from the scene – almost falling on the floor in my haste to escape from the horror of it. Just then Jason grabbed me, pulling me towards him, burying my head in his chest where I sobbed and sobbed. Lloyd meanwhile placed a non-consoling hand on my dad's shoulder, but he doesn't even notice: he's far too busy attempting to stem the flow of blood from my mother's mouth, which is now pouring down her chin and onto her nightdress.

These are the moments I'll remember. These are the things, I know, will haunt my dreams forever more.

These are the things, I know, will never leave me. I remember how the blood continued to pour from my mother's mouth, and how my dad simply could not stem the flow, not with a nightdress, a pillowcase, a tea towel. I remember thinking how strong Jason was – my little brother – how he sacrificed his own immediate grief for the sake of mine. I remember the fact that Sharon would be arriving at Eltham Station in the next thirty minutes: I'd promised to pick her up in the car. If I wasn't there she'd know what'd happened, and she'd be forced to walk that same route I took just over a week ago when my dad phoned me at work and ordered me to come home; she'll know that she'd never arrive in time. I remember in the weird calm that followed. I remember how my dad had attempted closing my mother's eyelids – the way they do in films – but how they refused to close as if in defiance of us all, how they refused to close as if in defiance of her death. I remember how my dad had requested we all go downstairs – how he wanted a few minutes alone with her – and how we all kept bumping into each other like the Three Stooges – Larry, Curly and Moe – all bumping into the bedroom door in our haste to leave the room. I remember how, afterwards, my dad had gathered us in the living room and asked us to promise him – demanding it of us – that we wipe from our memories the scene we'd just been witness to. "I don't care what you do," he'd said, "but I want you to forget everything you saw in that room." For his sake, we offer a collective nod, although we all knew that would be impossible. "It'll haunt you for ever more if you don't," he said. I remember the moment my dad went to the chest of drawers in the dining room and removed a small address book, and then how he went to the kitchen in order to start making the telephone calls. "Hello . . . it's Jimmy. . . I've some sad news to tell you . . . Doreen passed away today."

There are only a handful of people exiting the station at this time in the afternoon: the rush will start in about an hour's time, the trains out of London will be fuller; in two hour's time there'll be standing room only. As usual, Sharon is the last to emerge. She speeds up when she sees the car and waves. Half-heartedly, I wave back, only then realising that I'd forgotten to switch the cd player on, knowing that *she'll* know – *He always listens to music*, she'll be thinking. I lean across and open the passenger door for her. She lowers herself into the passenger seat, always flushed: handbag, workbag, flowers for my mother. She's always out of breath; she always needs a moment to sort herself out before she can put her seatbelt on – I always wait until I've heard the 'clunk-click' before putting the car into first gear.

"How is she?" she asks.

"She's gone," I say.

"What do you mean; she's gone?"

It's like my grandfather's death all over again. Not hearing the news. Not *wanting* to hear the news. "About half hour ago," I say. "Twenty minutes at most."

"But, she can't have . . ."

"She's dead," I said. "My poor mother's dead."

For the next fifteen minutes we just sit there – sat in the NO WAITING bay – the pair of us crying.

"I can't believe she's gone," Sharon says the words over and over. "I just can't believe she's gone."

When we arrive back at my dad's house – it's his house now – he's still on the telephone, still breaking news to people - "Hello . . . its Jimmy . . . I've some sad news to tell you . . . Doreen passed away today."

Sharon brushes past him in the kitchen, rubbing his arm, before placing the flowers on the side – she doesn't bother with the vase. She then goes through to the living room where she hugs and kisses Lloyd, and then Jason. "I can't believe she's gone," she says again.

"Have the undertakers been called?" I ask.

"They're on their way," Lloyd says.

"Is Anne coming?" Sharon asks.

"Yeah, she's on her way, too," Lloyd says.

"What about Lorna?"

"She's just dropping Josh over at her mum's, and then she'll be over," Jason says.

We all sit in the living room. In-between telephone calls, my dad makes a fresh pot of tea.

Ten minutes later the doorbell rings: two men are standing on the doorstep – both are soberly dressed. "It's the undertakers," Lloyd says, peering out through the net curtain. My dad lets them in – the pair of them look sheepish – and then immediately shows them up to my mother's room. A few minutes later he comes back downstairs again and shuts the dining room door. He walks to the window and looks out. "I told them to park their van outside the house," he says. "But, look, they've gone and parked it all the way down the road."

A few moments later we hear the front door open and close, and then we all avoid watching as the two men carry my mother's body down the street. No one mentions the fact that when they arrived at the house they didn't have a coffin with them, yet when they left they took my mother away in a coffin. *How did they do that?* I sat there thinking. Was it some illusion? Was it some form of slight-of-hand magic? Was it all smoke and mirrors? Just where do you buy a fold-up coffin?

Another ten minutes pass before the two men return. In the dining room we all stand behind my dad as they hand him my mother's wedding ring. He undoes a gold chain from around his neck and threads the ring through it, before clasping it and then hanging it back around his neck once more. I notice that both the undertakers have scuffed shoes. I'm disappointed by that fact. I've always been obsessive when it comes to clean shoes – we all have. When I was little, every day I'd wake to be greeted by a long line of highly-polished shoes which stretched from the bedroom door, down the passage, and ended at the living room. My dad would've already left for work by that stage – he was always at work.

"Mum?" I always asked. "Why does dad always clean all of the shoes before he goes to work?"

"Because he loves you," she'd always reply.

It's only now that I understand it.

"We'll take your wife to Woolwich," one of the undertakers said. "You can still view her there."

"Later in the week," the other one chimes in, "we'll move her to Well Hall."

My dad shakes both of their hands, but doesn't tip them.

We all watch from the living room as they drive my mother away.

"Dad?" I ask. "Did they give you a receipt?"

Wednesday 20th May 1998

<u>*Allder's Department Store, Eltham.*</u>

Today is going to be a day of practicalities – death certificate, funeral arrangements, flowers; a visit to Allder's department store, in the high street, in order to cancel my mother's store card, even though we all kept telling my dad not to worry, that there was no need to rush anything like that. My dad's insistent though – he knew he'd still be getting correspondence addressed to my mother over the next few months (the next year in some cases) – just wanting to get as much out of the way today. "When we get back home, perhaps I can get you to compose a letter, explaining what's happened, which I can send off to anyone that writes to her?" Even as he's asking I'm conjuring up just what I might tell them.

Dear Sirs

Mrs Bradley's gone. Please don't write to her again, ever!

Respectfully yours

The lady in the tiny payment office at Allder's is very sympathetic. Understandably though, she's awkward with it, getting herself in a bit of a fluster as she fills out the paperwork: at first she gets the wrong form, and then she makes a mess of filling in the details. "I'm really sorry," she says again, but we all smile – we appreciate the fact that she appears genuinely sorry for our loss.

Greenwich Town Hall, Woolwich.

We're directed to a typical, wood-panelled, waiting room, where we're informed that the Registrar won't keep us too long. Across from us an African woman and her proud husband are there to register their baby, and a youngish couple sit just along from them, nervous, waiting to find out about just what it is they have to do in order to get married: my dad, absentmindedly, makes some comment about the circle of life – births, deaths and marriages – but it's nothing like *The Lion King*, and the Town Hall is nothing like what you'd see in a Disney production.

The Registrar, when she finally deigns to put in an appearance, offers her sympathy, tells us how much each additional death certificate will cost, and goes about the business of enshrining my mothers details in a big book of parchment with a fancy fountain pen – the extra certificates are simply printed from the computer and look as if they could have been run up at home.

The Co-operative Funeral Home.

It doesn't take my dad take long to make a decision: he quickly flicks through the brochure, pointing to the second coffin on the page – not quite the cheapest, but chosen in the same way one would the second most inexpensive bottle on a restaurant wine list. "What do you think of that one?" he asks us, and we all nod our approval.

"Of course, we do have a collection of more luxury caskets," the woman offers.

"No," my dad insists. "That one's fine." By now he's simply going through the motions, so we all chip in, agreeing that the coffin he's chosen is perfectly adequate.

"It's all a rip-off, anyway," Lloyd attempts comforting him, knowing that my dad is a practical man, certainly not one ruled by emotions or guilt.

Lloyd's right, anyway; it's all a rip-off: the cars, the flowers, the pomp and ceremony. Even so, we're also aware that these are the things my mother wants – wanted.

One problem my dad has now is with the plot at the cemetery. It's all been paid for – my mother saw to that ages ago – but we're all worried about the location. "I don't want one up where your dad's buried," she had said that evening when were all sitting in her room listening to her relay her instructions for the funeral; that day Father John had come to the house and held that cup and saucer in that strange fashion. "I want one of those ones at the top of the hill . . . the one overlooking London," she had demanded. "Either that or one beneath a nice tree."

My dad enquires of the undertaker the possibility of choosing where the plot should be. The undertaker though, she already knows the answer I think, even if she claims that she's not certain, claims she's not really sure: she recommends we pay a visit to the superintendent's office up at the cemetery. This though, proves a waste of time, and only adds to my dad's worries.

Greenwich Cemetery, Shooters Hill.

The cemetery superintendent is kind enough to take us up to the area where my mother's grave will be dug – my

Granddad Jim's grave is about twenty yards away, although none of us mention that fact to my dad.

"This looks fine, dad," I attempt reassuring him.

"It's not where she wanted," my dad replies.

"Dad, we've not really got a lot of choice," Lloyd says, in an attempt at backing me up. On the way up to the plot the superintendent had explained how the cemetery was virtually full. In fact, there are less than fifty plots left in the whole cemetery. After that the cemetery will be pretty much mothballed, kept maintained, but only really used in the future for the burials of those with double plots – those joining their loved-ones somewhere down the line – like my dad someday, joining my mother.

Leaving the cemetery my dad seems really disconsolate. We all know what he's thinking: that he's failed somehow - failed my mother. He's wrong. We all know how much he cared for her - how much he loved her. Even so, for him, that doesn't seem to be enough.

The Anchor and Hope Public House, Shooters Hill.

After the cemetery we drive up and over Shooter's Hill and pull into a pub on the other side. My dad had mentioned something about us having something to eat together, but when we get there we only order drinks and ignore the menus. It's still pretty early and the pub is empty save for a chap sitting at the bar reading the paper in-between making small talk with the barmaid. It's obvious that my dad is still brooding over the plot in the cemetery. None of us mention it further, though. Instead we take collective tiny sips of our beer.

Just then the door to the pub opens - far more forcibly than is needed - and a man walks in. Whilst waiting for his drink, he's carrying out a one-sided conversation (argument) on a mobile phone. Having got his drink he comes and sits at a table far too close to the four of us, especially considering the sparseness of the pub: he seems really agitated, a little shaky maybe, like he's had an argument or is on drugs or suffering a serious drink problem. He slams the pint down, and then the phone. He nods to us. My brother, Lloyd, nods back, but has a look on his face that suggests he'd like to smash the man's face in – by the looks of the man, that wouldn't have been the first time.

Taking my dad's lead, we all ignore the man, although it's clear that he wants to engage us in conversation, either that or is spoiling for a fight – *yeah, well he'll fucking get one if he wants it*. He picks up his mobile phone, looks at it for a few seconds before slamming it down the table again. "Women, eh?" he suddenly declares. "You can't live with 'em, and you can't kill 'em."

I look at Lloyd, who I know is ready to fly across the table at him – we all are. My dad though, takes one last tiny sip of beer, puts his glass down on the table and declares, "Come on, let's go."

Wednesday 27th May 1998

This morning the chap next door, who is a Sergeant at Catford Police Station, put out traffic cones all along the road, ensuring that no one will park outside the house. Even so it still doesn't stop one guy from pulling up, and then crossing the road in order to take a closer look at the collection of second-hand vehicles in the car lot on the opposite side of the road.

"You'll have to move that," I call out to him, motioning the offending vehicle.

"Yeah, no problem," he replies, although he continues walking up and down the line of cars.

"You need to move it, now," again I call out to him.

Again, though, he offers up the same dismissive reply. "Yeah, in a minute."

"Oi, pal, we've got funeral cars coming," I growl.

It's only now that he acknowledges me properly, glancing over to where his car is parked, suddenly taking in the collection of flowers rapidly covering my dad's drive. "Oh, right . . . yeah, sorry." Immediately he comes back across the road, gets in his car, and quickly pulls away from the kerb.

Since early in the morning my mother's neighbours have been laying flowers on the drive. By nine o'clock people are already turning up outside the house – the funeral cars are not due for another hour – and there are already people waiting outside the church. "It'll be standing room only," I overhear someone say.

A few days after my mother died Denise, her next door neighbour, had knocked early evening just to let us know that my mother was being taken extra care of: she works at the local *Co-operative* Funeral Home and is taking care of my mother personally. My dad invites her in for tea, but she declines. "I've only just left her, but she looks really nice," she says, which I thought that was an odd thing to say - they normally mention how *peaceful a person looks*. Besides, she hadn't looked nice at all. Yesterday I went to see her in the chapel of rest: my dad had ordered us all there to see her one last time; hoping that this image of her lying in her coffin would help us lose the image of her during those last moments.

It doesn't. Instead, I'm now left with both images, the one of her final horrific moments, and this final one of her not quite at peace – the manner of her death, despite the make-up and the mortician's touch, still every bit in evidence upon her face.

At ten o'clock the hearse and two funeral cars arrive along with the rain.

"There's always something," someone says.

Once the flowers have been placed onto the cars there's this chaotic moment when no one's really sure what should happen next. Cars are slowing down – the curious, the respectful – but none of them actually stop. In the end Lloyd simply walks out into the middle of the road and holds both his hands up.

My mother gets her wish. She stops the traffic. The hearse pulls out into the road and we follow it, procession-like, walking the short distance around the corner from my mother's house to St. Luke's Church.

They'd been right. It's standing room only in the church. When everyone's settled – the entrance music having faded – Father John signals for us (Lloyd, Jason and I) to come to the altar, where we drape the church flag over my mother's coffin. I have to hand it to Father John, he really knows how to deliver the pomp and ceremony that my mother so craved for the service. Following his sermon Jason is invited to the altar to read a short poem he's written for the occasion, followed by Lloyd, who reads a long list of my mother's virtues. Both of the readings surprise me. Both are moving pieces, heartfelt, sincere - full of love for a mother that only a son can express. When my turn came however, I took my words to the pulpit, climbing the stairs, immediately thinking that I'd written too much; suddenly worrying that the eulogy was far too long: a week earlier Father John had cautioned me as to keeping it brief, "One side of A4 ought to do it," he'd smiled. He was obviously fearful that I wouldn't be able to deliver it – that he'd be forced to step in and attempt deciphering my grief-stricken handwriting. Stubbornly perhaps, I saw this as a challenge. On the eve of the funeral I managed to conjure up a dozen pages in defiance. The vague idea had been to pick some random moment in time, something from the past, and build a eulogy around that – my dad waiting in our new home during the 'big freeze.' It seemed apt somehow.

"I've been trying to write this book," I tell the congregation. The book though, this book I refer to, is not *this* book, even if the skeleton of that first attempt would eventually end up appearing here pretty much fully-fleshed. Back then, during the writing process – not that there was any real process to speak of – I was simply creating a collection of little family stories, none of it really matching: the things I remembered about childhood, happier times, at least compared to now.

"I remember the Apollo Moon Landing (1969)," I tell the congregation. "It actually happened in the middle of the day, with all my family, our neighbours, all of us, standing in respective back gardens in Ruby Street, looking skyward for signs of invisible spacemen . . ."

From the pulpit I can tell that people were ill-at-ease with my perceived lack of sentiment – there had been no mention of my mother so far. Throughout the church there hung an uncomfortable silence, a shuffling of feet, some sporadic coughing, people shifting uneasily amidst the crowded pews, until suddenly I began to explain how during the weeks leading up to my mother's death a life story had been told. Not just the life of my mother, but of a family struggling to establish itself in the modern world – a family that set off one day in search of a New Jerusalem - *One small step for man, one giant leap for mankind.*

"What good did it do us, eh? All this sending rockets to the moon? What did we achieve from it, the non-stick frying pan? Teflon?" At that moment, standing up in that pulpit with hundreds of family members, friends, neighbours, all transfixed by the words I uttered, I was so full of rage – so full of love, and heartache, and confusion. "They can put a man on the moon . . . yeah, they can do that alright . . . yet they still can't find a cure for cancer!"

At the conclusion there was complete silence. As I descended the pulpit steps I found Father John waiting for me. I attempted a smile. He shook my hand, and held me there in his grip for what seemed like the longest time. "Wonderful," he whispered.

As I walked back to the front pew, my legs shaking, Barbara Streisand's *Evergreen* played over the speaker system, and when I eventually sat down, trying to stop my whole body shaking from nerves and grief and pain, my dad, crushed by the words, squeezed my knee.

Evening

Most of the people have gone now, and my dad is saying goodbye to the last of the stragglers on the doorstep. In the living room we all sit, as if in some de-briefing exercise – discussing the day's events.

"Could you believe the amount of flowers?" Sharon said.

"Mum would have loved it," Anne, my sister-in-law, chirped in.

"And the amount of people at the church."

"People were standing up at the back," I said, "and along the side aisles."

"Father John said the only time he'd seen the church as full as that was when they had that memorial service for those kids killed in that car in Westmount Road," Lloyd, said.

Jason meanwhile, sits passive in the armchair: he doesn't say too much at the best of times, but today he seems even more introvert. During the service I noticed how he didn't cry, finding it strange: Lloyd and I were in floods, crying uncontrollably at various times during the day – in the church and at the graveside. Jason though, he seemed to take it all in his stride – bottling it all up and blocking it all out – acting as if nothing had happened, and that everything was fine in this tiny little world we found ourselves inhabiting.

With the front door finally closed on the last remaining mourners, my dad headed back to the kitchen to attend to the, already-boiled, kettle. He seems impatient: unbeknown to us, there are things he needs to do – requests from my mother – but first, tea. It's always been tea – first and last drink of the day, along with all those moments in-between, certainly over the last few weeks, when the silence of the passing hours threatened to overwhelm us all.

The tea made, served, drunk; the cups washed and dried, and put back in the cupboard, my dad sets about his task: without saying anything, he quickly goes upstairs and then returns a few moments later with a collection of little parcels – presents, wrapped as if at Christmas. For the grandchildren there are books – *The Wind in the Willows*, my mother's favourite. For the daughter's-in-law there is jewellery: for Sharon there is the eternity ring my dad had bought for my mother only a few months previous, along with a necklace and a note explaining how it had been presented to her by the staff at *The Tatler* magazine shortly before she was due to leave there and give birth to me.

Once again, I marvel at the ways she'd organised everything: following the service the grandchildren walked around amongst the mourners carrying a bulging pillowcase. In turn, all of the women present were invited to reach in and take something; pulling out pieces of my mother's jewellery, all of which my mother had painstakingly attached to small pieces of white card by way of a subtle ribbon.

On the other side of the room – chatting to people, but not listening to the kind words being offered – I observed this strange ritual (my mother's grand plan), as one by one the women took their gifts and instantly broke into tears; quickly walking away clutching a ring, a bracelet, earrings, a broach. I noticed, too, how throughout the process my dad had turned his back on the proceedings – finding the whole thing crushing, I'm sure.

I'm not sure that my mother had intended for him to do it all so quickly. There were other things she had asked him to do: sort out the family photographs; give back to us various ornaments and object dart – things we'd given her over the years, presents and the like:

things she had bought for the house; things she wanted us to have – there was a fancy fountain pen, something I'd won in a writing competition, and which I'd given to her, something she'd wanted to return to me in kind. My dad, I think, was just trying to get it all out of the way – *now*, the day of the funeral – in no mood to stretch out the agony.

A few hours later he sent us all home – even Lloyd wasn't allowed to stay.

"I've got to get used to being on my own," he'd said, but none of us knew what to say in reply, other than in promising to return again tomorrow: we'd arranged to go back up to the cemetery – lay the flowers out properly; collect all the floral sympathy cards.

"Perhaps we can go to the pub afterwards, just the four of us," Lloyd had suggested, the four men in the family, minus the women that held it all together. "Maybe have a bit of dinner somewhere?"

We all agree.

Late Evening

Sat on the sofa back in our flat in Camberwell, the sealed letter in my hand, Sharon finally confessed to me what my mother had said to her up in the bedroom that day, when I was cutting the grass. "She just worried about you," she said.

"Oh yeah, and why's that?" I say, far too sharply, half grief, half rage.

"She just knew what you were like . . ." I can tell that Sharon is uneasy with the confession - with the subject matter, "She said that, she hoped we'd get married." She knew that this was one of my biggest regrets, the fact that we never got married – we could have done it at the house, or at St. Luke's – I should have done it for my mother. "She said, she hoped you'd find a little bit of happiness for yourself." She wipes a tear away, always reluctant to talk about the subject. "She said she hoped you'd finally find what it is you've been looking for all these years."

My mother knew me too well, I think: like my dad, knew me better than I probably knew myself. "He's always seemed troubled," I'd often overhear her say. "He's always worrying, always sad, always feeling blue. I always knew, when he turned up on the doorstep, or at my work, that he had something on his mind," she'd say. "He was always visiting me at work." This was long before she became ill - long before she was made redundant – when she was still working for the print union, SOGAT, in Brixton Road. "He'd always turn up during the lunch break . . ."

I remember those visits only too well: I always turned up unannounced, had a cup of tea; I never said too much, small talk mostly. Throughout, I'd be looking at my watch, "I have to go, Mum," I always said, the words haunting me now.

"I'll put the kettle on," Sharon said.

Using a knife I carefully cut the seal on the letter - folded once on blue paper. Unfolding it I instantly recognise my mother's handwriting.

Dear Neil
My goodbye letter from me to you.
You are my second son and
I've always tried to make you special.
You have repaid me by being

so loving, and so close to me all my life.
I couldn't have wished for a better son.
I Love you very much.
All My Love Always
Mum
X

Sharon returns with the teas, but is halted frozen in the doorway watching me sob, the tears like heavy raindrops falling onto the letter. When the tears subside she comes and sits on the sofa next to me. "Why don't we drink this and then go to bed?" she says.

The Wedding

Black clouds had been closing in all the way from Eltham like some portent of doom, following our journey along the A2 to Wilmington. As soon as we pull up in the car, Jack and I, the heaven's open. "It's bleedin' typical," I said.

I look at my watch. "We're well early," I say: there's still another hour and a half to go before it's all made official. That's all it means, really - making it official. Oh, I know Sharon sees it as far more than that, but I'm still too much in a fog following my mother's death to really conjure up very much enthusiasm for a wedding. It was the same when she moved in with me – this was around the same time that my mother became really unwell – when my defences were well and truly down. At the time I thought she was mad: some days I wouldn't even wish me on my worst enemies, and yet here she was, throwing herself into the whole thing, supremely confident – taking it all in her stride – not really taking no *or* yes for an answer. In fact, for the next day or so, she simply went about 'moving in,' eking out from me little bits of precious space, feminising everything, whilst I sat there grouchy, but glad that she was there - even if I was far too stubborn to ever admit that fact: as she walked around her new home, putting down ornaments and object dart, I followed in her footsteps on the thin carpet, picking things back up again, moving them slightly to the left or right – the panic inside me subsiding little by little.

"Everything will be fine," I told her later, putting the cup of tea down on, newly purchased, coasters. "I'll make some more room," I said, "get rid of some of my stuff."

"I know everything's been up in the air," she said, "what with your mum . . ."

"Everything's fine," I said. "Everything's going to *be* fine." Even now I'm not quite sure just who it was I was trying to convince.

In the car park the rain was still coming down by the bucket load, and didn't look like dissipating any time soon. In the passenger seat next to me, Jack sat nervously playing with the knot of his tie. Throughout the journey, and for the last twenty minutes sitting in the car, we've not really said two words to each other. During the build-up to the wedding he'd seemed fine. Over the years he'd always got on really well with Sharon. He also knew better than anyone that the prospect of my forming any kind of mutual relationship with *his* mother was nigh on an impossibility – far too much water under the bridge for that to ever happen. Obviously I had regrets about what happened between us – I've always regretted terribly leaving Jack behind. I was haunted by that fact – but I never once regretted leaving enough to ever attempt reconciliation: there was no point – I would've only left again at some later date.

Over the years, despite everything that happened, I always thought we got on well – Jack and I. We always spoke pretty openly. I always thought that we had a good father-son relationship, even if that relationship was being constantly interrupted by problems of (non) access rights. Today though, as we sit in my little rusting car, waiting for the rain to stop, I'm not really sure what to say to him. He seems really quiet, although I've put this down to the fact that he's nervous.

"Have you got your speech?" I ask.

"Yes," he says, producing a piece of folded paper from his inside jacket pocket.

"Have you got the rings?" I know he's got the rings because I only just handed them to him a few minutes earlier.

"Yes," he replies, part bored, part apprehensive.

Looking at him now, he seems older. Not quite teenage looking, but older than the little boy whose photographs are scattered all around the flat: the little boy that came to visit every other weekend, and for one full week in the summer holidays, and for five hours on Christmas Eve - poor sod. During Christmas dinner he had to sit eating cross-legged on the floor – we all did – as I didn't have a table. Sharon though, she always made it really special, laying out the tablecloth on the carpet – the three of us sitting there pulling crackers and wearing stupid Christmas hats, everyone keeping one eye on the clock.

Today he just looks uncomfortable: I don't think he's ever worn a suit before. About a month ago I took him to buy an outfit and he immediately picked out a pinstripe affair, which makes him look like Marlon Brando in *Guys and Dolls*. "You look really smart," I tell him, and he immediately raises himself up in the seat and checks out his reflection in the rear view mirror. "You look like Al Capone." We both laugh.

For a few moments the rains stops, at least long enough to allow a mad dash from the car to the venue – some country club/health spa that Sharon had read about in a glossy magazine. Today is the first time I've actually seen the place (properly), although Sharon had insisted that we drive there the week before just so as I knew where it was come the big day. Even then though, I didn't bother getting out of the car. "It's nice," I said, viewing it through the trees, before quickly turning the car around in the car park and heading back along the long narrow lane that led to the exit.

As soon as we're through the door, both our collars up against the rain, a pair of registrars, a man and a woman, step forward and introduce themselves to me.

For the next few minutes we pass pleasantries, until, inevitably, the conversation is steered towards the terrible weather outside. "I should have known it would've rained," I said. Both of them laugh, although I'm not sure I get the joke.

As it turns out the weather will affect the whole day – the ceremony, the photographs, the mood – as news filters through of a huge multi-car pile-up on the M25. The male registrar asks if any of our guests would be travelling via that route. "I wouldn't have thought so," I say: Sharon's family all live on the other side of the river (Thames), and so I imagine they'll come through the Blackwall Tunnel and then follow the same route as us along the A2, as will the rest of my family.

"Not to worry," the Registrar says. "We've still got plenty of time, even if they're a little late."

Just then my friends, Mick and Gill, arrive, along with their two sons, Daniel and Joseph – the latter one's Jack's age, the pair of them born within a week of each other. They all look as uncomfortable as I feel, dressed up in Sunday best – none of us used to wearing suits.

"You like nice," Gill says.

"I feel like a right prat!" I say, and we all laugh.

They all rib me over the wedding – *will the bride turn up?* I don't let on, but I'm more worried about the *groom*.

Sharon's boss, Helen, turns up, along with another woman she works with. Helen has a shock of white hair – she's ultra cool. She carries an old-fashioned cine film camera, and quickly snaps a few seconds of footage. She's going to make a video: in the past she's directed music videos and will later head up the British Forces Television Service (BFBS), feeding back footage from Iraq and Afghanistan.

"What sort of video are you going to make?" I ask.

"A wedding video, what did you think?" she replies.

"As long as it's not like Duran Duran's *Wild Boys*, I'm not really fussed."

"Oh, you," she says, slapping me playfully on the shoulder, and everyone laughs again.

I introduce her to Mick and Gill and she immediately points out that Mick's flies are open – more laughter.

Just then I'm slapped on the other shoulder. Turning around I find two of Sharon's aunts, Lurda and Kathleen – they'd been there all along, sat in the lounge having something to eat. They smother me in kisses and attempt embarrassing me in front of the other guests. Introductions are made.

"Have you been drinking?" I ask the pair of them, half joking, half serious.

"No, of course not," Kathleen says, frowning like she's been insulted. "We've had a posh sandwich, and a nice pot of tea."

"That's all right then," I laugh, although I wouldn't have put it past them.

"This is a funny old place," Lurda says.

"Why's that?"

"Well, have you seen it through there?"

"No, what's up?"

Grabbing the sleeve of my new suit, she guides me through the bar area where they'd been tucked away, and then I follow her into a lounge/restaurant area which I find is full of women, all wearing white bathrobes – some have towels wrapped around their heads, others are wearing face masks – everyone's drinking champagne and tucking into sandwiches and meals, none of which look too healthy to me. "It's because this place is a health spa," I say, as if it really needs any kind of explanation.

Just then all the 'tribe' arrive: my brothers, my dad, my sister-in-law (the other one's up in the room with Sharon – doing her hair), my nephews, my nieces and their respective boyfriends. Introductions are made again, everyone fumbling to shake hands. I suddenly feel old. They all take the piss. They all compliment Jack on his suit and some comment that "I look like a right prat!"

Sharon's friend, Margaret, arrives with her husband, Michael, and further introductions are made – everyone's smiling, the decibel level getting higher. During small talk, my dad discovers that his family, years back, lived next door to Michael's family, in Austral Street – that same street where Charlie Chaplin once lived. Everyone agrees it's a small world.

Inevitably, conversation switches to Millwall's match with Brentford, with Millwall going for promotion. Under normal circumstances – and this feels anything but normal – we would've all been there. Suddenly Mick produces a small transistor radio from his jacket pocket, with one of those single earpieces attached. "I brought this, just in case," he says, and we all laugh.

"It's pissing down out there," Lloyd suddenly declares, craning his head to see out the window into the gardens.

"It's a sign," I say, not quite joking.

"We're all doomed," chimes in Mick, mimicking that Scottish undertaker in *Dad's Army*.

Everyone laughs again.

As if on call the male registrar suddenly appear again. "We have a slight problem," he says. It seems that the M25, the M20, and the A2 are all now blocked as a result of that earlier accident. "Any sign of your other guests?" he asks, checking his watch in a ritual that he will repeat over and over again during the next couple of hours.

"I'm not sure what's happened to them," I say honestly. "They should have been here by now."

"Well, not to worry," he smiles, "we've a little while yet before we need to start panicking."

"Will it cause a problem?" I ask.

As it turns out we need to be officially married by five o'clock or some such time, or else the union is not actually legally binding.

This is just perfect, I think.

An hour or so later the registrar appears again – for the last hour a few of us have been listening to Radio London in the hope of hearing news of Millwall's match, whilst others talk amongst themselves, and others, Sharon's aunt in particular, occupy their time sat at the bar. "We're getting pretty close to the deadline," he says, prompting the pair of us to look at respective watches.

"Forfucksake," I curse under my breath.

"Of course, we could always have the ceremony after five o'clock. We'd be happy to do that for you" he said. "That way at least you could have your photographs taken, a nice celebration, cut the wedding cake. Only you'd need to then visit the Registrar's office at the town hall and have the ceremony performed again formally."

"No, we'll do it now," I say. "I don't care who's here and who's not."

And so that's what happened, with everyone ordered to take their places – a message is relayed to the bride-in-waiting to make ready with the mascara and the lipstick, and one last flick with the hairbrush – the room falling into silent hush, save for the odd gentle heckle from behind. "There's still time do a runner," and "It's not too late to call the whole thing off," although they seriously didn't know how close I was to considering that particular option. The truth was, we should have made a run for it long before now. We should have jumped in the car and headed for the hills or Gretna Green or that Little White Wedding Chapel in Vegas, with Sharon adopting her middle name (Priscilla) and me dressed as Elvis – long before his bloated period – the *68 Comeback Special*. Too late. Before I can contemplate merits of *Heartbreak Hotel* or that thing that wise men say about fools rushing in, the first strains of Ennio Morricone engulf the flock wallpaper and the oak panels and corporate hospitality – please speak to one of our friendly staff it says in the glossy brochure or ask for a list of our tariffs.

"Ready?" the registrar whispers in my ear and gives my elbow a gentle squeeze.

"It's the wrong track," I say.

"Sorry?"

"This is *The Good, The Bad, and The Ugly*. It's meant to be *Once Upon a Time in the West*."

Behind me everyone's in hysterics, although I can't help feeling that the first song is somehow apt.

Just then Mick lets out a cry. "Yeeeeessssss!" Millwall had just secured all three points. Everyone laughs again, including the registrar, although his laugh is accompanied by a look in Mick's direction that 'the radio needs to be turned off *now*.'

I should have known it would be like this. Sharon wanted perfection, and so far it's been nothing but a disaster: half the guests have not arrived, it's still pissing down with rain, the photographer hasn't stopped giving me grief all afternoon about the fading light.

A few moments later though, Sharon is at my side, and calmness, finally, descends over me. Snatching a glimpse to my left I can tell she's been crying. I attempt a smile and reach out and squeeze her hand, and she let's out a sigh, as if to say 'phew,' prompting even Ennio Morricone to take the hint, bringing our music request to its operatic climax, and the signal for the games to begin.

"Dearly beloved," the registrar says, only it isn't a religious service: his opening address more along the lines of a greeting, as if he were the keynote speaker at a conference of insurance salesmen – his words only really making sense once he gets to the part about "Do you, Neil James Bradley, take this woman, Sharon Priscilla Doyle, to be your lawfully wedded wife?"

To be honest; I'm not quite sure how it even came about. I mean; it wasn't as if I'd gotten down on one knee and suddenly declared to her my undying love. Not even when we accidently became engaged – this was way back when my mother was still the picture of good health – was there any sort of romantic ritual. In actual fact it had followed a longish period when the pair of us had been apart: I was going through another one of those long periods when I refused, or was simply not capable of, coming out from under the black cloud that constantly seemed to follow me.

On the day we parted (again) I declared I'd needed 'space,' although, I realise now, that was really just a copout. As usual though, Sharon was great about the whole thing, tearfully taking a step back, but assuring me she'd wait for me, however long it took. At the time I was probably the most miserable I'd ever been. Only her absence from my life made me even more so.

Of course, I knew back then my mother had written to her - I think she knew, even better than I did, that I'd never meet anyone quite like her again. But then all of this was done in secret: the correspondence, the messages of support, the sympathy and good wishes.

After the inevitable drifting back together I bought her an engagement ring, but, even then, I warned her that it definitely was not an engagement. As always she nodded, and then went and announced to everyone behind my back that we were 'engaged.' I didn't mind, not really: my mum and dad bought us a set of towels. An engagement though, should usually be followed, at a reasonable length of time, by a wedding. Only there never was one. Not really as a result of any reluctance on my part – I would have married her in the few minutes after we'd first met. We just never got around to it, that's all. Sure, we talked about it from time to time, and were certainly both confident that it would happen 'some day.' Only it didn't. *We* didn't. In fact, it wasn't really until the last few weeks of my mother's life that I realised I should have gone through with it - for Sharon's sake, and for my mother's. Only I'd left it too late, that events - my mother's illness - had overtaken us, with any hope of a wedding ceremony draining away along with my mother's health.

As we shuffled back down the smallest aisle in the world, our hands entwined, the strangeness of new gold rings on respective fingers, and exited the room with a joint sigh of relief, we find the smarmy photographer waiting for us.

"Smile," he commands, even though he looks as if he's about to burst into tears. "Oh, surely you can do better than that," he prompts, although it's clear he's still worrying over the fading light. "You have to understand, because of all the delays, we really only have this very short window of opportunity," he declares, although I had the feeling he'd been rehearsing his lines in a 'don't-blame-me-if-the-pictures-turn-out-crap' type way. He attempts taking a few more pictures, although just then the other guests (finally) arrive. For the next few minutes there are more kisses and fumbled handshakes, with everyone talking over each other and comparing times of arrival.

"The traffic stretched back for miles," someone said.

"We were here nice and early," proudly claimed another.

"It looked like there was a body lying in the road," says someone else.

NEIL BRADLEY

Explanations and congratulations offered, we find ourselves ushered into an anteroom where waitresses serve champagne and orange juice and sparkling water. There follow more shaking of hands and pats on the back and kisses for the bride type congratulations. "It was a lovely service," someone said. I nod, although I'm still not sure whether they're being sarcastic or not.

Across the room I spot Jack with a glass of champagne in his hand. I give him one of those 'what do you think you're playing at?' looks, but don't take it any further than that: at the conclusion of the service, at least that part of the ceremony when we stopped to sign the register, he suddenly burst into tears, and I was torn between stepping forward and signing on the dotted line or putting my arm around *him* in an attempt at consolation. Who knows, perhaps he thinks things will suddenly change between us, although I realised they had changed years before now, when I first decided I was unhappy; when I first realised I was useless as a father and as a husband, and that the only way I could think of getting out of it was to take a walk halfway across Blackfriars Bridge and climb up onto the wall – the view downriver pretty apt I felt at the time.

Just then the photographer steps forward again demanding further photographs: by now he looks like the Doctor Frankenstein in that old black and white movie with Boris Karloff, only instead of screaming, "It's alive, it's alive," he keeps mumbling something about, "the light, the light."

Another picture, another pose, this one the three of us, Jack, Sharon and I, sitting on a carpeted staircase – I think it's meant to look candid. It's the only photo where we actually look like we are laughing or happy: I was taking the piss out of the photographer, who now seemed even more regretful than me over the wedding.

"Smile," he demanded, very camp, very Austin Powers.

"Idiot," I said under my breath. All afternoon he'd been giving me grief.

"I really can't stay much longer," he'd kept telling me.

"He's charging us the cost of a small family car, and he can't stay here much longer," I said. "I feel like *not* smiling just to spite him."

"Shhhhh," Sharon shushes me, poking me in the ribs. "He might hear you." She laughs all the same though, the pressure gage lifting slightly, allowing the tiniest bit of steam to escape.

Jack meanwhile, is laughing hysterically, although I suspect it has more to do with the champagne. "How many glasses have you had?" I demand to know, although this only makes him laugh even more.

Hearing us laughing, the photographer is suddenly buoyed, mistakenly believing that it's his winning charm that has prompted the laughter. Warming to the challenge, he starts barking out further instructions, which only makes Sharon and I laugh just as much as Jack. "That's the spirit," he says.

For the next twenty minutes or so he happily snaps away, although by now it seems like it's been a long day, with everyone's patience wearing more than a little thin. The photographer though, is having none of it. "We'll have to get outside soon, if we're going to get any kind of daylight whatsoever."

Outside it looks black, although I can't tell whether this is due to further brooding rainclouds closing in or whether night has suddenly decided to bring the curtain down on the whole sorry mess.

There follows a collection of group shots, followed by a last couple of photos of Sharon and I standing in the garden looking back in the direction of the camera. Despite everything, we both smile, even if the eventual picture will look like it was taken at midnight.

Back in the room where the ceremony was held we find everyone sat down at a collection of small tables – everyone famished. Sharon and I enter to sporadic applause, although all we really want to do is sit down and eat!

During all of this meanwhile, my dad has been aiming worrying glances in the direction of Jack, who's suddenly looking a little green around the gills. In fact, no sooner had we sat down, which signals the waiting staff to begin placing down the starters, my dad starts tugging at my sleeve. "Have you got a carrier bag?" he asks, although initially I'm not sure what it is he's talking about. The next thing I know though, he's grabs the nearest carrier bag – it's the one containing all the cards and the well-wishes and the decorative horseshoes and wooden spoons and balls and chains – leans across the table, and holds it precariously beneath Jack's chin. Unfortunately, he's not quick enough to prevent Jack from being sick all down himself, into the bag, over the wedding presents.

In the next few moments everyone – Sharon, my dad, my new mother-in-law, wedding guests - are reaching for napkins, and moving chairs out of the way, and a waitress is attempting to serve more starters.

"Look," I said to her, "just take all this stuff back to the kitchen!"

The hotel manager steps forward, "Is there a problem?" she asks without the slightest hint of irony.

"We need a little more time," Sharon intercedes. "We have a slight problem with one of our guests," she says, as if it really needs further explanation. Meanwhile, Jack is being led out of the room, half staggering, half carried, in a drunken stupor by Lloyd and Jason.

Someone laughs at the sight of him, but then, seeing the look of thunder on my face, immediately falls silent again. The whole thing's a fucking disaster.

Taking pity on us, the hotel manager offers to delay the serving of the starters by another fifteen minutes or so – because of the earlier delays we're already running about three hours late. "That would be great," Sharon says, although I can see she's crushed.

"Why don't you just go an talk to the guests," I tell her. She nods agreement, but then immediately runs off in the direction of the women's toilets, where, next door, my dad, my brothers, Michael, are attempting to sober Jack up.

"Who the fuck's being giving him booze?" I demand to know.

"I could see he was going to be sick," my dad said.

All of us are panicking – everyone except my brother, Lloyd. "Just relax," he says, holding Jack's head under the cold tap, although it's clear to everyone that I'm way beyond the relaxation stage.

"We should have just gone away, the pair of us," I said. "We should have just got married on our own."

"This is what Sharon wanted," Jason said.

"She didn't want *this*!"

Thirty minutes later we're all back seated again, and the starters are re-served, everything looking a little more withered than it did half an hour ago.

"How is he?" Mick asks, in reference to Jack.

"He's still drunk," I say. "He's upstairs laying on the wedding bed . . . Lloyd's with him . . . I'm only grateful he's got a television to watch."

"He didn't look well," someone says.

"Ah, bless," from someone else.

"Yeah," I attempt light-heartedness. "I'll be blessing him when he comes back down again."

Following the starters, which pretty much go untouched, the main course is served, although anyone requesting a 'medium-rare' has no chance: Sharon barely touches hers, and it takes me nearly an hour eat half of mine.

"That was lovely," I hear someone say. Looking around the small room I note most have demolished theirs, although I put this down to ravishment, rather than a taste for fine food. Others nod in agreement, and throughout you can hear the buzz of small talk, interspersed with the occasional shriek of overloud laughter.

"Are you okay?" Sharon asks every few minutes or so.

"I'm fine," I say, although I can tell she doesn't believe me. "Are *you* okay?" I ask in return.

"Fine," she says, although she's a worse liar than I am.

Following the sweet and the coffees, it's time for the speeches, although by this stage I'm in the mood to bypass that particular tradition in favour of an early night. Even so, one or two guests, perhaps sensing my

'Plan B,' begin tapping their glasses with cutlery and demanding, "Speech, speech."

Of course, in our case it's very much a modern day wedding, with everyone arriving with baggage from previous respective lives: it's Sharon's mother that gives her away and who will deliver the speech traditionally reserved for the father of the bride. Then there's Jack, the groom's son, playing the role of best man, along with my dad putting his two-pennethworth in. He's always been good like that – he always gives a good speech – always managing to say plenty of nice things about everyone, about the pair of us, Sharon and I. As usual, he makes a proclamation about how the two families have suddenly become one, this despite the suspicious looks being exchanged back and forth in the respective directions of those two families: everybody's weighing everybody else up, trying to work out just where it is they figure in the new hierarchal pecking order.

During Sharon's mother's speech though, the words of welcome are suddenly drowned out by Sharon's aunt, Kathleen: all of those pre and post wedding drinks suddenly kicking-in – the champagne, the table wine – liberally poured out in a collection of glasses that surround her dinner plate and wedding fancies and place names and scattered confetti. In fact, before Sharon's mother can even get through the written words of welcome her sister attempts drowning out the speech. "Give it a rest, will you," she demands, snarling, as other guests start looking around the room, probably looking for an escape route. As with everything else that day though, my poor, new, mother in law attempts ploughing on regardless, although even she is eventually forced to admit defeat as her sister calls out for someone, anyone, to bring her another drink.

"Who is she?" my sister in law, Anne, demands to know.

"Someone should take her outside," someone else says.

"Someone should punch her," someone else half-jokes, prompting laughter from that side of the tiny room.

"Speech!" someone else demands from the floor, although I'm not sure if this is mischief making or a prompt for me, the reluctant groom, to attempt making myself heard over Sharon's drunken aunt.

"Better just get on with it," my dad says, although I can tell he's fuming at the behaviour of this particular drunken member of the family I've just been joined together with in happy matrimony.

"Perhaps you should wait?" Sharon said anxiously.

"Sod it," I say, rising to my feet and bringing the room to order by way of a large silver knife, which I wrap against a pint glass and ring out a death knell.

I had it written down, of course - the whole speech. No prompt cards for me. I knew exactly what it was I wanted to say, and the tone I wanted to say it in. For weeks now I'd been agonising over it, making subtle little changes, editing and re-editing (Stephen Knight would have been proud of me). It was simple, just give the reasons for finally submitting to the marriage, aim a few well timed jokes in the direction of one or two of the guests, and then give a long list of Sharon's attributes - the fact that she was so like my mother, which I know she, and my dad, certainly, would appreciate. Before I can get a quarter of a way through though, Sharon's aunt lets forth once again with a drunken tirade. "Oh, give it a rest, will you," she demands, freezing me to the spot like some stand-up comic whose been abused by one too many hecklers. "This is *so* boring."

I look around the room, everyone embarrassed. I exchange glances with the people around me on the table: Sharon on the verge of tears, her mother looking like she wants the ground to open up and swallow her whole, so mortified is she at her sister's performance; my dad, looking just like he did at the hospital following his last bout of heart surgery - grey. As far as I'm concerned the whole thing's ruined - I should have gotten married when my mother was ill. I should have just done it then. We should've just run away somewhere - come back the next day and presented my mother with the wedding bouquet.

"Why don't you just get on with it," Sharon's aunt shouts out again. "I need another drink," she demands without irony as everyone else in the room concludes that the last thing she needs is another drink, EVER. "For fuck'sake, just get on with it!"

And so that's what I did: abandoned the speech, remaining on my feet long enough to thank a few of the people that needed thanking - my dad, Sharon's mum, Sharon, obviously. Unfortunately, I couldn't thank the best man as he was still upstairs, laying on the wedding bed in a drunken stupor - he'd been sick in the wastebin. My poor brother, Lloyd, had volunteered to sit up in the room with him, eating his wedding dinner on his lap - it was the most sensible decision anyone of us had made that day.

The festivities dispensed with, the coffee's half drunk, people get up to stretch their legs, most of them letting out a huge sigh of relief that this madness has finally been brought to an end.

"Go and have a chat with everyone," I tell Sharon, who is just sat there looking down at her lap. I squeeze her hand, and lean over to kiss her. "Go on, it's fine," I say.

She leaves the table and heads for my family and friends side of the room. Her mother follows. One or two of the guests leave the room - the toilet or outside for a cigarette - and I'm left alone with my dad. "What a nightmare," I say, and he manages a smile, which I accept with gratitude. He gets up and leaves the table too, and I'm alone, sat there thinking about the disaster that I've just been witness to - the disaster that I've just been a part of. I should have gotten married sooner. Away from this circus, that's for sure.

Mick comes over and puts a pint down in front of me. "Well, that went well," he said, and I can't help but laugh.

"Thanks," I said.

Mick's wife, Gill joins us. "Where's the lush gone?" she asks in reference to Sharon's aunt.

"Fuck knows," I shake my head.

"She certainly likes a drink," Mick said without irony.

"She was chatting up Daniel," Gill said. "He's only fifteen!"

"What a fucking nightmare, eh?" I attempt a half-laugh.

"At least Millwall won," Mick says, always seeing that silver lining.

We all laugh at that.

"Come on," he said, "come and sit over with us."

"Sure," I nod. "In a minute."

He squeezes my shoulder and returns to the table. He always seems happy. He's got a real simplistic way of looking at things. He never overcomplicates anything, certainly not the way I'm prone to do. I couldn't ask for a better friend than him. Over the years we've both been witness to the good times, and the very worst - him losing his dad, me, my mother.

I was just trying to do the right thing. I couldn't get that thought out of my head. *I should've known it would turn out like this.* I was just trying to give Sharon what she wanted, but it all turned to mush. How can we ever celebrate the anniversary of *this* day in a year's time, in ten years, in twenty? Even later, as we faked one last smile, as we faked cutting the cake, I was still contemplating that same question. It was like my mother's death all over, when my dad ordered us all to purge it from our memories - the things we'd been witness to that day. And he was right, of course. Only this time it I didn't need him telling me. How on earth would I want to preserve the memory of this day in a wedding album?

This morning, on my way over to my dads, I decided to drive round to Ruby Street - just off the Old Kent Road, sat in-between the, romantically named, Ruby Triangle and the Old Kent Road Gasworks – where, as a family, we'd all been so very happy.

Pulling up in the car I tried to explain to Jack the reason for the detour, but he seemed disinterested, or preoccupied, I'm not sure. After that we drove to the cemetery with the intention of standing over my mother's grave for a while, only the visit was cut short as the wind got up and the clouds darkened and the inevitable rain threatened once more.

"Come on, let's go," I said. Immediately Jack turned on his heels and marched off in the direction of the car, although I lingered just long enough to rub my fingers across the picture of my mother that adorned the headstone. "See you later, mum," I said. I always said that. *See you later, mum.* I was always in a hurry to 'get off.' I was always in a hurry to be elsewhere.

At my dad's there was a welcome air of calmness. On arrival I found him stripped to the waist having just shaved: I can see the remnants of shaving foam on both his earlobes. Around his neck is a gold chain, and my mother's wedding ring still threaded through it.

"Do you want tea?" he asked by way of greeting.

Around ten o'clock that evening Jack made his first appearance at the reception: people applaud, and everybody ribs him over his drunken antics, even though I'm not sure I see the funny side. "Just leave him be," my dad advises though. "Just try and enjoy what's left of the evening."

It's an odd reception. There's no dancing – we have a stereo, but the room is far too small for anything like that, and so most people just sit around talking. Fortunately, everything appears much more relaxed now, mainly due to the fact that Sharon's aunt has disappeared from the room – apparently she's joined the Scottish wedding in the function room down the corridor. Hopefully, she'll meet a nice chap named Angus and he'll whisk her back to his tenement castle up in Edinburgh.

A couple of hours later the taxi's start arriving, along with the mini-coach my dad arranged to transport my side of the family to and from the wedding.

"The bus is here," he tells us.

There follows thirty minutes of handshakes and kisses, best wishes and congratulations. I notice Jack lingering in the doorway. I motion him over and give him a bear hug, attempting to convey to him that nothing had changed between us. As the mini-coach pulled away from the entrance though, and I caught one last glimpse of him (not really looking back), I knew it had. I knew that after today the bond between us would become less and less, until all I'd be left with are photos and vague memories of access visits when, every other weekend, I attempted creating normality out of all the absurdity of the three way relationship between his mother, him and I. The truth was; I was rubbish as a husband, and rubbish as a father. Nothing was going to change that fact. Sure, I tried. Sometimes I tried so hard to keep it all afloat that it was the only thing keeping me from leaping off that bridge into the Thames, or taking a very large handful of tablets my GP had insisted would . . . what was it he'd said . . . *help me sleep?* He never once realised that I didn't need tablets to help me sleep. Sleep was the one thing I was really good at. Sleep, my bed, was the only place I could escape it all, unless of course my dreams, my nightmares in reality, shook me back awake again.

"Are you okay?" Sharon asked, squeezing my hand, knowing what was on my mind.

"It's been a long day," is all I said.

"Let's go back inside," she suggests.

Back in the room - the scene of the crime - the hotel staff are already clearing away the debris, although immediately upon our return they make their exit. Before leaving the manager offers to take care of the cake and anything else we need putting aside for collection tomorrow.

"Thanks," I say.

"Can I get you both a drink?" she asks.

"Coffee would be great?" we say in unison.

We sit down in two chairs and drain our first real celebration drink – flat champagne.

"Mr Bradley?" Sharon smiles.

"Mrs Bradley," I smile back.

Paperback Writer

Tuesday 19th May 2009

Even from the car I can see my dad sat on the bench opposite my mother's grave. I can't believe it's been eleven years. I take the flowers from the boot of the car. It's only now that he notices me. He waves. I wave back. I wind my way down the hill through the labyrinth of graves that surround my mother's, and then place the flowers in a vase my dad has already filled with water. I step back and admire my floral handiwork, before taking a seat on the bench next to him. "It's turned nice now," I say, looking up at the sky.

"Still writing?" my dad asks.

"Yeah," I smile, even though we never actually discuss just *what* it is I'm writing.

I mention how a women on the course had brought in photographs to accompany a piece of life writing she'd written, which showed various members of her family riding horses in top hats and holding riding crops.

My dad laughed. "Your great Nanny Bradley had her own horse . . ."

"Really?"

"Yeah, it pulled the veg cart!"

For the next few minutes we sit in silence. Occasionally he'll point to a robin sat atop a headstone or to a pair of fox cubs that chase each other amongst the graves.

Following my mother's death my dad underwent a course of bereavement counselling, which had been paid for by the Daily Telegraph, but which had ended as soon as my dad was presented with a personal bill – it wasn't the cost that had stopped him continuing, but rather the working class shackles that prevent any of us from discussing our emotions with others – especially outsiders. Instead he found solace in the past, in old photographs, melancholy music, with frequent trips back to places of familiarity – his old stomping ground – the area of his courtship to my mother. For him it was all about filling up units of time – filling up the hours with constructive little chores – housework, Telegraph, sleep: for a time he attended evening classes – *Conversational Spanish* and *Basic Computer* – but all that fell flat after he was told he'd need to take an exam. "Can't I just repeat the course?" he'd asked. They didn't understand. He wasn't looking for academic accreditation. He was looking for company - an escape from loneliness.

I check my watch – the cemetery closes at eight during the summer months – they'll be ringing the first bell soon.

"Did you submit your portfolio?" my dad asks.

"Yeah," I said.

"So, what happens now?"

"It gets read, and then it gets marked."

"And then?"

"Nothing," I say. "It's all over after that."

"Is that when you graduate?"

"Yes," I nod: I think that's the thing he's been waiting for the most – graduation. Sharon's the same - the pair of them more concerned about the end process, the cap and gown, the photo on the mantelpiece.

"I was reading this piece in the *Telegraph* about John Betjeman's muse," he said casually, as though this is a subject matter we always talk about. He makes me laugh. Ever since I've being doing the degree he's taken a keen interest in the arts, in literature, in poetry. "I suppose, a muse is a bit like an artist's model?"

"Yeah, I suppose so."

Looking across from my mother's grave I can see my grandparent's grave also: my grandmother finally passed away a few weeks after the Millennium celebrations (13th January 2000), although during those remaining years she still spoke about my granddad every day – still asked what time he'd be coming home, still wondered why he was working so late: at the time of my granddad's death, I couldn't even start to imagine what was going through my dad's head, what with my mother dying, *his* mother well into the onset of Alzheimer's, his father gone.

The plan had been a simple one: my paternal grandparent's were going to leave their flat at the Borough and move closer to my parents. My mother, who'd been made redundant from the print union, SOGAT, was going to look after them; pop in everyday, do their housework and their shopping; bring them the three gallon of milk they requested each day for putting on the three ton of muesli they consumed – all about the 'roughage.' A few years previous their GP had given my granddad an M.O.T. – blood pressure, water works, that sort of thing – and had told him that his cholesterol was a little high, and that he should cut down on cheese and salt and every other thing that had been a staple food on their shopping list. My dad though, had cursed the doctor, "He should keep his opinions to himself," he'd said, "What does he (talking about my granddad) need to worry about cholesterol for? He's in his eighties, and he'd never heard of cholesterol until the doctor mentioned it!"

After that, just as my dad had predicted, my granddad became obsessed with everything health and food wise: he had an obsessive personality at the best of times, so the last thing he needed was something else to obsess over. "They should just eat what they want to eat," my dad shook his head. "It's far too late for them to start worrying about any of that stuff."

My granddad though, he did worry about it. He worried about everything: he worried about his diet, he worried about his neighbours, he worried about his sister – he obsessed over all this stuff – *feeling sorry for himself*, my dad thought. "His sister, Joanie, gets oxygen, so now he wants oxygen," my dad said. "I explained to him, "she gets oxygen because she's got emphysema," but he won't listen."

"I still think I should have oxygen," my granddad had countered.

"You've got a pump for your asthma."

"She gets two bottles of oxygen a week."

"That's because she can't breath." It was pointless my dad arguing with him.

"The woman downstairs gets *Meals on Wheels*."

"You can have Meals on Wheels; if that's what you want."

"I'm not eating that rubbish."

"Well, why'd you bring it up then?"

My granddad ignored this argument. "And she gets *Home Help* . . ."

"Well, you can have *Home Help*, if you want it."

"I'm not accepting charity."

"It's not charity; you have to pay for it."

"I'm not paying for it . . . I'm a pensioner!"

It continued like this for months, years even. My mother went up every week with their shopping; did all their housework, made them a bit of dinner, and took their laundry home with her. A couple of times a week I popped in, each time bringing them eight pints of milk – my dad said it would be cheaper getting them their own cow.

Upon leaving my granddad would always reach into his pocket and give me a twenty-pound note for the milk. "It's only £1.70," I'd say.

"Take it, take it," he'd insist.

Just before my mother became ill my grandparents had moved to a sheltered flat, just down the road from my parents house. The plan had been that my mother would look after them. Only my mother had become unwell, and they had to fend themselves a little more. However, my granddad started complaining – he had no idea that my mother was unwell (this had been kept from the pair of them) – suddenly claiming that he didn't like living there, claiming that he'd never wanted to move from his other flat.

Understandably, my dad exploded, all of the frustration he felt at my mother's illness pouring out of him. "*She's* dying, and you're worrying about yourself," he'd raged, telling him about my mother, telling him all the things he'd wanted to say to him over the years: my dad was one of the most dutiful sons a parent could wish for, yet for years he lived in my granddad's shadow. It's clear that he spent every waking hour attempting to live up to my granddad's ludicrous expectations. And yet my granddad was full of flaws: he drank, he gambled; he could moan for England.

"Some days he'd have to walk home from Catford Dog Track, because he'd gambled all his money away," my dad shook his head at the memories of it, "or he'd have to be carried home because he'd had too much to drink!"

He told me that following the war my granddad hit upon the notion that he had cancer of the tongue. "He drove us all mad," he said. "Night after night he'd be at Guy's Hospital . . . they must have thought he was some kind of lunatic . . ."

"And did he?" I ask. "Have cancer of the tongue, I mean?"

"Of course not," my dad shook his head again. "That didn't stop him going back up that hospital every single night . . . do you know; he claimed that it was caused by the sediment in beer . . . he even took to scrubbing his tongue with bleach!"

"What?"

"It didn't stop him drinking it, though . . . it didn't stop him drinking beer."

These things were a revelation to me. I always thought my granddad was miserable – in an Alf Garnett type way. But then that was no different to how my dad always seemed miserable to me – the way I would become equally as miserable as the pair of them. Even so, when I was a kid at least, my granddad always seemed like a comical character – always full of affection for his grandchildren. Then again, he never gave too much away.

"What did you do in the war, granddad?" I would always ask him.

"You don't want to know," he'd always say. The trouble was though, I did want to know: I found out later that, during the Blitz, he'd been posted along the Thames on the heavy ack ack guns. When war broke out he'd joined the London Regiment, although even this was typical of him – he was not doing out of London pride, but rather the fact that he'd discovered that those in the London Regiment, when not on duty, and when not billeted, were allowed to return home at weekends.

"What was the war like?" I'd always persist.

"It was bloody 'orrible," he'd always declare.

When he was finally posted overseas, he was involved in the shelling around Belsen, and had arrived with the Americans to discover the grizzly secret of the concentration camps.

My dad told me that he'd never spoken to him about the war, although he'd managed to overhear little snippets, and was told certain things by his aunts and uncles. My dad assumed that he'd constructed the whole 'cancer of the tongue' thing as some kind of defence mechanism, and that what he'd really been suffering all these years was some kind of post-traumatic stress disorder. This perhaps makes sense: I remember one day watching the Remembrance Day commemorations with him – he was so venomous about the whole thing: he hated Remembrance Sunday, he hated all those men marching past the Cenotaph with their medals and their bowler hats. "The Glorious Dead," he spat out the words. "There was no glory in any of it."

In the 1930's `` he'd joined the Communist Party. During that period he'd suffered long spells of unemployment, and like most men at the time such extreme political affiliation seemed to make perfect sense to him. Even so, it was clear his heart was never really in it. "Come the glorious day, I'll probably end up manning a barricade somewhere, rather than being given some cushy job in the town hall!" he always said.

My dad told me that he'd lost his job once – more than once by all accounts – because he could never get out of bed on time. My dad was always warning us, my brothers and I, "If you're going to be active in the union, in the workplace, you have to get to work early; you have to work hard, you can't give them any excuse to sack you."

My brother, Lloyd, was the same: full of all the same demons as my granddad, especially as far as 'getting a beer down his neck' was concerned. He was militant in the workplace – as we all were – always causing arguments. Like my granddad though, he could never get out of bed in the mornings, and so he, too, got the sack. My dad though, he was a shining light – a beacon. He knew better than anyone how the game was played. He always described it as a 'game.' "It's not a war, it's just a game," he'd always say, "and a stupid game, at that."

When we were younger though, my brother and I, we really did think it was a war. "All that anger," my dad would counter though, "it won't get you anywhere." He was always full of that wisdom. "You bang the table at the end of the meeting; you don't bang it at the beginning," that was another one of his. "All about showing your poker face. My dad rarely raised his voice, but he always seemed to achieve more in negotiations than we ever did.

"Your granddad was a pain in the arse," he told me later – much later, when all of this was done and dusted – when my granddad was in the ground, my grandmother, also, my mother in a grave within touching distance of theirs.

Following their argument - once my granddad found out about my mother's illness – his whole demeanour changed: he was really apologetic, and made a renewed effort in terms of his independence, which seemed to be working well for all concerned. However, within a few short weeks he suffered a heart attack, and had died instantly.

It was a Sunday morning, and my dad had paid his usual visit. When he arrived my granddad had done his usual disappearing act into the kitchen in order to go through his tea-making exercise: over the years the kitchen had become a sort of sanctuary for him – away from my grandmother's Alzheimer's. A few weeks previous, my mother had rigged up a net curtain in the kitchen door frame, offering some form of escape from my grandmother's incessant questions: since the move she'd become steadily worse, suddenly believing that she was on her holidays, staying in some hotel or holiday camp. "They're a lovely crowd," she'd say. "We've had a lovely time. Everyone was singing," her memory now clashing with things she'd heard on the television or my granddad's radio in the kitchen.

With my granddad out in the kitchen, my dad was left sitting with my grandmother on the sofa in the living room. She was holding his hand. Stroking the back of it, and asking him questions about school – he had no idea what age he was meant to be.

When my granddad returned with the tea my dad noticed how, "He looked different, somehow. There was a look about him . . . I knew something wasn't quite right . . . It was almost as if he knew," he'd said. "Just then he sort of pitched forward, crashing through the coffee table, smashing his glasses, cutting his eye, his head."

It was really tragic, that whole episode, especially in terms of the timing, my mother being unwell like that, and what with my granddad's and my dad's cross words. I know my dad has always felt guilty over it, even though he really had nothing to reproach himself over. He told me that he knew that there'd be no saving him. Even so, he turned my granddad onto his back, already he was lifeless, and then quickly phoned the ambulance. As he waited he attempted the 'kiss of life,' attempting kissing the life back into him – all to no avail.

My grandmother meanwhile, had not the faintest idea what was going on: as soon as my granddad hit the deck she was up out of the armchair wanting to 'spend a penny,' wandering around the tiny flat in a daze or a sort of fog – these days she could manage to get herself lost just making the short journey from the living room to the bathroom.

On her way back she actually stepped on my grand-dad. "Mother, what are you doing?" my dad had demanded in-between blowing puffs of air into my grand-dad's mouth and rhythmically massaging his chest.

"What's he doing down there?" she demanded to know, the evidence of her own eyes, the witnessing of my granddad falling through the coffee table, still not registering with her. "He's never looked like that before," she said. "He looks all blue."

Of course, if my mother had been alive, if my mother had lived, my grandmother would have stayed with them, my parents would have looked after her – that had always been the plan. On the day my granddad died though, my dad was already making plans to put her in a care home.

"You can't look after her, dad," we'd all said. "Mum's not well; you can't look after the pair of them." My dad though, I know, was crushed. You could tell that his whole world has collapsed around him and that he was incapable of doing anything to prevent it. "Dad, you can't feel guilty about this," we'd pleaded, but you could see the guilt on his face. The whole thing was a tragedy – a kitchen sink drama writ large.

At the funeral the priest couldn't even remember my granddad's name, let alone deliver anything near to telling his life story – he doesn't want to know. He's got his eighty quid, he's more than happy. He's like Father McKenzie, at the funeral of Eleanor Rigby, wiping the dirt from his hands as he walks from the grave – none of us were saved, certainly not that day.

Sat alongside my mother (she was on her way to becoming permanently unwell at that stage) and my dad in the cold chapel, it's clear everything's going wrong, and my dad, always a 'fixer,' is unable to fix any of it. Throughout the service he appears broken, sitting helpless – impotent, even. He's always been a fixer, a man with the ability to fix things. He's like Mr Wolfe, in *Pulp Fiction*, turning up in that sports car. Only he's turning up in a Nissan Micra. "What the problem?" he'd always ask.

Way off in the distance we hear the bell ring, signalling the fact that the cemetery will close in the next ten minutes. As I make my way back up the hill to the car, my dad lingers by my mother's grave: when I look back I see him lip-syncing some words that only he and her can share, and I quickly turn away again.

Back in the car I turn the key in the ignition and sit waiting patiently as my dad stands another few minutes, this time at his parent's grave. Behind him in the distance I can see Guy's Hospital, the GPO Tower, St. Paul's Cathedral – free from the architectural shackles that once blighted its surrounds – once more restored to Sir Christopher Wren's glorious vision as viewed from the upper windows of Cardinal's House on Bankside. I let out a little sigh. Our whole life seems to be out there on that horizon, I think, the whole history of our family – a twenty-minute train ride from London Bridge, in the space of a few inches of horizontal skyline

MA in Creative and Life Writing

People will often ask – friends, family members - "You're not writing about *me* in that book of yours, are you?" Of course, they don't really mean that. What they really want to ask is, "You're not writing anything *bad* about me in that book of yours, are you?"

"I don't know where you get it from," they always say, also. "No one else in the family's ever written," as though it's something I should be ashamed of. This though, I've long since put this down to a mistrust in anyone that wants to 'share their feelings,' especially when the intention is to share those feelings with a 'wider audience.' More bizarre still however, despite their misgivings at *my* writing, is the way in which they all claim that they wish they could write like me: that *they* could put into words the way they're feeling. None of them though, see it for what it really is – a curse. They don't seem to realise that the dead, memories of the dead, stay with throughout the days and nights – that they never leave me - that they're constantly in my thoughts. Some foolishly think that by my writing it all down it somehow makes it easier. It doesn't. It just means I have a written record, that's all. It certainly hasn't resulted in me attaining, despite hating that particular term, any form of 'closure.' Perhaps that was the reason I initially chose fiction: writing about people that I didn't know or who, indeed, did not exist - conjuring up these fictional 'others.' Then again, this might also be the reason, if only in fictional form, as to why I've always seemed content to write about the dying or the dead - the reason, despite struggling to believe in a higher being or heaven or any notion of an afterlife, that I've constantly attempted to capture a workable concept for a heaven I refute the existence of – attempting to make right what 'death' has so often made wrong in terms of my loved ones.

Certainly in *The Brass Angel* I attempted writing a workable description of heaven – a heaven of sorts – a heaven I perhaps wished for, rather than having any real conviction with regards to it, for those that I've known and loved, and who have died. But then, isn't that what creative writer's are meant to do?

I remember my initial plan for the MA portfolio had been to write two different versions of my paternal grandfather's death: one factual (the account that is presented in this book as Funeral Two), and a fictional version, long since intended for my novel (*The Brass Angel*).

Discussing the idea with Stephen Knight he wondered if I'd be tempted to alter the outcome – write it so my grandfather would have been 'saved,' that he doesn't die at the end?

"No," I'd smiled bitterly, answering the question instantly. Unfortunately, life's not really that simple – even fictional life. In fact, my only concession would have been for me (Jimmy, in the novel) to have arrived on time at my grandfather's/Charlie's bedside – for me/ him not to have gone through the agony of that hospital blunder when they simply announced, "he's gone."

Just why the content of the portfolio changed, just why the direction of my writing changed, I still, to this day, have no real idea. I know Stephen Knight was taken by surprise the first time he read an extract from the piece that would eventually become the main body of the portfolio. Then again, I'm not sure I helped myself sometimes, especially in terms of the tutorial system (part-time students have two tutorials per term – one with a personal tutor, and one with a guest tutor). Of course, it would be easy to blame my change in direction solely on the criticism I received in terms of the novel, but surely that can't be the whole reason that I suddenly started writing about the build-up to my mother's death? If I'm honest, that really came about by accident, although, perhaps that's what's meant to happen: you tell a story by accident. This certainly seemed to be true in my case.

Of course, there were some on the MA that managed to use the whole time constructively, professionally even, by sticking to their guns and simply using the course as a vehicle - a means to an end - to complete their novel or memoir or long envisaged collection of poetry. Others though, myself included, seemed none the wiser, or at least no closer to the finish, quickly losing momentum and certainly finding themselves no nearer to the completion of respective literary projects that have nagged away at them through pregnancy, divorce, illness, mundane jobs or careers which have long since lost their sparkle. In my case the things I thought it would resolve, the loss of my mother certainly, and the way I felt at her loss, remain just as they were, only now I have a record of it – allowing others perhaps an insight into what it is I feel, or at least what it was I *felt,* during those certain/

uncertain days in 1998. Throughout my struggle to capture (in words-on-paper form) that short period though, I was always concerned that it would immediately be pigeonholed as some form of 'misery literature,' even if I was repeatedly reassured that it wasn't, or that I didn't want to write something that garnered sympathy and little else. In fact, the worse thing would be for people to feel sympathy for me: that was *never* my reason for writing it.

At a reading event one evening I remember asking Blake Morrison if he'd ever regretted publishing the account of his father's passing away (*And When Did You Last See Your Father?*) so soon after the event: certainly from a professional point of view, I suspect, he can have no regrets, especially in terms of its continuing success. His response though, was more to do with the fact that, with hindsight, he may well have written it differently, which, I'm sure, will always be the case when one is allowed the time to reflect upon ones own work? By contrast the account of my own mother's passing wasn't truly tackled until nearly eleven years after the event – even though it was delivered as if written in the moment – and was only really prompted by the experience of the course, the reconsidering of my own writing style, and the stories I suddenly wanted to (re)-tell.

Of course, in many ways, Blake Morrison may well have written his, and I mine, by writing it as a form of 'therapy:' writing something that not only does what it says on the tin but also allows the writer that 'closure' that so many people – a modern age phenomena – seem to crave these days. The trouble is, I've never done 'closure' very well: for me 'closure' means a factory, a printing works or a coal mine, rather than the conclusion of a journey in mental health. Then again, following the submission of the main portfolio, I certainly felt that I'd solved one or two things, even if much of what I envisaged I'd resolve, when I first engaged in the life-writing genre, remains unresolved: my novel for one remains unwritten or at least in first draft form, despite sporadic attempts at reinvigoration. Within weeks of the portfolio submission though, I was lost again.

I see Maura Dooley in the coffee bar at Goldsmiths. "I've read your portfolio," she whispers: I'm sure she's not meant to let on.

"Oh, yeah?" I say surprised, smiling, knowing that I owe her so much,

"It really made me cry," she said, giving me a sympathetic look, confirming that I'd finally achieved what it was I'd unintentionally set out to achieve.

"I'm sorry," I smile again, reaching out and touching her arm.

"No; it was wonderful." I know that she genuinely means it. I know her mother is not well. I know that some-where down the line I'll probably read something she's written about her mother's passing. I know that one day I'll share the same bond with her as I do Stephen Knight and Blake Morrison: this unhealthy obsession with death.

A few months later it's confirmed: Master of Arts in Creative and Life Writing. I'm not sure what I expected. Nothing has really changed. I don't suddenly feel different; the euphoria I felt upon handing in the final portfolio has dissipated, and once again I feel the same way as I've always felt.

"You have the ending to your book now," my mother had said. Maybe that was the problem. Maybe, having finally committed her death to paper, I worry that my memory of her will suddenly start to fade. I worry that having written it all up that I'll have nothing left to tell – no pieces of me left to give away.

Blake Morrison's view was the same – he was always advising me about 'not giving everything away too soon,' believing that these deaths, these memories of those deaths - these little tales of family folklore - were all perfectly good sources for a writer, but how one should never, both from a creative and a business point of view, attempt telling the whole thing – something I know I've always been guilty of: what Maura Dooley described as "over-egging the pudding." It was always fascinating watching Blake dissect the long pieces of text I always tended to submit; watching the way he broke the whole thing down. "That's one book," he'd smile, highlighting one particular chunk with a pen. "Your trouble is that you're always trying to get everything in . . . everything but the kitchen sink."

"Everything, but the kitchen sink drama," I smiled back.

"There are at least four different stories in this piece," he said: I think his view was that these stories were like coal dug out from the mine, and that I should always be looking for new seams. I think he saw them more as commodity than separate pieces of memory and that I should be exploiting each of them individually. "I know you've got hundred's of these little stories," he once commented.

Whenever we discussed my work in tutorials I was always going off at a tangent – a bit like Ronnie Corbett, sat in the armchair wearing a golfing jumper, never quite getting to the end of the joke. I think Blake thought I expended far too much energy – used far too many words – simply in order to deliver a single punchline.

And so that was it – Graduation in 2009 – even though I'm still not quite sure what it was I'd achieved: the novel still lays in tatters, although hopefully I'll conjure up enough energy one day to return to it - finally write that airport novel that everyone at Goldsmiths thought me so capable of. Okay, so that's a little unfair. In fact, I readily admit that it was a life-changing experience - perhaps not in professional terms, but certainly in terms of discovering things about myself and, far more importantly, others discovering things about me also. In many ways the hope when writing is that you can somehow manage to surprise people. In my close circle of family and friends that was certainly very much the case. I just wish I'd never written what it was I ended up writing. No, I wish the reason for my having to write what it was I ended up writing had never presented itself to me. I wish my mother had never died, that's all.

Even so, my dad and Sharon have always seemed suitably proud. For them there was a sense of great pride, I think: the fact that I went to university, the fact that I was attempting doing what it was I was eventually did. I'm not sure, but I think they saw a change in me - a spark perhaps. I think they saw the same change in me that I'd seen in myself. With others though, I sensed there was always an element of suspicion, a worry perhaps that I was getting 'ideas above my station.' One good friend of mine even joked that I was like *Good Will Hunting*. "Yeah, Good Will Hunting,"

I replied. "Only without the boyish good looks and the mathematical genius!"

Of course, that *Good Will Hunting* joke was meant as a compliment. Others though, are not so light-hearted, which I mention it to Stephen Knight during a tutorial. He nods knowingly. *People think I've changed*, I tell him - some members of the family, some of my friends - the people closest to me. I've not changed though. *Their* perception of me might have changed. But I've always been like this. I know I've always felt different. I know I've always had this feeling at the back of my mind that I needed much more than the life I've lived.

It might sound clichéd – Stephen was always warning me over my use of cliché – but I think the course saved me; that education saved me. Writing certainly did. It might well be difficult for others to grasp – those who were always expected to go to university or those that were condemned never to - but just being on the course allowed me to be the person I was always meant to be. Just being on the course allowed me an insight into just what it is that has so troubled me all these years; just why I hated the jobs I've had, just why I loathed my wasted years at school.

And yet, studying has not come without a cost. "Weren't you working on a novel?" my fellow students would often ask.

"Yes."

"How's that going?"

"*It's not*," is what I *want* to say. "It's . . . er . . . its changed direction somewhat," is what I usually tell them: how could I explain to them the fact that I was in possession of this (sixty thousand words strong) bundle of confusion, which had been occupying my attentions on and off for the past three or four years? How could I tell them that I was no nearer finishing now than I was at the beginning? How could I tell them that the criticism I'd received in terms of my novel had knocked my confidence to such an extent that I suddenly found myself drowning amidst waves of uncertainty? In the same respect though, how could I tell them, very much as a result of that criticism, that I'd suddenly been granted a moment of clarity; that things had suddenly become much clearer to me?

One day, almost by accident – certainly as a result of the criticism of my novel - I wrote that life-writing piece: the start of that journey from work to my mother's bedside (Stephen Knight often claimed that much of my literary output was life-writing not so cleverly disguised as fiction). This though, despite being well-received, suddenly presented me with new problems, especially – as it dealt with my mother's death – the fact that people from my background just don't like to talk about *that* sort of stuff. Indeed, even after I'd overcome my initial reluctance to commit such personal memories to paper, I still wasn't quite sure exactly what I had, where the story would lead, or what form it would take. Of course, in my head I think I knew what it was I was attempting to do, even if much of it I was struggling to get down on paper – even if I couldn't explain it to my dad, couldn't explain it to Sharon, couldn't explain it to Maura Dooley or Stephen Knight or Blake Morrison. Initially, I thought it was about the relationship with my mother. However, as the months went on, I suddenly started to suspect that it was more to do with everyone: my dad, my wife, my family and friends – about my relationship with all of them. Naturally, my mother's presence, not just because of the theme, was still at the very heart of it.

During a tutorial with Blake Morrison I attempted explaining away the million and one thoughts that occupy my mind when writing - especially against a backdrop of someone that has no formal qualifications, no prior experience of academia, and no real concept of English literature – worrying that my vocabulary was not large enough; worrying that I was not 'clever enough;' burdened by an overwhelming fear of failure – knowing that some people couldn't wait to see me fall flat on my face, yet also knowing that *this* was the most important thing I would ever write.

"Okay, so what is it you're planning?" Blake Morrison asked.

"I'm not sure," I say honestly. "I have a concept of what it is I'm trying to achieve."

"And that is what, exactly?"

"I think I'm trying to give an insight into what it's like struggling to write a novel, or a memoir. I'm trying to capture what it's like having your confidence knocked, and the feeling of wanting to give up, yet knowing that, if I do, I'll be accused of another five minute wonder . . ."

"A five minute wonder?"

"That's what my dad always said whenever I took up something new. "That'll be another five minute wonder." No matter what it was - violin lessons, the saxophone, the guitar - they always ended up on top of the wardrobe gathering dust, my dad shaking his head, *another five minute wonder*!

"When I was younger I always thought that he was miserable – whenever he came home from work he always seemed to be in a mood. How could I tell this man that I wanted to be a writer, even if, at the time, I didn't want to be anything – other than left alone?

"It's funny, but it was the course that made realise that my dad was once a young man. It was talking to him about creative writing that I suddenly realised that he was once younger than I am now - that he was once filled with the same burning ambition as I am now. When I was younger though, I just didn't see it. "Doesn't anybody bother turning a light off in this house? It's like Blackpool illuminations in here," he'd always moan."

Blake Morrison let out a laugh. "All father's are like that," he said.

"Oh, don't get me wrong, he's always encouraged me."

"Well, that's good isn't it?"

"Of course it is. I'm not knocking him," I said. "He knows me better than anyone."

"So, what's the problem then?"

"This can't be a five minute wonder."

"The writing, you mean?"

"Absolutely, the writing. This is the one thing I *can't* fail at. This is the one thing that has to last longer than five minutes."

"And it will, I've no doubt about that."

"The trouble is, the more I plough on, the more I feel . . ."

"Alienated?"

"Exactly. That I don't fit in anymore. . . the people I know . . . the people around me. They think I've changed. They think, *I think*, that suddenly I'm too good for them now."

"That's always going to be a problem for someone from your background."

"I haven't changed. I've always been like this. Just being here has convinced me of that fact. Even so, I suddenly feel like I don't fit in with those people that perceive themselves to be in the class above me. I don't fit in with the people from my own background, who seem resentful that I no longer wish to appear like them. And yet none of them can see; I don't want to be like *any* of them. I don't want to change the way I talk, the way I dress, the way I write. People just can't see that though. None of them see the real *me*."

Tutorials, especially the earlier ones during the course, always seemed like rounds of boxing to me. Sometimes I don't think I helped myself. Sometimes I think there's this rage inside of me, this burning desire, which I always struggle to explain away. It's like electricity. Only, the electric's on the blink! That's why I don't think I ever used the tutorial system to its fullest advantage: always resistant, always viewing it as another form of industrial relations, always fighting the urge to argue rather than to take on board the criticism. Of course, it hasn't helped that I've had to work full-time – it hasn't helped that I've been forced to divide my time between the reading list, assignments, home life and the mundane nature of work. As such I've had to develop a rather haphazard approach to writing, picking up a pen or sitting down at a keyboard as and when the precious time allowed: I write on the bus on the way to work every day, free-hand in a note pad. Before I start work I type it all up. During my lunch break I do a rough edit and then type it all up again. On the train journey home (I get a bus to work and then a train home) I do another edit. The next morning, I start the whole process again, writing all the new stuff up in a pad. I often joke that I'm like Virginia Woolf, only I'm doing it on a travel card. I'm attempting to do it whilst some idiot in front of me engages in a one-sided mobile phone conversation for the entire length of the journey. I'm attempting to write while some young kid blasts 'gangsta rap' from the back seat of the bus. I know what he's up to. He's hoping I'll turn around and confront him. But he doesn't realise how busy I am. He doesn't realise how ironic and how insignificant his choice of music is. He doesn't realise how important these scribbled words in a notepad actually are to me. Then again, sometimes I'm not sure even my family or my friends realise just how important all of this stuff is to me, so what chance has he got? In fact, I don't think he, *they*, any of them, realise just what it is that's going on inside my head, why all of it distracts me so; why I'm so troubled by all of it – this need in me. Not that I can really blame them. "I mean, *writing*, it's not really a proper job, is it?" That's what they normally tell me.

Maybe, on some level, they're right: not so long back I might well have offered up a similar argument. Today though, I realise they couldn't be more wrong. Today, now, it's become far more important than that to me: far more important than any job - it's certainly far more important than the long list of dead-end jobs *I've* had over the years. One problem I've faced though, is viewing it as a job: forcing myself to divide my time equally between life and solitude. I think that's another thing that people don't really understand, the fact that, on the whole, writing can be a truly lonely business: it requires solace, it requires selfishness; it requires removing oneself from a life of domestic bliss - an evening on the sofa with Sharon. To counter this *she's* taken up the piano: I think she feels excluded. And yet she rarely disturbs me. She just writes the cheques on the monthly degree instalments. She brings me a cup of tea. She kisses me on the ear. She believes in me – far more than I actually believe in myself, I think, sometimes.

"How are you getting on?" she asks.

"Great," I lie.

"Let me know when you want dinner."

Throughout the writing process she has been an all-too-willing participant in terms of offering up initial feedback on my work: often she'd be sitting there happily watching television and suddenly have her viewing of *Friends* or *ER* interrupted by my request for a sympathetic ear. "Can I just read you this?" I'd always ask. "Can you just let me know what you think of it?"

"Of course," she says, always the willing recipient of my latest scattered thought process: she's always been great like that – truly supportive.

One night I read her the latest extract from my portfolio. She never actually offers up any real criticism, other than to rub my arm and give her usual reply, "It sounds good, honey." I think we all need that sometimes.

"Do you have a study or an office where you write?" Blake Morrison asked me that once.

"When I lived in my flat at Camberwell I typed at an ironing board!" I laughed.

About a year ago *his* study actually featured in The Guardian's *Writer's Room* series: of most note is his father's stethoscope and his pacemaker. The accompanying photograph revealed a cramped little space full of books and clutter: *I'll never read that many books*, was my first impression. The article did get me wondering though, just what he'd make of my study (a converted back bedroom in reality): the music collection and the films, the framed photographs on the wall – Tony Bennett, Tommy Steele, David Bowie, John and Yoko, Twiggy "Twig the Wonder Kid" Lawson, Alan Bennett, Bryan Ferry, Brian Eno, Tony Hancock, Sid James, Charlie Drake. It made me wonder whether, if he were to see it, he'd understand me better; perhaps understand better just what it was I was trying to do.

I show the Guardian article to Sharon. "That's a weird thing," she says in reference to the pacemaker: on a shelf in my office there's a pair of my grandfather's broken glasses: the ones he was wearing when he had his heart attack; the ones he was wearing when he fell crashing through the coffee table. One of the lenses is missing and there are specks of blood on the bridge: they remind me of John Lennon's blood-spattered glasses following his murder.

"Did you read the bit about the desk?" I ask her.

A few weeks into the course Sharon bought me this old desk from work (I think she wanted the ironing board back) – she paid these two blokes to deliver it in a van. "One day, maybe you'll get your office in *The Guardian*," she smiles.

During the writing of my academic essay I read her an extract from Blake Morrison's *And When Did You Last See Your Father?* I explained to her Morrison's theory that his father actually died the moment he stopped being the person he (Morrison) so well remembers; the larger than life character - his father in rude health.

Sharon just smiles, as she always does – she's so proud – so very easily pleased. I explain to her how I could use the quote to highlight an aspect of my mother's passing: consider perhaps the last moment *she* was truly alive – in polite, rather 'rude,' health. "It sounds good, honey," she says again.

When did I last see my mother? There were moments, of course, between bouts of chemotherapy, between morning sickness that lasted all day, between the taste buds disappearing and my dad trawling the supermarket shelves for exotic fruit my mother might just have a hankering for. There were moments when she looked perfectly healthy; when she looked like the woman she always was – the woman in the photographs, the woman in the kitchen, the woman that often came to me in dreams.

I still describe them as 'dreams;' all the time I sleep they remain deserving of such description. When I wake though, when I discover my mistake, they instantly turn to nightmare.

Most dreamful nights the scenario's the same - some domestic scene. My mother is always present in the room. Sometimes other family members swell the number - other family members that have now passed on. Often the dreams are like real life - they're certainly not dream-like. Nothing really happens, normalcy reigns, conversations pass, all is mundane domestic bliss. Towards the end I always say the same thing. "I have to go, mum." For a mere second I notice the disappointment crossing her face - a betrayal of the merest hint of regret. And just then I wake up and the nightmares begin.

She's gone.

Through the darkness I peer at the clock that illuminates upon the ceiling like the Bat Sign – trouble in

Gotham City. Lying beside me, Sharon is barely visible beneath the quilt, soundly sleeping away another night of unbroken sleep, curled up in a foetal ball taking up no space whatsoever in the bed.

"I have to go, mum." It's not the sleep I dread, but the waking up – those frequent moments when I wake to find her gone, her presence in my sleeping life these past eleven years a cruel dream.

When did I last see my mother? She was sitting in the armchair – his and hers. My dad, having made the tea, sits alongside her, a lamp between them on a nest of tables illuminating their features, affording them a warm glow. Sharon and I sit together on the sofa.

"Have you been out?" I ask. I always asked that: my mother had been made redundant from the print union, SOGAT – an ironic sign of the decline in print union membership – and so her days were filled with trips out, happily trawling museums and stately homes, biding her time whilst my dad worked his way towards retirement and that place in the sun they'd always talked about. If my mother had still been working I would have asked *have you been to work?* - the question more akin to an opening gambit, the way the British open all conversation with talk about the weather.

"Have you been out?"

"We've been to the hospital," my dad said.

"Oh?"

"Your mum's been suffering back pain."

That was the last time I saw my mother – during those few moments when we arrived on the doorstep unannounced, during those few moments when my dad veered off in the direction of the kitchen and we entered the warmth and sanctity of the living room; during those few moments that we made our greetings, those few moments when kisses were exchanged and we made ourselves comfortable on the sofa. That was the last time I saw her – through the eyes of a child and the eyes of a man; the woman that raised me so perfectly, the woman that had the ability to blow dark clouds away from above my head; the woman that seemed so refined, so gentle to me, smiling as my dad enters the room, and places down the cups, and then takes his place in the armchair by her side.

That was the last time I saw my mother – smiling that smile of hers – that moment before the spirit of optimism left her body and I went and ruined it all by asking, "Have you been out?"

Funeral Four –
James Lloyd Bradley

Wednesday 13th January 2010

Snow. This had not been predicted – there had certainly been no mention of it on this morning's weather forecast – yet suddenly there had been this downfall, which started around eight o'clock and fell heavily through the rush hour.

I'd not been in work long, and had just made a cup of tea for myself, and switched on the computer, when the telephone rang. I looked up at the clock – ten to nine: from around eight thirty it will ring incessantly all day. Ignore it, I think, although it rings and rings and rings – I'd forgotten to switch on the answering machine.

Reluctantly I'm forced to pick up the receiver. "International Office," I say, in reference to the International Office at Goldsmiths College.

"Is that you Neil?" It's Joan's voice, which sounds weird to me – familiar/unfamiliar - as I've never spoken to her on the telephone before. In the background I can hear a siren – police or ambulance or fire engine. "It's your dad," she says, "he's had a heart attack."

"What?"

"Your dad's had a heart attack," Joan repeats the news. "We're in the ambulance now. We're going to Kings (College Hospital)."

"Okay, I'll meet you there," I say, my head already in a spin, not really sure what to do next.

As I'm talking the guy I work with, Joe, is just walking through the door, cursing to himself, brushing snow from his hair and his shoulders and the sleeve of his coat. "Where did that come from?" he demands to know, indicating the falling snow outside the window. "They never mentioned it on the radio. They said it was going to be nice. Cold, you know, but nice. They never said anything about snow." Each morning we go through this little ritual: talk of the weather, our respective journeys into work, the latest story on the news – we can both be pretty miserable.

"My dad's had a heart attack," I say, motioning the telephone.

"Oh, shit, is he alright?"

"They're taking him to Kings . . . I've got to go there now."

"Get your coat," he says, "and I'll drop you there." The poor sod, he's only just walked through the door. Worse still, he only lives around the corner from Kings and now he's being made to drive back there again.

"Cheers, Joe," I say, quickly swallowing a mouthful of tea, switching my computer off, and pulling on my coat. Before leaving I make a quick telephone call to Sharon, asking her to ring my brothers: let them know what's happening.

The journey to Kings College Hospital is slow, partly due to the weather, partly due to the traffic, which is still heavy at that time of the morning. Throughout the journey Joe and I make small-talk, with him attempting to reassure me: that my dad is going to be okay, that he's had heart attacks before, that he's going to the best place.

"You're right," I nod in agreement, even if I'm not convinced. Even so, I'll remember this little scene. I'll remember the journey. I'll remember the snow. I'll remember the telephone call. I'll remember Joe's little kindness.

"So, how did you find out?" he asks.

"Joan rang me . . . she was in the ambulance . . . she was panicking."

Joe knows about Joan. It's a topic we've discussed often, and he always asks how she is, whenever he asks the same with regards to my dad.

Joan was my mother's best friend. A good few years after my mother died, she lost her husband, Bill, my dad's best friend, under similar circumstances – young. For most of his adult life Bill had worked for a heating and ventilating company – lagging pipes. When he retired he got no pension from the company. A few months after retiring though, he became unwell, with hospital tests soon revealing 'asbestosis' of the lungs – his lungs became so thin that they eventually just disintegrated. Bill had always been a tall man – he looked like Dean Martin – until he suddenly became smaller, somehow, thinner, certainly – skeletal like.

At his funeral Joan had asked me to deliver a eulogy – Bill was really like an uncle to me – which I did, and which I themed around the reason for his demise – the unfairness of it – the obscenity of it. Amongst the congregation were a dozen or so men from Bill's old company: from the pulpit I could see the terror on their faces – they'd all worked with Bill. They'd all worked with asbestos. "Dead men walking," was how I described them. It was a cruel thing to say – the cruellest – but I was so angry.

After I'd delivered the eulogy the vicar complained that he'd have to cut short the ceremony, as I'd spoken for far too long. In fact, even before Bill's farewell song had been played, and with the coffin not yet through the red velvet curtains, the vicar and the undertakers were attempting ushering the mourners from their pews. "You'll have to leave," the vicar smiled. "There's another funeral waiting to come in."

Bill's family had hunted high and low for the song, only getting their hands on it the night before the funeral. "But I wanted to hear his song," Joan had protested, although it was obvious that her heart wasn't really in it.

My dad, on the other hand, was furious. "Just sit there," he'd demanded of Joan and her family, and of those in the pews behind, yet even as the opening bars were offering hints as to the song's identity all of them were being unceremoniously ushered out of the chapel, with the next funeral already making its way through another door. "What a life, eh?" my dad had said at the time, shaking his head in disgust.

As we pull up outside the hospital I spot Sharon standing on the opposite side of the road. In-between thanking Joe for the lift, and promising to let him know as soon as I hear any news, I attempt motioning her to cross at the lights – not attempt crossing in front of the traffic, it's too dangerous what with the snow, the speed they go, the fact that she's panicking over my dad. Too late, before

I know it she's playing chicken with a bus and a lorry and a motorbike. "You should have crossed at the crossing," I said furiously, once she'd reached me, worrying – she never looks. She'll get knocked down one day. Her mother's the same. Whenever we've been out I'm always grabbing her arm. "You didn't even look," I'd always admonish her.

"Was that Joe?" she asks, ignoring my rebuke with regards road safety.

"He dropped me off," I said. "He'd only just walked through the door."

"That was so nice."

"Yeah, it was," I agree, and we both stand there momentarily, waving in the direction of Joe, doing a U-turn in the road and heading off back in the direction of work.

"Sorry," Sharon says, although I'm not sure if this is about crossing the road in the middle of the traffic or about the news of my dad. Briefly we kiss amidst the still falling snow, and then I immediately put my arm around her shoulders and lead her through the doors to the Casualty Department.

Inside it's a similar scene to the one at Greenwich Hospital all those years before. The place is packed, although this time around there is more of an air of calmness, which I put down to the snow and the still early hour of the morning. Even so, on the giant televisions hanging from the walls, they're actually showing an episode of *ER* – keeping people amused during their four hour wait to see a doctor – the irony of the broadcast seemingly lost on everyone other than ourselves. "Can you believe that?" Sharon asked amazed. "They're actually showing *ER* in a casualty waiting room!"

Even I have to laugh at the absurdity of it: it puts me in mind of that spoof film, *Airplane*, with the in-flight feature film some airport disaster movie with planes crashing and everybody perishing in a ball of aviation-fuelled flames.

We walk to the reception desk, where a receptionist appears, and asks if she can help us.

"We're looking for a James Bradley . . . brought in by ambulance . . . not long ago," I say.

She checks the computer, and then checks again.

"His name, again?"

"Bradley. James Bradley. Heart attack."

She checks the computer again, and comes up with the same blank. "Just wait there a moment, I'll check out the back," she says, like some shopkeeper checking in the stock room.

Five minutes pass. Ten minutes. Sharon and I exchange frequent glances, in-between watching snippets of muted *ER* on the television screen: George Clooney is saving someone, as he always does. In fact, even when he doesn't we forgive him his bad luck. It's George Clooney after all – we all know how caring he is. We all know that he would have done his best. Who wouldn't want George Clooney saving them?

The receptionist returns, a little more urgency to her. "We do have a James Bradley," she says. "He's upstairs at ECU."

"ECU?"

"Emergency Cardiac Unit."

Sharon rubs my arm. "Is he okay?" she asks.

"All we know is that he bypassed casualty and went straight there. That's why we didn't have him on the computer," she explains, pointing us in the direction of the ECU – it's on the first floor in the same building. "Take the lift," she tells us.

Quickly we walk down the corridor, but when we reach the lift we're greeted by a throng of people – doctors, nurses, visitors, a few suspicious types – all swarming around the lift doors, most of them looking upwards at the unlighted arrows giving little indication as to whether the arrival of the lift is imminent.

"The stairs," I say, pointing to the staircase to the left of the lift doors, which we proceed to take two at a time.

When we arrive on the next floor we see the ECU directly in front of us. I buzz the intercom, but get no reply. I buzz again, craning my head to see through the tiny square of glass in the door. Still no reply: it's like that time with my granddad all over again, only this time I know my dad's here, or at least he was the last time someone checked. I buzz again.

"You're supposed to stand in front of the camera," Sharon says, pointing to a sign above the intercom: PLEASE STAND IN FRONT OF THE CAMERA, the sign says, which below someone has a taped a rider: WE WON'T BE ABLE TO SEE YOU OTHERWISE!

I buzz again, only this time I stay marooned to the spot, looking into the camera, my body frozen as if in the few seconds when you await your passport picture being taken in one of those photo-booths. Still no one answers the door. "This is ridiculous," I say.

"Wait," Sharon says pulling me away from the camera and back to the square of glass, "I can see Joan."

Through the window I can see her sitting on a chair, alone in the corridor, clutching her bag and my dad's coat. I tap on the glass, but she doesn't hear me. I tap again, waving my hand in the small window attempting to attract her attention.

Sharon buzzes the buzzer again, and stands statuesque in front of the camera.

"Hold on," I say. "I think she's seen me." Through the little window I can see Joan coming towards the door, where she quickly pushes the button that grants us entry to the unit. Immediately, she gets tearful. Sharon hugs her, and I kiss her on the cheek, giving her elbow a squeeze: she's obviously shaken by the whole thing. "You alright, Joan?" I ask, although it's a ridiculous question.

"What happened?" Sharon asks.

"He cut himself shaving," Joan says.

"Shaving?" Sharon asks, confused.

"He couldn't stop the blood," Joan said.

"What, and this meant he was having a heart attack?"

"Yes, but you know what your dad's like . . ." she turned to me and shook her head, as if to suggest you're all the same, the men in your family. Stubborn. "He just carried on," she continued. "He had a shower, and then he went upstairs to get dressed," her hands were shaking as she retold the tale, and she kept looking off down the corridor in the direction of where, I assume, my dad has been taken. "When I went upstairs he was sitting on the bed. He seemed really calm, only he told me he was having a heart attack, and that I needed to phone for an ambulance!"

"Oh, wow," Sharon rubs her arms. "You poor thing."

"Trouble was, I was so nervous . . . I couldn't remember the number . . ."

"Nine, nine, nine," Sharon says instinctively: she'd remember the number – she can remember everyone's telephone number, even the number plates of the cars they drive – she's a bit weird like that.

"So, where is he now?" I ask.

"He's down there," Joan said, pointing off down the corridor. "I think he's having surgery."

Just then a large woman approaches, the ward sister: glasses, dark blue hospital scrubs, and those white clogs everyone that works in a hospital seems to wear. "Are you Mr Bradley's son?" she asks of me.

"Yes."

"And are you his next of kin?"

"Yes," I said, although I'm not sure that I am, technically. Besides, Joan's here, and I don't want her overlooked. To be honest, none of us are really sure anymore where we fit into the family hierarchal structure: Joan's his 'partner' now – that's what she'd be described as - although with them it seems to be more a companionship borne out of joint grief. I'm his middle son, although Lloyd is technically the next of kin, even if he's not arrived yet. Besides, he never visits him anyway – never picks up the phone to him, or knocks at his door . . . *I live the closest, if that helps?* I want to say.

The sister doesn't really need to know the ins and outs. "Your dad's had a heart attack. But he's in good hands," she attempts reassurance, before explaining the procedure: my dad's had four heart attacks so far, so we're well versed in terms of the latest techniques and possible outcomes. "We've managed to clear a blockage in his main artery, but he's still very unwell."

Just then my dad is wheeled past us on a trolley: he looks grey, that combined with his white hair, giving him the appearance of an actor in some black and white hospital drama from the 1950s. On his bottom lip there appears to be a massive blue welt, which I assume is from the shaving cut Joan had mentioned. As he's transferred from the trolley to the bed, the sister explains how, "The next thirty-six hours are the most critical." She squeezes Joan's hand, and then announces that "You can go in one at a time, but you mustn't wear him out."

I'm the first to go in. Joan insists. I think she's always felt awkward around all of us, not wanting to step on anyone's toes. The first Christmas they were 'together,' if that's the right description, my dad made Christmas dinner for everyone: in the years after my mother died he never bothered too much with the celebrations. During the festivities though, Joan stood in the kitchen, not really wanting to interfere, not wanting to sit down and eat with us, not wanting to take my mother's 'place.'

"Go on, Joan, you go in first," I demanded, but she wouldn't hear of it.

"No, you go. You go," she says. "I'll see him later." What if there is no later though? What if something happens? What if . . .

Cautiously I approach the bed, never really knowing what to say under such circumstances. Besides, we've never really gone in for all that 'touchy-feely' stuff. If Lloyd had been here, he would have walked up and kissed him. He doesn't ever visit anyone, but on occasions like this he's always big on that sort of thing. Jason, by contrast, is even worse than me, and will usually just plop himself down in the nearest armchair – he always seems self-conscious, although he has a similar sense of humour to us, if only he could learn to let it out a bit more often.

"How are you feeling, dad?" I ask, making a half-hearted attempt at rubbing the back of his hand.

"Better than I did," he says, although it's clear, despite the casual way he delivers his reply, that he's really not well.

"Joan said you cut yourself shaving?"

"Yeah, it was only a little knick, although I knew straight away it was a heart attack," instinctively he reaches up to feel the welt on his lip, which appears to be turning bluer as we speak. "I've cut myself shaving a million times before . . . only this time it was different . . . it just wouldn't stop bleeding . . . it was pumping blood out of my lip." As he was relaying the story Jason arrives, and then Lloyd, and then the rest of the family – each one recounting their own versions of how they heard the news, along with their respective journeys to the hospital in the snow.

"How are you, Joan?" I can hear them all asking.

No sooner had we all had our respective few minutes with our dad at his bedside the sister approaches again, informing us that the ECU is being closed with immediate effect, and that we'd all need to leave.

"What's going on?" I ask.

"We've got the norovirus," the sister said apologetically. "Not here, but up on the wards. That's why we're shutting this unit down. We can't afford to get it here."

"No," everyone says in unison.

"We're already started turning patients away," she shakes her head. "Your dad was really lucky; he was the last patient to get here and be allowed in. Another half an hour and he would have had to have gone elsewhere."

At this stage we're not really aware of the significance of that fact, however, it transpires that if you can manage to get to this particular hospital, within a reasonable time period, your chances of surviving a heart attack are greatly improved, with patients operated on immediately: angiogram, angioplasty, stents. With other hospitals in London it's more a case of 'stabilisation' – a finger's crossed and hope you don't die type approach - followed by corrective surgery at some later date. Of course, with the former approach there are always risks involved. But it was always worth the risk. I know that's how my dad always viewed it. "You have to put your faith in the hands of the experts," he always said.

"So where's my dad going, now?" I ask.

"He's going upstairs to one of the wards."

"But haven't they got the virus up there?"

"Unfortunately, yes."

It's like Greenwich Hospital all over again. I mean; what is the point? We have all this new technology, all these medical breakthroughs, and then someone cleans the floor with a dirty mop, or doesn't bother washing their hands.

"Can we speak to him before he's moved?" I ask.

"Just you and your brothers," the sister says. "Only a few minutes."

Lloyd, Jason and I approach the bed again - Joan has already said her goodbyes, and Sharon has taken her off to get a coffee.

"How are you feeling?" we all ask again, although it's obvious to all three of us that he looks far from well: his skin is milk white and the welt on his lip has turned from blue to an ugly black.

Just then the porters arrive to transfer my dad to the ward upstairs. Lloyd leans over and kisses him, and then Jason, although I get caught between the two porters and the trolley that they're about to transfer him to. "I'll see up on the ward, dad," I say, and he nods.

"Come on, let's go," Lloyd says, turning on his heels and heading for the exit. Jason follows, but I linger in the doorway, observing my dad being shifted from one bed to another: between the two porters I just catch a glimpse of his face, peering behind one of the men and catching my eye. He nods again and smiles. I wave to him and leave.

Years ago, when he was much younger than I am now, I visited my dad at Guy's Hospital. This was some time during the 1960s, I'm assuming; it can't have been the 1970s, I wasn't tall enough for it to have been the 1970s. Besides, I'm wearing little tailored grey shorts with red braces, *long white socks with sandals*, if you please. To add insult to injury, my mother insists that I wear a clip-on bow tie, which gives me the appearance of a very camp member of the Hitler Youth.

Arriving on the ward, an outtake from *Carry On Matron*, I can find no sign of my dad amongst the ordered regime of sparkling clean floors and symmetrical "Male Only" beds – no MRSA here, no norovirus, the NHS, then at least, still very much the envy of the world.

"Dad's not here," I say, looking from bed to bed in search of my absent father.

"There he is," my mother says, ignoring me, waving as if in recognition, quickly setting off down the ward like most women with little time to spare between work, housewifery and worry - conscious of the time restrictions and the matron's bell ringing a halt to family visitation rights. My brother, Lloyd, and I though, we stay rooted to the spot, watching fascinated as my mother walks about halfway down the ward and suddenly greets a complete stranger in the bed with a kiss, a copy of *The Boxing News* and a bottle of *R. Whites* Original Cream Soda. As far as we can tell, the man in the bed is an Indian – not a red Indian, but rather the turbaned kind - looking like an extra from Ali Baba and the Forty Thieves. *That's not my dad*, I thought.

"Dad's gone," Lloyd whispers. "Something to do with the operation," packed off to heaven, with my mother on the lookout for a new dad for the pair of us.

Ignoring our suspicions, my mother beckons the pair of us, luring us towards the bed with a waved hand, luring us towards the strange man that hides beneath the crisp sheets and the warm blanket, luring us towards an Indian she claims to be our father.

Creeping forward, I take a peak. *He's wearing the same pyjamas as my dad*, he has the same yellow dressing gown strewn across the foot of the bed keeping his feet warm. *My dad never wore a turban though*; the giant beehive bandage looks ridiculous on his head – his features much better suited to a flat cap or trilby.

As I draw near the man in the bed suddenly holds out his arms towards me, as if in greeting, but which I mistake for a gesture similar to that of Boris Karloff in *Frankenstein*. Immediately I back away.

"Give your dad a kiss," my mother demands, although this only prompts me to back away even further from the bed - *that's not my dad*.

As if to confirm this fact the man in the turban suddenly throws back the covers and gingerly swings his legs over the side of the bed, as Lloyd spies the scene with wide-eyed fascination, and I simply look on in terror. Attempting to bring his feet to the floor – he has short legs, so his toes point downwards like a ballerina – my mother gently navigates the man's feet into newly-purchased slippers (you had to have new slippers when you went into hospital apparently). She then picks up the dressing gown and drapes it around his shoulders heavyweight boxing style, which is somewhat ironic when considering the fact that it was boxing that has led my dad here in the first place: as an amateur boxer he took one too many blows to the left ear, causing life-long hearing problems, hence the reason he's now wearing a turban. This time around it's for surgery to correct some imbalance in the middle ear, which I assume is similar to the middle *eye* - my dad the Martian Pater.

A few moments later my dad, the man in the turban, Boris Karloff's monster incarnation, stands, or at least attempts standing. For a few brief seconds he staggers back and forth, holding his arms aloft in a similar Karloff pose, before toppling backwards onto the mattress. Immediately there are a flock of nurses flittering around the bed, fluffing pillows and smoothing down sheets, and grabbing my dad's elbows, "Going for a walk Mr Bradley?" they ask, everyone being jolly together.

I'm shocked. *He's drunk*, I thought to myself. *He's wearing a turban, and he's drunk.*

On the second attempt he manages to stay on his feet a good while longer, leaning heavily on the nurses as if crutches.

Mumbling to himself Frankenstein monster-like, *smoke good, drink good*, he suddenly attempts shuffling across the ward in my direction. This though only serves to terrify me even more, as I back away from him, finding myself between two beds on the opposite side of the ward; they too have these strange pyjama-clad men, both of whom reach out towards me like zombies. Terrified, I squeeze myself through behind the beds and the bedside cabinets, attempting to hide behind the giant curtains.

Turning my back on the scene, I press my face against the far window, emitting a tiny mushroom cloud of steam upon the glass - if I'd have turned around again I would have seen my dad being led back to bed, I would have seen the disappointment on his face following my rebuttal. Instead I choose to stare down at the giant miniature railway set, which snakes off in all directions from beneath the dirty glass ceiling of London Bridge Station below. To the left of the station, across London Bridge, on the other side of the Thames, I can see the Monument, not yet suffocated by the office buildings that will soon surround it – my dad and I had made hundreds of trips to the top over the years, climbing those 311 steps to the viewing cage beneath the solid gold ball: my dad claimed it was solid gold, although staring at it now from the hospital window I begin to have my doubts.

To the left of London Bridge I can see Southwark Cathedral, the church where my parents were married. Once I went there on a school trip, during which we were all told off for messing about, for running around and screaming in a place of worship. We were all told off for sticking our hands through a crack in the tomb of the unknown bishop - our eyes closed in terror as we thrust our tiny hands inside and fingered the velvet shroud. When we came to leave the organist played the theme from *Rollerball*, and we discovered that a ghost had stolen all of our gloves.

When I turn back from the window I see that my dad – the man my mother claims to be my dad – is back in bed, his eyes closing, his bandaged head sinking back into the collection of NHS pillows.

Just then the bell rings, signalling that visiting time is over. Reluctantly, I kiss the man in the turban goodbye, although he's sleepy eyed and seems to barely notice the gesture.

As we pass the nurses station a nurse offers Lloyd and I a sweet from a giant tin, whilst my mother lingers at my fraudulent father's beside. A few moments later I race my brother to the lift. My mother follows, catching up to us, tearful. She lets me push the button.

Early Evening

There's no ringing of the matron's bell anymore. No *Carry On Matron*. No visiting hours. In fact, no one's allowed in. We've been sat here for hours – all day – although the lack of seats has meant we've had to do it in rotation. We're still waiting for news: news of the norovirus, news of my dad. We're still not allowed on the ward, and news of my dad has become less and less (we're out of sight, literally, and now very much out of mind).

From time to time a doctor will arrive, or a nurse, or a porter. "That one didn't wash her hands," someone comments, despite a sign on the ward door demanding: YOU MUST WASH YOUR HANDS BEFORE ENTER-ING – over the last few hours it has become almost a mantra.

"None of them have washed their hands," another will say.

"That last one was drinking a coffee and eating a sandwich," Lloyd says, shaking his head in rage. "He was a doctor, he should know better."

"No one's been near or by with a mop," someone else comments.

Every now and then I break away from the family group, taking a walk along the corridor and peering through the tiny pane of glass in the door to the ward. Halfway down the ward I spy my dad in one of the beds, although from my vantage point I can't tell if he's awake or asleep. He's certainly not moving. "It's all a bit touch and go, I'm afraid," the ward sister had told us regarding my dad's condition, although we're not sure if that's a medical opinion or she's simply preparing us for the worst. Either way, it can't end like this, surely?

In his second memoir (*Things My Mother Never Told Me*) Blake Morrison imagines what his mother's death will be like – in the final moments before she actually dies – allowing his poetic self to take over from a journalistic instinct to capture the witnessed truth, which was the case with his memoir regarding the death of his father (*And When Did You Last See Your Father?*): in that book he captures the death almost clinically, although the description of his mother's passing is truly poetic, much better aided by time and the writer's luxury of reflection.

Understandably perhaps, under the circumstances, I too wonder what will happen next, with my dad? Whilst Blake Morrison chooses to capture his mother's death as a poet, I now worry that I won't be afforded the luxury of such literary choice. In fact, my biggest fear now is that my dad, as a result of the norovirus, will die alone, leaving me no choice *but* to imagine what happened at the end – what those last moments were like.

And When Did I Last See *My* Father?

We'll be milling about in the corridor – stuck outside the ward as a result of the norovirus – unable to be at his bedside. Just then there'll be some minor commotion. An alarm will sound or the light above the ward door will flash red intermittently. From further down the corridor will come a doctor pushing a trolley with electronic equipment and they'll enter the ward – they won't wash their hands as instructed, as time will be of the essence.

Sensing a shift, as a family, we'll gather outside the ward door, craning our heads to see through the small glass pane – all of us fearing the worst.

Some time later the ward sister will come to the door and inform us of the sad news, and she'll offer us her apologies, and then she'll invite my brothers and I to come onto the ward in order to spend a few moments in my dad's company. Before we can do so however, she'll make us don gowns and facemasks and demand that we wash our hands as a result of the norovirus – the most bitter ironies of all.

That night we'll leave the hospital, taking away my dad's possessions in a carrier bag, just like had happened with my Granddad Joe and my Granddad Jim, leaving us to hate hospitals like we always did. For a few minutes we'll linger in the hospital car park, working out who's going with whom, and then we'll make our way back to my dad's house, where we'll sit around his dining room table, drinking tea, looking at all the photographs. In the living room my dad's chair will remain empty – all of us knowing that the safety net has somehow been removed, and that we're all on our own now: my dad was always great like that. You could always rely on him when you were in trouble, when you were in debt, when you needed advice or a handout. He'd always lecture us, as all dad's are prone to do, I suppose, but the problems would always be solved, the bill's paid - we'd all survive.

Another cup of tea and then we'll begin the process of ringing round the same way my dad had done after my mother had died – the bearer's of bad news. "Hello . . . this is Neil . . . Jimmy's son . . . I'm afraid I've some sad news . . . dad passed away today."

The next day we'll all meet up again. The funeral arrangements are already made – my dad's arranged the whole thing – we just need to fill in the blanks. My dad already has a plot with my mother up at the cemetery; there's a hearse and two funeral cars, already bought and paid for. It's typical of my dad. "If you want a third car, you'll have to pay for it yourself," I remember him saying a long time back.

If we're all in agreement, he can go to St. Luke's. He's actually catholic, but I don't suppose it really matters. I'm sure he won't mind either way. It's more about the 'send off' than anything else. Father John won't be there to perform the service however (he left to take up a new position elsewhere), which is a shame: for all his doubt, my dad always liked Father John – he'd often said that if he were ever to be tempted back to the church it would be the likes of Father John that'd make him do it.

After the funeral we'll have all the dilemmas over the house, the contents, the money. It was different when my mother died: my dad was there to carry on (or not) and the house remained intact – there was no clearing out or 'going through' to be done. Now though, it will be impossible, his presence in the house too fresh. Besides, where would we start? I've no doubt someone will want the furniture: the contents, the fixtures and fittings. His clothes will go to the charity shop. Bag upon black bag will be filled up, and loaded in the car, and then driven up to the high street and distributed amongst the various good causes: the British Heart Foundation, Cancer Research UK, etc. With each new bag though, the house will become more and more devoid of life, devoid of my dad's presence in it, until all that's left is an echo: an echo of the part my dad and my mother made in our lives.

"It's all so sad," Sharon will say, and I'll nod agreement, but not have the words to reply. These will be saved for the moment I climb the steps to the pulpit in eulogy, in the same way that I did with my mother, along similar lines, only far more masculine in delivery – a masculine eulogy for a man whose traits were always often far from masculine. I'll speak of his life – his life at work, his life with my mother, his life as our father.

Sinatra will play afterwards, or Tony Bennett – much cooler, I think – and after that we'll accompany his coffin to the cemetery, where he'll be reunited in the ground with my mother once more the way he always hoped and claimed he'd be one day.

Of course, I worry about my brothers – the family – and about what will become of us all. We won't argue, but there's bound to be some resentment's - our dad's house: the contents, the photographs and the odds and ends – it'll be make or break for us as a family. I worry *that my dad's passing will signal an end to our relationships – that the bond we once had will dissipate, and that we'll no longer make an effort, no longer worry whether we continue to see each other or not, realising now that it was my mother, and then my dad, that was the glue that held us all together. Sharon was right. All so sad.*

Later that evening (back at Eltham)

I reverse the car up onto the drive and switch the engine off, although we both sit there for the longest time making no attempt to move. It's been a long day, starting off with unexpected snow and that nightmare journey to work, followed by yet another one of those 'bad news' telephone calls when your world is suddenly turned upside down.

"Come on," Sharon says eventually, unclipping her seat belt and motioning for me to do the same. Reluctantly I follow her lead, removing the key from the ignition and reaching for the door handle.

"Watch your feet," I say, as I step out of the car and test my grip on the icy drive – it's not a day for humour, but we both laugh as we slip and slide our way up to the front door.

As soon as I connect the key with the front door lock I can hear the telephone ringing from within – Sharon's mother. Immediately the door opens Sharon's grabbing for the telephone, filling her mother in on the day's events, whilst I head to the kitchen – my place of sanctuary – and fill the kettle. Through the kitchen window the garden appears to glow beneath a thick layer of snow, covering up a multitude of 'things-to-do,' which, regardless of the weather, will probably have to wait a little while longer now.

As soon as the kettle clicks I pour over-boiling water into two cups, and suddenly find myself lost in a fog of steam. For a few moments I stir the tea bags in respective cups, over which I pour far too much milk, which means that I have to leave the tea bags immersed in the water far longer than I would normally, squeezing them with the teaspoon, leaving tiny flecks of tea film floating on the surface of the water.

"It's ready," I call to Sharon – she's finished her telephone conversation, but has slipped upstairs and is busy changing into her bedwear. When she comes back down again a few minutes later she immediately heads for the bathroom and locks the door. Even from the kitchen I can hear the bathroom cabinet opening as she reaches for a collection of bottles: handcream, facecream, nightcream – those feminine touches that remain a mystery to me. I sit myself down on the small step that leads down from the dining room onto the cold kitchen and drink heavily from the cup – it has red hearts on, which is somewhat ironic under the circumstances. As usual my mind wanders off, although I'm quickly brought back to reality as Sharon's gentle fingers suddenly caress the back of my neck. I half turn and offer up the cup of tea. "I've already brushed my teeth," she says by way of a refusal.

I put the cup back down on the floor beside my feet. "I'll be up in a while," I say.

Taking the hint, she leans down and kisses me on the forehead and is immediately off upstairs, leaving me to stew alone in the scant light shining down from the weak fluorescent bulb above the cooker hob.

I sit there for another thirty minutes or so, draining the last of the tea from both my cup and hers. I stand up and rinse the cups out in the sink and place them on the draining board to dry. I remove two fresh cups from the cupboard and fill those with new tea bags - save me doing it in the morning. I switch the light off above the cooker, but still see clearly by way of the snowy garden. I check the back door's locked.

The Wedding (Reprise)

I'm not sure when I became so unhappy. I'm not even sure that I *am* unhappy – I'm not sure that unhappiness is a permanent fixture of my life. What I do know though, is that there have been long bouts - as well as more frequent shorter bouts - of unhappiness, especially during the years following my mother's death. Often, it's all I think about – that period when everything seemed to go wrong: my mother dying, or my grandfather dying, at that time, under those terrible circumstances. And then, of course, there was *that* terrible wedding day. Even now I can't view that particular day as being anything other than a disaster. Not because of the things that went wrong – the terrible weather, the drunkenness, the delays; each new disaster that befell it – but rather the things, naively perhaps, I hoped it would put *right*.

For Sharon, who I knew felt the same, the memories of that day are different, or at least she's conveniently managed to block out that same view in her futile attempt at preserving to memory, what she so hoped would be, the perfect wedding. But then, who could possibly blame her?

Not that I helped. "How could it have been that?" I kept demanding of her. "How could you have possibly thought it perfect?" Too much had happened, especially in a relatively short space of time, for it ever to have been that. There had been far too much tragedy in the family for me to approach that wedding with anything other than a feeling of foreboding: at the back of my mind was that nagging feeling that I'd left the whole thing far too late for it ever to have any real meaning.

Even now I wonder had my mother been there, had she still been alive; had my grandfather not dropped down dead, literally, a few months previous; had my dad not been consumed with heartache, that the whole thing might well have been, I don't know what, joyous?

For the pair of us though, Sharon and I, there was more a feeling, even if we didn't share that feeling at the time with each other, of great relief: relief that it was over, that it was done and dusted, that we could now attempt simply getting on with our lives, hoping against hope that those past events would not overshadow our future life together. In the years that followed then, we did our best to ignore all those previous portents of doom: Sharon settled into the flat and the strange rhythm of married life, settled into the burden of being that second name on the rent book and on the council tax register and on the electoral roll. For the most part the transition was painless, although both of us were aware of that unhappiness eating away at me - of those dark clouds constantly forming over Camberwell Green and that cramped, tiny little flat we shared there.

Sunday 11th April 2010

I look at my watch for the tenth time in as many minutes, and check the knot of my tie in the hall mirror. "Are you nearly ready?" I call up the stairs.

Just then Sharon appears at the top of the staircase –
a new dress, new shoes, a stylish wrap around her
shoulders, her hair perfect, as always. "How do I look?"
she asks.

"It's nearly eleven," I say: she knows how she
looks, even if I don't offer up the required complimen-
tary reply.

"Have you got the keys?" she asks.

"Yes."

"Have you locked the back door?"

"Yes."

"Have you got the envelope for the vicar?"

"*Yes*."

"You don't think we're too early?"

"Just move," I say exasperated, but smiling.

She kisses me. "You look nice."

"You too," I say genuinely.

Outside the sun is beating down, and we make the
short walk along the road, heading in the direction of
St. Luke's, shading our eyes from the glare of the sun and
those sat in cars in traffic. As we pass my parent's house
we both glance to the right, taking in the fresh coat of
paint, a few new flowers and plants in the earth that ran
along the path leading up to the front door.

It's funny, but I always thought I'd end up in that
house, hence the reason we'd never bothered looking at
properties before: the pair of us never having any real
desire towards home ownership, content in the knowledge that it would probably happen some day. One
day though, my niece had been out looking at houses
and we'd offered to drive her around, give her a second
opinion on all of the over-priced properties on her list.
"We'll just have a quick look at this one, if that's alright,"

she'd said, handing over the estate agent's A4 sheet, with its brief description and grainy photo. "It's way out of my price range, but it's just along the road from granddad's house."

Pulling up outside the house Sharon and I immediately exchanged looks: nine doors away – a house, in all the years I'd be driving over there, the few years when I was younger and the few months following my divorce that I'd lived there - I'd never even noticed before.

Upon entry to the house we discovered an empty shell of a building. Inside everything was painted white; there were new carpets, a new bathroom, and the tiniest kitchen you've ever seen. Apparently some builder had bought it cheap, 'toshed it up' with paint, installed a cheap bathroom suite and kitchen units - it can't have cost a lot more than ten thousand pounds (and I'm being generous) and put an extra fifty grand on the asking price. It was perfect.

As my niece followed the smarmy estate agent around, feigning interest in a house she could not afford and had no intention of buying, Sharon and I couldn't help but look at everything in a sort of silent wonder. Could it really be possible? Could this really be the place? Could this be the final piece of the jigsaw? "I know Terri can't afford it," I whispered, as the estate agent got his sales patter up into overdrive, "but can *we?*"

"I wouldn't have thought so," Sharon said, even though we went right ahead and bought it there and then – one viewing, no survey, no guarantee that we'd even get a mortgage, let alone raise any kind of deposit on it. At the time I think Sharon was even more surprised than I was at the way I took control – made an offer, organised a mortgage, booked a removal company (which turned out to be bogus, although that's another story). In fact, following that initial first view to frantically ringing around for another removal company, with all of our furniture and belongs sat on the pavement at Camberwell Green, we were both surprised at just how quickly the whole thing happened: in little over a month we'd made the biggest decision of our lives, and had unwittingly discovered, what would turn out to be, what, paradise?

It'd been ten years since the wedding, a long time passed and an awful lot of water under the bridge. And yet still the memory of that day remained with me – nagged at me, chipped away at me – almost to the point that it threatened to spoil this new-found life we'd finally managed to carve out for ourselves. Only one thing for it then, as far as I could see, do the whole thing again, only this time around do it for ourselves, with minimal fuss and for all the right reasons.

Understandably perhaps, even if it had been chosen for its convenience more than anything else, we chose St. Luke's – that church around the corner, that same church at which my mother's service was held.

For a few weeks previous we'd been putting in regular appearances, although we both struggled with the concept - Sharon as a result of her ingrained Catholicism, and me simply because for too many years I'd struggled with the concept of God as a life-style choice. The vicar there, Elaine, though, was always very welcoming, as had been Father John, the man whose shoes for many years she struggled to fill. When we tentatively approached her, not really knowing what it was we wanted - a blessing of sorts we both supposed - she couldn't have been more helpful, especially when we explained to her the fact that we wanted little or no family involvement, no celebration, again, no fuss. She was fine with that though, suggesting we come along on the Sunday closest to our tenth anniversary. "Just pop along after the mass," she'd suggested. "We usually get one or two people mingling around afterwards, drinking coffee, but I can shoo them away pretty quickly if they won't take the hint."

Sharon and I laughed at that, both surprised at how simple the whole thing was in terms of its organisation – both agreeing that *this* was the wedding we should have had in the first place: sun shining, in a church; doing the whole thing for exactly the right reasons – love happiness, a desire to spend the rest of our days together.

Standing at the back of the church, as the last of the Sunday morning congregation stragglers finally take the hint from the vicar to 'sling their hooks,' I'm struck by the rays of sunshine flooding through the stained glass windows – *it's perfect*, I think.

"We'll do it up at the small altar, if that's okay with you?" the vicar said, smiling, knowing how important it was to the pair of us.

Walking up along the main aisle we pass the pulpit where I'd spoken such words of grief and tribute to my mother – the venue suddenly seeming more than fitting somehow. Back where it all started (or ended).

The vicar welcomes us, and reads a few lines from the Bible, before asking us both to kneel – to kneel before a God I had serious doubts about, and Sharon worried as to her Roman allegiance to. Even so, the service was perfect, partaken of for exactly the right reasons. At the end the vicar shook both our hands, I slipped her a discrete envelope containing a donation for the church roof fund or a new pipe organ or whatever it was the painted barometer was slowly climbing its way towards, and then we went home – back to the enchanted cottage.

Stepping out into the garden, with the sun shining, and with everything just starting to come into bloom, we both laugh at the simplicity of the service – the event – we'd just been party to: in secret, like some (not) guilty little sin. We take a few pictures and some video footage. We both look self-conscious, although we smile all the same - it's a day of celebration after all.

We walk up and down the garden, stopping occasionally to look at new buds or the progress of shrubs and plants that were bedded last year and the year before that. At the end of the garden we stop and stand in silence for a few moments, our hands entwined, looking back at the house, even though I can't help but look to my right, up to a bedroom window of a house nine houses along.

Sharon squeezes my hand – she knows me far too well – and then leans in and kisses my neck. "I'll go and put the kettle on," she says. As she enters the house she passes my dad standing in the shade just outside the kitchen door. He waves to me and smiles: even from here he looks better than he's done in a long, long while. I wave back, still marvelling at his fighting spirit, the way he seems to get knocked down, but then get's straight back up again – always just getting on with it – with little fuss. Sharon, of course, still marvels at the shock of thick white hair that sits atop his head, laughing over the fact that none of us, his three sons, were blessed with such heads of hair, despite mine, what's left of mine, gradually turning the same colour as my dad's. The colour seems to be back in his cheeks also, and there's certainly no sign of the heart attack that appeared certain to bring this book to its unhappy conclusion. Now, he looks genuinely happy for the pair of us. I walk down to the garden to meet him. "Do you want wine, or a beer, or something?" I ask.

He shakes his head and smiles. "A cup of tea would be nice."

The Carrier Bag

Years Back

My dad is speaking in hushed tones on the telephone – shaking his head with the shame of it. "He says he wants to be a writer," he tells whoever's on the other end of the line. "I think he might be having a breakdown or something. Either that or he's smoking the funny fags, or has gone gay!"

I always found it curious, my dad's response to my 'wanting to write.' When I was at school he got himself elected as a school governor at the secondary school I attended – a position usually reserved, especially back in the 1970s, for doctors, solicitors, architects, and the like. Naturally, my dad was proud of this new position, especially boasting the fact that he was a toilet cleaner by way of his 'profession.'

Compared to most of the other dad's I knew – the dads of the boys I went to school with, the dads of those lived on the same council estate as us, he was always really enlightened – he was certainly always challenging the 'system,' believing that we had the right to be whoever and whatever we wanted to be. And yet, years later, when I made that declaration about wanting to write, he'd seemed so dismissive – worried, even – worrying that such a pursuit would bring me, *him*, nothing but trouble.

I'd been writing for about a year, with none of it making much sense, although I'd suddenly started having a lot of letters (to the editor) published in a variety of men's magazines: *Arena, FHM, Maxim, GQ*, and was happily stockpiling an array of prizes for my efforts: Sharon got a *Mont Blanc* pen, my mother another pen of similar value and stature.

At the time, everyone – my mother, Sharon, my brothers – seemed really proud, if somewhat surprised, although my dad continued in his reluctance to even talk about the subject of my writing, let alone embrace the concept. Or, at least, so I thought.

One day, by chance, looking through the drawers in my parent's dining room cabinet I discovered a collection of magazines in which I'd had letters published, and for which I'd been awarded prizes.

"What's all this?" I asked.

"Your dad bought those," my mother said, smiling from the kitchen.

"What?" I said, incredulous: I simply couldn't envisage my dad in the local newsagents, leafing through the pages of those magazines in search of evidence of my 'craft.'

"Don't mention it to him," my mother warned.

It was strange, although very working class, his buying those magazines in secret, although, even in recent years, whenever I've written anything my dad's praise for my work had always come via a third party – Sharon, usually.

A few weeks after the discovery of those magazines I was back over at my parent's house, making prepara-tions to drive back to Camberwell Green, Sharon and I having enjoyed Sunday lunch with the pair of them.

My dad meanwhile was out in the hall preparing himself for a walk up to woods with the dog: putting on a thick scarf, ski hat, heavy coat, wellington boots.

"I'll see you later, dad," I called to him: he'd already made his goodbyes and was heading for the front door.

"There's a carrier bag in the dining room for you," he called back.

I wait until I hear the door close behind him before getting up from the sofa and going into the dining room to investigate. Upon the dining table was a Daily Telegraph carrier bag, which looked as if it were full to bursting. "What's this?" I called to my mother

She's sat in the armchair, smiling. "Your dad got you some stuff from work."

Opening the bag I discover a collection of pens, reporter's notepads, Post-It notes, along with an entire years worth of the *Daily Telegraph's Arts and Books* section: he'd saved everyone for me – all any aspiring writer needed, surely?

"What is it?" Sharon asks, and I hold up the pads and pens towards her, shaking my head at my dad's gesture – the physical proof of his approval in terms of my 'craft.'

Sharon looks over at my mother, and they both share a smile.

"Come on," I say. "Let's go."

As we busy ourselves with putting on our coats and gathering together our belongings, my mother waits in the hallway by the front door.

"Bye, Doreen," Sharon says, kissing my mother.

"Bye, mum," I say, copying the gesture. "See you next week."

As we walk the short walk down the garden path my mother stands watching us. We turn and wave. She waves back and then closes the front door on another Sunday. Sharon grips my hand and we walk around the corner to where the car is parked. Everything seems hopeful.

In Loving Memory
of
The National Health Service

All of us should mourn the dismantling and inevitable loss of this great institution – Clement Attlee's Spirit of 45, when Britain first caught a glimpse of that wonderful New Jerusalem

<u>Coming in 2014</u>

The Brass Angel – **An (Airport) Novel by Neil Bradley**

This is the story of an angel that thinks he's a man, and a 'Ministry of Terminations' that makes every attempt to convince him otherwise. Just who is right?

Jimmy – the Circus Boy - is a loner, a dreamer, who one days stumbles upon the love of his life in a lift.

Sarah – the girl with no name - is a loner, a dreamer, who one day stumbles upon the love of *her* life in the same lift, only for him to immediately disappear the morning after their first date.

Charlie is Jimmy's grandfather, who keeps encountering angels stood at the end of his bed in the middle of the night, or sat at his kitchen table in the early morning hours, forcing him to pour an extra cup of tea. Oh, and he's about to suffer a heart attack.

Sergeant Harrison is Charlie's best - a retired policeman who divides his time equally between sitting watch over Charlie's hospital bed and conducting a search for Charlie's missing grandson.

Frank McGovern is a drunken Fleet Street hack that's become so cynical with the world that he's happily drinking himself to death. That is until one day he's paired with Jan Halligan, a bright young reporter on the newspaper, who will eventually force him to look at life afresh.

Danny, 'The Angel Boy,' is a young boy that very nearly drowns, only to be saved by a mysterious stranger wearing a long, black coat and a bowler hat, who he claims is an angel.

Agent Green is a long-time employee for the Ministry of Terminations, a little-known government department, who one day starts to suspect that his colleague, a very confused Agent Winston, is not all he appears to be.

The Brass Angel is the story of love, life, family, loss, death and the civil service!

Lightning Source UK Ltd.
Milton Keynes UK
UKOW03f1619100314

227889UK00001B/3/P